SHAKESPEARE THE HISTORIAN

Shakespeare the Historian

Paola Pugliatti
Professor of English
University of Florence

First published 1996 by
MACMILLAN PRESS LTD
Houndmills, Basingstoke, Hampshire RG21 6XS
and London
Companies and representatives
throughout the world

ISBN 0–333–63329–6

A catalogue record for this book is available
from the British Library.

10   9   8   7   6   5   4   3   2   1
05   04   03   02   01   00   99   98   97   96

Printed and bound in Great Britain by
Antony Rowe Ltd
Chippenham, Wiltshire

 Published in the United States of America 1996 by
ST. MARTIN'S PRESS, INC.,
Scholarly and Reference Division
175 Fifth Avenue, New York, N.Y. 10010

ISBN 0–312–12840–1

For Simone and Luca,
'and with it all my trauells history'

Contents

Acknowledgements

The long incubation of this book meant that for a number of years I enjoyed the generosity of many friends.

In 1985 a research group that had been working for years under the direction of Bill Dodd on various problems concerning drama was dispersed owing to the changed academic destiny and destination of most of us. The group comprised Guy Aston, Keir Elam, Lino Falzon, Pino Martella, Roberta Mullini and Romana Zacchi. Before we set out towards our various exiles, I submitted a project on Shakespeare's histories to them for discussion; the main idea of this project was centred on the genre peculiarities that I then thought those plays to possess. My project was indeed 'discussed', and I was kindly but firmly dissuaded from proceeding in that direction. I resisted the advice for as long as I could, but at last I gratefully, if silently, acknowledged its soundness.

Bill Dodd continued to play an invaluable role, implacably pointing out what he thought was unsound or purely speculative or contradictory and suggesting more readings and longer brooding over my texts.

Pino Martella posed basic philosophical questions on such unanswerable issues as 'what is historical drama?' or, worse, 'what is history?', to which he nevertheless supplied many unorthodox, and therefore extremely exciting, answers.

Jeanne Clegg was my first reader. Although I then suspected and still suspect that sympathy and affection coloured her reading, her encouraging remarks produced a significant suspension of the utter disbelief I was then experiencing about what I was writing and opened the possibility of dialogue.

Marcello Pagnini and Alessandro Serpieri read parts of the book and made many constructive remarks while encouraging my then timorous first steps.

Agostino Lombardo provided a precious opportunity by suggesting that I contributed a text to his series 'Piccola Biblioteca Shakespiriana'. His advice and the need to contain the text in the format of the series ('piccola') were an invaluable help in making clear many of the still cloudy issues that I was then developing in my lengthier text.

The Fellows of the Shakespeare Institute at Stratford-upon-Avon granted me an EEC scholarship in 1989. Their amicable hospitality and the 'personalised' bibliographical help of Susan Brock, in the best possible framework for the study of Shakespeare, revived my enthusiasm and helped me to reshape my entire project.

The Committee of the Fifth International Shakespeare Congress and the Italian Ministry of Education granted funds which allowed me to attend the Tokyo Congress in August 1991. The paper I read on that occasion appears now, with variations, as Chapter 9 of this book.

The staff at the London University Library and at the British Library were invariably helpful and as competent and kind as one might desire.

Giovanni Marchetti's 'green finger' with the computer was nothing short of magic and Keir Elam's precious linguistic suggestions offered a last-minute rescue. To both I am sincerely grateful.

Earlier versions of Chapters 8 and 9 have appeared in *The Year-book of English Studies* and in *The Journal of Medieval and Renaissance Studies* respectively, and an Italian version of Chapter 6 was published in a volume edited by Mariangela Tempera, *King John dal testo alla scena* (Bologna: CLUEB, 1994). I am grateful to the editors for permission to reproduce those parts of my articles which have not been substantially reshaped.

Finally, Filippo, Simone and Luca never complained about my long absences from home and the organisation of their *ménage à trois* left very little to be desired. What I most appreciated, however, was that they both did not and did, make me feel indispensable.

List of Abbreviations

CE   *Cahiers Elizabéthains*
ELH   *English Literary History*
ELR   *English Literary Review*
HT   *History and Theory*
MLR   *Modern Language Review*
PMLA *Publications of the Modern Language Association of America*
SQ   *Shakespeare Quarterly*
SS   *Shakespeare Survey*

Unless otherwise specified, all references to Shakespeare's plays are taken from the Arden editions.

Introduction

It is one of the generally accepted ideas concerning the reign of Queen Elizabeth I that the year 1588, with the defeat of the Spanish Armada, marked the end of a long nightmare and inaugurated a period of optimism characterised by a sudden surge of nationalistic feelings.

Historical generalisations are in a sense useful, in that they reduce otherwise complex issues to a manageable size. But, for this very reason, they contribute to producing and perpetuating stagnant views, which end up dominating our perception of the phenomena. This has certainly been the case with the Armada, which has long been associated in our historical imagination with two things: in the first place with a brilliant and incontrovertible victory and in the second with a sudden change, which is thought to have affected all aspects of national life and culture, particularly in the capital of the kingdom, the political heart of the nation.[1]

Among other things, the hagiographic picture of the Armada also affected for many years interpretations of the emergence of a theatrical genre, the history play, a fact which has generally been explained by the sense of optimism and unity and by the sudden wave of nationalism and patriotism that is said to have followed the defeat of the Spanish.[2] Although challenges to this view appeared from the 1940s on,[3] the idea that this victory was fundamental to the rise of the history play has been slow to lose its spell; though it is now commonly agreed that 'To suppose that the passion for history plays stemmed exclusively from national euphoria following defeat of the Spanish Armada in 1588 would be absurd.'[4]

Indeed, more recently, historians have begun to look more closely at the glorious achievement of the English fleet off Gravelines on 29 July; they have shown, for instance, that the outcome of the battle remained dubious for weeks even to those who had fought it and that a general sense of dejection followed that fatal day, especially among the crew, who realised much more clearly than anyone else that their efforts had only produced a partial victory. 'Most of the English sailors', Wernham suggests, 'were disappointed'; and he adds that 'part of the trouble was that all were a little dispirited,

1

and more than a little surprised, at their failure to destroy the Armada in battle'.[5] (Another cause of trouble was that the heroes of Gravelines waited for a long time to get the wages that they had so bravely earned.)

As regards the general enthusiasm of the population, we know that the 'spontaneous' response was – as happened in other circumstances – artfully orchestrated: carefully prepared propaganda had preceded the battle from the early spring, when news that Philip II was preparing to invade England with his army started to circulate. It was entrusted mainly to the parish churches, where prayers were read and where the parishioners were invited to join in imploring God's assistance. After news of the English victory became certain, the 'enthusiasm' was, again, officially induced by thanksgiving services aimed 'to marshall opinion and to interpret God's blessings as an overwhelming endorsement of the Elizabethan regime'.[6] While the nation celebrated, however, the heroes of Gravelines still wondered whether the Spanish might come back. Moreover, 'the navy's senior officers, especially Howard and Hawkyns, were struggling with the problems of sick and destitute sailors, and angrily pleading for supplies to feed them and money to pay them. They were not in a mood for self-congratulation. Nor was the country especially grateful for what the navy had done. Howard was criticized for the way he fought the battle, and for failing to destroy the armada.'[7]

But, above all, the effects of the victory were not as long-lasting as the success of the history plays, however ephemeral these may in the end have been as a literary genre. As Hurstfield argues,

> The memory of 1588 along with the Tilbury speech apparently had a more lasting effect on later generations than upon contemporaries who, when the immediate glory faded, still had to endure privation, inner conflict and a bloody struggle, a dreary, indecisive war of attrition. The conditions came increasingly to resemble, not St Crispin's day but, if we choose modern examples, the daily circumstances of 1917 or 1943.[8]

But challenging the traditional view of the effects of that victory also means undermining an argument that has been used to account for Shakespeare's initial steps in the theatrical trade, for it means reassessing the idea of his celebrative intent and conformist attitude. In the Armada scenario, the young man from the provinces, determined to make his living in the theatrical trade, is overwhelmed, on his arrival in London, by the enthusiastic atmosphere that followed the victory. He thus immediately seizes the chance to try out his dramatic skills on a subject of enormous general interest and topical import; he senses too that the audience's 'horizon of expectations' has recently brought the theme of national history into the foreground, and foresees that his first attempt at representing the nation's past will bring him commercial success and may even prove politically rewarding.[9] Moreover, if – as is probable – the young playwright's first appearance on a London stage was *The First Part of King Henry VI*, performed at the Rose on 3 March 1592, the picture may be further corroborated by the evidence of the play's theatrical success and therefore, indirectly, of the young man's flair for artistic and commercial affairs.

This scenario is very appealing, since it is tempting to use a well-established frame of events such as the Armada story in order to fill in, at least in part, the 'lost years' of Shakespeare's career. Therefore, any attempt to reassess the matter will mean expunging important traits from the portrait that some critics have painted and indeed cherished of the young provincial suddenly taken, on his first contact with the metropolis, with the opportunity to celebrate the regime, and so intent on becoming from the very start its accomplice. It should be stressed, however, that although the historical genre was perhaps the most short-lived one in the whole history of English drama, it was anything but ephemeral and short-lived within Shakespeare's career, since it accounted for almost a third of his known production (not to mention his possible collaboration on both *Sir Thomas More* and *Edward III*), and was subject to intense development for almost half his professional career, being finally taken up once again at its very end.

Whatever the reason, or reasons, that determined the writing of his first play, therefore, Shakespeare's interest in the historical past of England hardly has the appearance of something contingent; and even though a particular event or the general atmosphere may indeed have played a role in his choice of a historical subject, the fact is that he remained faithful to the genre and experimented with it more regularly than with any other of the dramatic forms that appear to have attracted his attention. But quite apart from this, it is simply very difficult to imagine any real celebratory intention behind his first plays. Indeed, as J. D. Cox has remarked, although the *Henry VI* plays were written immediately after the Armada, 'they are

extraordinarily bleak. Why the young playwright would commemor-
ate a great national victory with a penetrating and dispiriting analysis
of how England lost her French possessions and collapsed into civil
war is not clear.'[10]

Besides, the celebration of a particular event requires an immediate reaction and clarity of intention; and even if one were to accept
Tillyard's view of the first tetralogy, its celebrative conclusion in
Richard III was presumably not even projected immediately following the Armada victory, while no hint at that pacifying conclusion
could be gleaned from any of the *Henry VI* plays.[11]

Clearly, things must have been more complex than would be
suggested if we were simply to evoke a sudden awakening of
patriotic feelings. Rather than a single decisive event, it seems more
plausible to hypothesise a number of interacting factors – intentions, needs, desires, pressures and inducements – behind the in-
creased production of works on national history both inside and
outside the theatres in the 1590s; by the same token, it seems reasonable to seek a similar set of interacting factors in order to explain
the sudden demise of the genre after 1600.[12]

Discussing the 'increase in the emotional immediacy of the plays'
subject matter' that 'seduced playgoers between 1587 and the end
of the century' and the fact that in those years 'the mood was . . .
right for the drums, swordplay and noise which suited the larger
stages and the natural daylight of the open playhouses', Andrew
Gurr says that, whatever the reasons for the appearance of historical dramas, 'the minds of men in company at plays in the 1590s
needed stronger meat for their affections than the 1580s had given
them.'[13] As Tucker Brooke remarked, the wave of history plays
coincided with a period of difficulty for playwrights and managers:
the increase in the number of theatres, in fact, 'produced an abnormal
demand for new plays which continually threatened to outrun the
possible supply'.[14] Naturally, the commercial need to have new
plays written and produced may have suggested the new, almost
unexplored, source of intricate plots that national history offered.
But, above all, we should not overlook the fact that important political problems were much to the fore in those years, and that the
climate was, therefore, propitious for the discussion of public issues.
The exceptional importance that the regime attributed to the victory
over Catholic Spain, which was even presented as 'confirmation of
the special destiny reserved for God's Englishmen as the new "elect
nation" ',[15] shows that the Queen needed further legitimation of her

rule. Moreover, Elizabeth was ageing, and the need to avoid the conflicts that might derive from a gap in the succession was becoming more and more pressing.

But, although public issues may have been crucial in determining the history-play vogue, certain personal considerations and even contingent circumstances should also be taken into account. Thus, the very appearance of a shake-scene with a penchant for history on the London stage, the success of one particular performance before one particular audience, and the discovery, thanks to that particular performance, that national history might prove to be the 'strong meat' that the audience expected from theatrical entertainment, may have been among the immediate stimuli that led some dramatists to use the inexhaustible store of ready-made and easily accessible stories that the chronicles of England provided. Thus, a simple event may have played an important role within the network of needs and interests – whether they be social, political or commercial – that concurred to encourage the theatrical exploitation of political myths in those years. In this respect, the Armada script has no greater claim to truth than any other account, and therefore there is no compelling reason to accept the *a priori* view that Shakespeare showed political opportunism in choosing a national historical subject. On the contrary, there is ample room for different interpretations: we may, in particular, hypothesise that the young playwright had a genuine intellectual attraction towards history and towards the methods of truth-representation that it involves, and thus assume that the issues at which he tried his hand at the outset of his career were in fact among his abiding interests even before he arrived in London, interests which he would develop intensely over the years and which would be revived in one final endeavour at the closing of his career as a playwright.

But the choice of national history may also have been encouraged by the need for social validation and advancement, a kind of currency that playwrights were certainly in need of. Thus Nashe's comment on a play that was presumably the first part of *Henry VI*, his appreciation of the fact that it resuscitated 'brave *Talbot*, the terror of the French' and the encouraging estimate of 'the tears of ten thousand spectators at least, (at severall times)',[16] apart from providing a record (although it is difficult to say how reliable this is) of the enthusiastic reception of the play, appears to have been dictated principally by the need to defend playwrights and plays, especially when these dealt with the representation of England's past: a need that was certainly Nashe's concern when a few lines later he pronounces his defence of historical plays (by which he means those 'borrowed out of our English Chronicles'), saying that they 'shew the ill successe of treason, the fall of hastie climbers, the wretched end of vsurpers, the miserie of ciuill dissention, and how iust God is euermore in punishing of murther'.[17] After all, by the time Shakespeare wrote his first play, 'the drama still savors of idle and frivolous amusement; but history is joyfully hailed as an open-sesame to learning and culture, . . . a teacher of virtue and patriot-ism, and a stimulus to material and professional success'.[18]

However, as is shown by the very fact that Nashe needed to mount a defence, the topic was by no means a safe one: the choice of historical narratives, in fact, brought with it a number of risks.[19] Those risks were clear in the mind of John Hayward, who suffered imprisonment in 1600 and whose second edition of *The First Part of the Life and Raigne of King Henrie IIII* (the first edition had been published in 1599) was suppressed apparently because, having dedicated it to Essex, the author was accused of collusion with the Earl; but probably also because the story of the deposition of Richard II was notoriously a topic that much upset Elizabeth. Years later, in dedicating to Prince Charles his *Lives of the III Normans, Kings of England* (1613), Hayward reports a passage from a conversation he had had with Prince Henry that sounds like a comment on his personal ordeal:

> men might safely write of others in manner of a tale; but in manner of a history, safely they could not: because, albeit they should write of men long since dead, and whose posterity is clean worn out; yet some alive, finding themselves foul in those vices which they see observed, reproved, and condemned in others, their guiltiness maketh them apt to conceive, that, whatsoever the words are, the finger pointeth only at them.[20]

It is a fact that Shakespeare decided to start his theatrical adven-ture by tackling the hazardous narration of the darkest age of the public past of England. His plays spread knowledge of that age via what was the most effective, popular and intrinsically historical of representational media. To an audience that may have been com-posed, as recorded by Nashe, 'of ten thousand spectators at least, (at severall times)', he disclosed, or recalled, with the immediacy that only theatre can achieve, the darkest and crudest fragments of

that history, even the forbidden story of the deposition and killing
of King Richard II. Other playwrights of that period exploited the
political myths derived from the English chronicles, and some of
them even wrote good plays; but, certainly, Shakespeare's interest
in history shows a constancy and a consistency which has no parallel
in any of them. Yet only recently have Shakespeare's history plays
started to be considered also as contributions to the field of historiography, as phenomena which – although peculiar, because dramatised – should ultimately be associated with the practice of historical
exegesis. Larry Champion makes a general claim for the historical
plays written between 1580 and 1640, arguing that they 'form part
of a general movement toward what amounts to a new mode of
historical inquiry', less didactic and providentialist and less intent
on the propaganda of the Tudor regime.[21] But, although agreeing
with many of the assumptions of Champion's book, I cannot go
along with him in attributing equal historiographical import to all
the plays – Shakespearean and non-Shakespearean – of the period.[22]
Besides, I believe that the 'new historiography' which in certain
cases came from the playhouses, far from being part of a 'general
movement', remained unnoticed by historians and that, as was the
case with Machiavelli's realism and Bodin's idea of historiography
as a quasi-scientific enterprise, it did not influence the practice of
Tudor and early Stuart historiography. It is indicative of the greater
alertness of theatrical practices in seizing on and using intellectual
novelties that Machiavelli's doctrines had more influence on the
stage than on history books.

Arguing for Shakespeare's sense of the 'pastness of the past',
Holderness claims that in Shakespeare's history plays we find 'a
grasp of history more akin to the new historiography of the seventeenth century' than to either Christian providentialism or Italian
humanism, and even affirms that the novelty of Shakespeare's attitude towards history lies in his perception and communication of
'the uniqueness and disparity of other societies'.[23] However, Holderness seems to be more concerned with content and attitudes than
with methods and procedures. Michael Hattaway has suggested a
perspective that is nearer to my argument, connecting Shakespeare's
idea of history to his style – or styles – of writing. Commenting on
the *Henry VI* plays, Hattaway says that 'the variety of styles found
throughout the sequence . . . need not be taken as evidence of multi-
ple authorship and revision, but rather of perspectivism, a dramatic cross-examination from differing points of view, embodied in

different dramatic styles, of the issues raised and events enacted on the stage'.[24]

One word, in particular, clarifies the notion around which I have been trying to build my reading of Shakespeare's dramatised historiography. *Perspectivism*, in the rapid but perspicuous definition that follows the comma in Hattaway's text, is the feature that strikes me as the most conspicuous novelty in Shakespeare's history of England, and as the one which constitutes the dramatist's significant contribution – one that has hitherto failed to be acknowledged fully – to an indirect criticism of contemporary historical sources.

The same notion of perspectivism – or of what in other contexts has been called *contrariety* and more recently *polyphony* – may, of course, be used to describe the whole of Shakespeare's canon, and to qualify 'Shakespeare's habitual recognition of the irreducible complexity of things':[25] it is maybe little more than a different way of referring to the 'negative capability' that Keats attributed to Shakespeare.[26] In my view, however, perspectivism is to be understood as active criticism rather than scepticism or pessimism, and therefore as a sign of involvement rather than of aloofness. Clearly, the 'cross-examination' of political issues 'from differing points of view' was by no means simply a matter of style; it was, on the contrary, a daring enterprise which involved more than one risk.

In the pages that follow, my effort will be to show some of the many ways in which these risks were run.

Notes

1. J. E. Neale opens his account of the event with a sentence that even betrays emotion: 'There was a prophecy, long rife among Englishmen, that 1588 was to be a year of wonders. It proved to be the year of the Invincible Armada.' *Queen Elizabeth* (London: Jonathan Cape, 1934), p. 294.

2. Here is how F. E. Schelling explains the appearance – and disappearance – of history plays: 'The English Chronicle Play began with the tide of patriotism which united all England to repel the threatened invasion of Philip of Spain. It ebbed and lost its national character with the succession of James, an un-English prince, to the throne of Elizabeth.' *The English Chronicle Play* (New York and London: Macmillan, 1902), pp. 1–2. Certainly, the effects of that event on literature, both in England and Spain, cannot be overlooked. See, for recent discussions

of the topic, S. Onega, 'The Impact of the Spanish Armada on Elizabethan Literature', in J. Doyle and B. Moore (eds), *England and the Spanish Armada* (Canberra: ACT, 1990), pp. 177–95; and for Spanish literature, P. Gallagher and D. W. Cruickshank, 'The Armada of 1588 Reflected in Serious and Popular Literature of the Period', in Gallagher and Cruickshank (eds), *God's Obvious Design. Papers for the Spanish Armada Symposium, Sligo, 1988* (London: Thamesis Books, 1990), pp. 167–83.

3. Quoting C. Tucker Brooke's idea that Shakespeare's historical plays resulted from the 'triumphant exhilaration' which followed the victory (*The Tudor Drama* [New York: Houghton Mifflin, 1911], p. 299), L. B. Campbell remarks that 'with the exception of *Henry V* and perhaps *Henry VIII*, Shakespeare's plays were written, not about the admirable rulers of England and their times, but rather about those rulers who had sowed the wind and reaped the whirlwind'. *Shakespeare's Histories: Mirrors of Elizabethan Policy* (London: Methuen, 1980 [San Marino: The Huntington Library, 1947], p. 11). Tillyard stated that the Armada 'at most . . . encouraged a process already in full working'. *Shakespeare's History Plays* (Harmondsworth: Penguin, 1962 [London: Chatto and Windus, 1944]), p. 101.

4. R. Smallwood, 'Shakespeare's Use of History', in S. Wells (ed.), *The Cambridge Companion to Shakespeare Studies* (Cambridge: Cambridge University Press, 1986), pp. 143–62, 147.
   Only recently have the reasons for the sudden disappearance of historical drama been the object of discriminating critical attention (but the performance of history plays was not discontinued as completely as their writing). Leonard Tennenhouse attributes the decline of history plays, along with that of Petrarchan poetry and romantic comedy, to radical changes in the strategies deployed to idealise political authority. See 'Strategies of State and Political Plays: *A Midsummer Night's Dream, Henry IV, Henry V, Henry VIII*', in J. Dollimore and A. Sinfield (eds), *Political Shakespeare* (Manchester: Manchester University Press, 1985), pp. 109–28 and 'Rituals of State: History and the Elizabethan Strategies of Power', in *Power on Display. The Politics of Shakespeare's Genres* (New York and London: Methuen, 1986), pp. 72–101. Richard Helgerson attributes the shift in genre preferences and the change in the conditions of playing to the Essex revolt in 1601 and to the death of Elizabeth, but adds that 'how the particular changes are linked to one another, which are cause and which are effect . . . , are questions that lend themselves to no easy resolution'. *Forms of Nationhood. The Elizabethan Writing of England* (Chicago: University of Chicago Press, 1992), p. 198.

5. R. B. Wernham, *After the Armada. Elizabethan England and the Struggle for Western Europe* (Oxford: Clarendon Press, 1984), p. 2. Neale characterises the defeat of the Spanish as 'a disaster beyond expectation' (op. cit., p. 300).

6. D. Cressy, 'The Spanish Armada: Celebration, Myth and Memory', in Doyle and Moore (eds), op. cit., pp. 157–76, 161.

7. D. Howarth, *The Voyage of the Armada. The Spanish Story* (London: Collins, 1981), p. 239.

8.   J. Hurstfield, *The Illusion of Power in Tudor Politics* (London: The Athlone Press, 1979), p. 19.

9.   The notion of 'horizon of expectations' is discussed by H. R. Jauss, who argues for a rewriting of literary history as a history of the reception and influence of literary works. *Literaturgeschichte als Provokation der Literaturwissenschaft* (Universitäts-Druckerei GmbH, Konstanz, 1967); English transl., 'Literary History as a Challenge to Literary Theory', in *Toward an Aesthetic of Reception* (Minneapolis: University of Minnesota Press, 1982), pp. 3–45. The expression, however, was first circulated by H. G. Gadamer: *Wahrheit und Methode* (Tübingen: Mohr, 1965); English transl., *Truth and Method* (London: Sheed and Ward, 1975).

10.   *Shakespeare and the Dramaturgy of Power* (Princeton: Princeton University Press, 1989), p. 83. See also the opinion of M. Hattaway: 'I want to claim that at the beginning of his career Shakespeare was not a pillar of the establishment . . . but himself a radical.' 'Rebellion, Class Consciousness, and Shakespeare's *2 Henry VI*', CE XXXIII (1988), 13–22, p. 13.

11.   For Tillyard, the theme of the first tetralogy is that 'of order and chaos, of proper political degree and civil war, of crime and punishment, of God's mercy finally tempering his justice, of the belief that such had been God's way with England' (op. cit., pp. 200–1). On *Richard III* as a closing of the tetralogy Tillyard says that 'An Elizabethan audience would take the dramatist's final amen with a transport of affirmation' (ibid., p. 202). I do not intend to argue that Shakespeare was wholly unaffected by the pattern described by Tillyard: rather, I believe that that pattern coexists with other models. However, as Rossiter has argued, 'the Tudor myth system of Order, Degree, etc. was too rigid, too black-and-white, too doctrinaire and narrowly moral for Shakespeare's mind' and, therefore, 'while employing it as a FRAME, he had to undermine it, to qualify it with equivocations: to vex its applications with sly or subtle ambiguities', *Angel with Horns* (London: Longman, 1961), p. 59; see also, on the same point, pp. 44 and 54. However, although we may disagree with the doctrinaire monologism that Tillyard attributes to Shakespeare, we should consider that his book was the first work to direct our attention compellingly towards Shakespeare's history plays as a corpus of political texts. In fact, the prevailing opinion before the Second World War was still that of Pollard, for whom Elizabethan literature in general and Shakespeare in particular had nothing to do with politics. *The History of England from the Accession of Edward VI to the Death of Elizabeth, 1547–1603* (London: Longmans, Green and Co., 1905), p. 440.

12.   Lucia Folena argues that, although the change in representation and culture coincided with the accession of James Stuart, we should consider 'the establishment of a direct relationship of causality (the culture changed *because* power had changed hands) as at least suspicious, in its mechanical paleohistoricism, and possibly even susceptible of being reversed, since the transformation in representation could be seen as

having created the ideological conditions for a relatively painless dynastic transition.' *'Mirrours more than One'. Fables of Alterity in Renaissance Culture* (Padua: Unipress, 1990), p. 190, n. 1.

13. A. Gurr, *Playgoing in Shakespeare's London* (Cambridge: Cambridge University Press, 1987), pp. 132, 135. Emrys Jones, in turn, mentions the reprinting, in the years between 1587 and 1590, of a series of works (Holinshed's *Chronicles*, the translation of Dolce's *Giocasta, The Misfortunes of Arthur* and, more importantly, *Gorboduc*) that, he believes, contributed to the vogue. *The Origins of Shakespeare* (Oxford: Clarendon Press, 1977), pp. 23–4. The argument is, however, circular, since it does not explain the revival of interest in these works. F. E. Schelling, in fact, uses the same argument to support his idea that the history plays sprang from the patriotic feeling aroused by the Armada (op. cit., pp. 31–2).

14. Op. cit., p. 300.

15. D. Cressy, op. cit., p. 157.

16. T. Nashe, *Pierce Pennilesse His Supplication to the Divell* (1592), in *The Works of Thomas Nashe*, ed. R. B. McKerrow (London: Sidgwick & Jackson, 1910), p. 212.

17. Ibid., p. 213.

18. L. B. Wright, *Middle-class Culture in Elizabethan England* (Chapel Hill: University of North Carolina Press, 1935), p. 297.

19. A. Patterson remarks that 'Historiography, in the sixteenth and early seventeenth century, was no academic discipline but a matter of public interest', and recalls that 'the government regarded English historical materials as subject to its own control'. *Shakespeare and the Popular Voice* (Oxford: Blackwell, 1989), pp. 77–8. See also Patterson's earlier book, *Censorship and Interpretation* (Madison: University of Wisconsin Press, 1984).

20. Quoted by J. Manning (ed.), *The First and Second Parts of The Life and Raigne of King Henrie IIII* (London: Royal Historical Society, Camden Fourth Series, vol. 42, 1991), p. 1. This edition contains Hayward's announced but unpublished continuation of *The Life and Raigne*. Two accounts providing different interpretations of Hayward's story in connection with Essex's rebellion are in Mervyn James, *Society, Politics and Culture* (Cambridge: Cambridge University Press, 1986), pp. 416–65 and Leeds Barroll, 'A New History for Shakespeare and His Time', *SQ* XXXIX (1988), 441–64.

21. *'The Noise of Threatening Drum': Dramatic Strategy and Political Ideology in Shakespeare and the English Chronicle Plays* (Newark: University of Delaware Press, 1990), p. 130.

22. Among these may be mentioned *The Famous Victories of King Henry V* (1586), *The Misfortunes of Arthur* by Thomas Hughes (with Bacon, Trotte, Fulbeck, 1588), *The Reign of King Edward the Third* (Marlowe?, Kyd?, Greene?, revised by Shakespeare?, 1590), *The Life and Death of Jack Straw* (1591), *The Troublesome Reign of John King of England* (1591), *The Famous Chronicle of King Edward the First* by George Peele (1591), *The Troublesome Reign and Lamentable Death of King Edward the Second* by Christopher Marlowe (1592), *Woodstock* (1592), *The True Tragedy of*

Richard the Third (1594), *Locrine* (1594), *Sir Thomas More* (1595, by Munday, Dekker, Chettle, Heywood, Shakespeare), *Sir John Oldcastle* (1599) and *Thomas Lord Cromwell* (1600). The datings of all these plays are uncertain, although they all appear to have been written between 1586 and 1600. References are from A. Harbage, *Annals of English Drama: 975–1700* (London: Routledge, 1989), 3rd edn, revised by Sylvia Stoler Wagonheim.

23. G. Holderness, 'Prologue: "The Histories" and History', in G. Holderness, N. Potter and J. Turner, *Shakespeare: The Play of History* (London: Macmillan, 1988), p. 18. Holderness has returned to this issue in a recent book, *Shakespeare Recycled. The Making of Historical Drama* (New York and London: Harvester, 1992).

24. M. Hattaway, 'Introduction' to *The Second Part of King Henry VI* (Cambridge: Cambridge University Press, 1991), p. 1. Tillyard wrote that the style of *1 Henry VI* is 'hesitant and varied' and argued that 'if a young man attempts a big thing, a thing beyond his years, he will imitate others when his own invention flags' (op. cit., p. 161).

25. N. Rabkin, 'Either/Or: Responding to *Henry V*', in *Shakespeare and the Problem of Meaning* (Chicago: University of Chicago Press, 1981), pp. 33–62, 61. M. M. Reese, in what is one of the first substantial correctives to Tillyard's view, spoke of 'many-sidedness' of vision and of 'two-eyed scrutiny'. *The Cease of Majesty* (London: Edward Arnold, 1961), p. viii.

26. On Shakespeare's 'negative capability' in relation with political issues, see A. Serpieri, 'La retorica della politica in Shakespeare', *Il piccolo Hans* XIII (1977), 111–36.

Part I
History 'with Parted Eye'

1

Meaning, the Author and the Reader

We need more light to find your meaning out.
Love's Labour's Lost, V.ii.21

Owing to their relationship with reality, political texts almost inevitably raise questions about the source of the production of meaning and about the author's attitude towards the issues raised and the events reported. Indeed, however much it is dismissed, covered up or even ostracised with theoretical arguments, the issue of intentionality tends to emerge in all critical readings, if only as a perspective that the critic intends to correct or exclude.

When openly stated and discussed, the issue of the author's stance and opinions in Shakespeare's histories has produced an extremely wide and varied range of evaluations: from Tillyard's idea that Shakespeare's history plays straightforwardly supported the monarchy's interests by contributing to the celebration of the Tudor myth, to the recent evaluations of the plays by new historicists and cultural materialists as providing the same kind of support, albeit via the sort of moderate criticism that they see as serving the ends of the regime, to the few readings that have striven to satisfy what Stephen Greenblatt has called 'a perennial longing since Romanticism to discover that all great artists have allied themselves, if only indirectly or unconsciously, with the oppressed and revolutionary masses'.[1]

However, ever since authors became unwelcome guests at the great feast of literary criticism, the issue of aims and attitudes has almost turned into an ideological taboo, and uneasiness with such notions as 'author', 'meaning', 'intentions' or, worse, 'opinions', has become an uncomfortable and encumbering companion to literary reflection.

Long before Stephen Greenblatt set up the issue in terms associated with the cultural poetics approach, various forms of author deletion, albeit formulated with diverse aims, had been theorised and absorbed by literary scholars. Wimsatt's indictment of the 'intentional

15

fallacy', the formalists' notion of art-works as self-contained artifacts, Booth's idea of the 'implied author', the logocentric claims of
the 'nouvelle critique' which consigned positivistic biographism to
the past, Eco's idea of the 'Model Author' meant as a set of 'circumstances of enunciation', reader-response theories, the prescriptions
of narratology, are all experiences that, however different in kind
and aim, have contributed to the dissolution of the authorial per-
sona and removed from the real person the responsibility for the
production of meaning and for intentions, reallocating it among a
number of diverse, even less stable factors – the text, the cultural
context, the reader, the horizon of expectations, and so on.

The hesitancy with which we pronounce the names of those who
are supposed to have written the works that we read has brought
us to the point where we put inverted commas around those names,
so that the sole authority to which we are inclined to attribute 'intentions' has become the text, obviously seen as just one of the
elements of the context (but, especially in certain cases, awareness
of the text's instability makes it difficult even to refer to textual
objects with full confidence).

There are, indeed, certain names that are less easily pronounced
than others: the more the cult of a certain author's personality has
developed over the centuries, the more we hesitate to mention the
object of this cult. That Shakespeare is 'Shakespeare', and occasionally 'Shakespeares',[2] is so widely understood that no explicit inverted
commas are now needed to stress the idea (although it may be
doubted whether in our private, uncontrolled and unmonitored
readings we invariably rescind all contracts with authors or with
the image we have of them).

It appears, however, that awareness of this issue has not made
things any easier for us: various forms of retrieval as diverse, in
fact, as the forms of deletion, have appeared in various contexts.
Thus, the author has reappeared as a theoretical construct, as an
implied strategy, as an arranger and organiser, or simply as the
(unconscious?) vehicle of ideology, of cultural and social demands,
pressures and constraints; as an entity, in other words, to which we
can attribute, though once again in inverted commas and in a less
personal and private way than was the case in the biographical
tradition, intentions, aims and stances; and even biographism has
made its reappearance on the stage of literary criticism.[3]

A few critics seem to consider this issue as preliminary to the
treatment of their subject. Introducing his book on *Shakespeare's*

Dramatic Transactions, Michael Mooney makes his purpose clear: 'Indeed, one of my intentions is to persuade readers that we can begin to write about authorial intention and communal effect';[4] Holderness shows awareness of the impediments created by the disappearance of the author and of authorial intentionality, which 'render impossible any straightforward definition of what "the author" "meant" '. He declares that it would be unwise 'completely to surrender . . . the genuine possibility that some kind of authorial "mastery" shaped those texts, and shaped them deliberately to particular ends' and concludes with a timid return to an authorial principle which 'is in fact "Shakespeare", the *inferred* author; a volatile, flexible, changing construction, engendered, and constantly reborn and rewritten, by the plays'.[5] More recently, Richard Wilson has argued that 'the logical end of historicism is the nature of the author, not indeed as the owner of meaning beloved by nineteenth-century literary biography, but as a cultural construct determined by the representational practices of a particular historical era';[6] and Stanley Fish affirmed that 'we have not done away with intention and biography but merely relocated them'. Reading, Fish affirms, is always biographical reading, only the 'sources and agencies' may have different specifications.[7]

One of the most explicit returns to Shakespeare, the author, and to his intentions is to be found in Annabel Patterson's book *Shakespeare and the Popular Voice*. As Patterson states in the 'Foreword', her book 'calmly reinstates certain categories of thought that some have declared obsolete: above all the concept of authorship' and that of 'intentions'. 'It is disingenuous, at best', Patterson says, 'to substitute for the concept "Shakespeare", someone who certainly existed (however inadequate our biographical account of him), the concept of "the text", something which, thanks to the revisionist bibliography of the past two decades, we now recognize *never* existed as a stable entity.' To this, Patterson adds a few lines of censure of 'the avant-garde proscriptions against talking about authors and intentions' and concludes: 'I have no difficulty in positing Shakespeare as a writer whose intentions, if never fully recoverable, are certainly worth debating.'[8]

Developing her project of 'local' reading, Leah Marcus affirms that 'we need to bring back, among many other methodological tools of the old historicism, an idea called the Author's Intent or putative intentionality. It is a construct, of course, and always has been. . . . But it is a very useful construct, particularly when it is demoted from its traditionally privileged position as the overriding determinant of meaning.'[9]

But even certain forms of author dissolution, displacement or fragmentation seem to derive from the sense of a lack that the formalists' version of the cancellation of the author had produced. Indeed, the transposition of the author into one of the agents of 'social energy' is not so much a dissolution as a retrieval under different conditions and in different terms.

Stephen Greenblatt's catalogue of abjurations opens with two points (1. There can be no appeals to genius as the sole origin of the energies of great art; 2. There can be no motiveless creation) that encapsulate the substance of the problem. That 'individuals are themselves the product of collective exchange' and that the motives for creation are to be found in various kinds of exchanges and currencies, serves to specify the relationship between the two statements; that 'there can be no autonomous artifacts' marks the distance between cultural poetics and formalism; while that 'there can be no expression without an origin and an object, a *from* and a *for*',[10] evokes that variegated field of literary studies which have stressed the relevance of reader-response and of social demand as a source of artistic production.[11]

In the same essay, Greenblatt traces his theoretical journey back to 'the close-grained formalism' of his literary training, a journey that appears to have developed independently from other experiences, mainly European, which may well have been shaped by a similar tension and directed towards similar ends but which ended up by being indiscriminately pigeonholed in the rubric of structuralism – namely, as part of what present theoretical trends, especially in the Anglo-American context, see as the expression of reactionary positions. But structuralism, or whatever it was that existed before post-structuralism, not only produced ideas that are worth recalling but also, and perhaps above all, brought a radical liberation of literary studies, and so rendered possible an experimental attitude that would have been quite unthinkable without that break. It also, I believe, laid the foundations for the appearance of a more resourceful kind of historicism.

Different cultural traditions (not unaffected by different national editorial and academic policies) have all developed similar issues, expressing a similar interest in a more complex and comprehensive kind of historicism. In European contexts, the text–context coalescence, or continuity, has been elaborated principally on the basis of ideas borrowed from mature developments in semiotics, from prag-matics and from textual studies.[12] Some of these issues are connec-ted with the historical reappraisal of meaning and the author.

Reacting to the eminently logocentric statements by Jean-Louis Baudry, who argues that the author is only one of the particular manifestations of the general *écriture*,[13] Marcello Pagnini, in an essay on literary enunciation, goes back to a set of arguments which he developed earlier in his book *Pragmatica della letteratura*.[14] Arguing for some form of 'presence' of the empirical subject (author), at least as regards those elements which the subject absorbs 'from the cultural systems that determined its format', Pagnini suggests that we may retrieve the subject in the form of an 'epochal and cultural subject', that is to say, as that part of the individual which comes 'from the cultural systems that determined its shaping': what can and should be grasped, in other words, is 'the subject as historical model'. It is true, Pagnini argues, that the information which comes from a given culture tends to shape the subject according to its prescriptions; however, individuals are not only the 'objects', but also the 'subjects' of history: historical mutations, in other words, are a combined effect of immanent material forces and of the individ-ual's reactions to the current cultural system: 'The set of normative systems of a given epoch and the set of textual behaviours adum-brate together, dialectically, the image – distinct enough, one would think – of an "author".'[15]

The statement that 'individuals are themselves the product of collective exchange' (Greenblatt) is not far from the idea that 'cultural systems control the subject's formation' (Pagnini) or that the author is 'expression and interpreter of cultural codes' (Segre). Although different from the point of view of the kind of language used and from that of the conceptual frame outlined, these essays all appear to give expression to basically the same tensions. In particular, just as Greenblatt tends not to disown the experience of formalism, Pagnini and Segre do not repudiate that of structuralism and proto-semiotics; on the contrary, they seem to argue that it is precisely against the background of those experiences that a new hold on the author and on the historicity of the problem of meaning can be elaborated.[16]

In what can be considered a concise, early manifesto of cultural poetics, Greenblatt explains the shift from the old to the new his-toricism while, once again, declaring the centrality of the experi-ence of formalism even in a reshaping of historical enquiry: 'The

earlier historicism tends to be monological; that is, it is concerned
with discovering a single political vision, usually identical to that
said to be held by the entire literate class or indeed the entire population', while the new historical practice 'challenges the assumptions
that guarantee a secure distinction between "literary foreground"
and "political background" or, more generally, between artistic production and other kinds of social production'.[17]

However, the construction of contexts remains a thorny problem.
Basic questions about the elements that may, or should, be pertinently considered as constituting the context have been given
a variety of answers. Greenblatt's suggestion that we look at the
'borders' of cultural practices and Dollimore's plea for the 'marginalised and subordinate of Elizabethan and Jacobean culture'[18] have
occasionally been challenged for submerging the canonical texts 'in
a sea of pamphlets, contemporary memoirs, biographies, travel accounts, letters, court records, household accounts, marriage manuals,
and public speeches',[19] especially since the reading of those marginal texts is ultimately aimed at shedding light on those textual
practices that occupy the centre-stage of Elizabethan and Jacobean
culture.

The task is rendered more arduous by the presence and weight,
in any interpretative enterprise and in any attempt to recapture
historical contexts, of the reader's own text; the awareness of different types of cultural conditioning in the way we construct our fantasies about the past poses an alternative: should one strive to cancel
one's own text or should one, on the contrary, use it to advantage?
Indeed, one of the questions which arise for the reader of Shakespeare's history plays concerns precisely the way in which he himself resolved this aporia, how he dealt with the pressure of cultural
conditioning: was he, when writing about the past of his country,
enquiring into the historical contexts and perceiving and presenting
them as alien to his own, or was he 'adapting' those past events to
the interpretative needs of the present? The remark of Graham
Holderness that from Shakespeare's history plays there emerges a
new grasp of the otherness of different societies, somewhat mod-
ified by the statement that in his historical dramas 'events and problems of the fifteenth century are addressed via the beliefs of the
sixteenth',[20] is an acknowledgement of the fact that the choice between cancelling or foregrounding one's own historical text was
also, inevitably, the choice that confronted Shakespeare when he
was writing about the history of his country. In this respect, the

critic's task when dealing with those texts is similar to the play-wright's: in both kinds of enquiry, temporal and cultural displace-ment, the interpolation of texts of a different nature, the weight of the historiographical and critical tradition, the pressures and condi-tioning effects exercised by events, tend to defer indefinitely our grasp on the final object, especially when it has to be searched for outside the world of written texts, in the fleeting world of 'facts'.

Certainly, these are the contradictions which perturb all historio-graphical practice; but at certain times in the critical afterlife of recorded intellectual production, the kind of transactions taking place inside a given interpretative community have tended – wrongly, I believe – to eliminate one or the other of these contrary impulses. During the last decade, there has been a tendency to affirm the idea that the only kind of non-conservative historicism – indeed the only kind of reliable historicism – is the one which tends to interpolate the reader's historical and ideological filters. Moreover, the theoret-ical consciousness of the many transactions which make up texts and of the many tensions which are at work in cultural contexts has produced intimidating instructions which, if taken literally, might rule out any possibility of description and even reading of texts. One of these statements prescribes that 'analysis must concern itself not only with the contextual and contingent history bearing upon the originating moment of a text's production, but also with the subsequent history of that text's strategic mobilization and ideo-logical incorporation by different cultural forces in different social formations'.[21]

My own position is that we should acknowledge, and even ex-ploit, the contradictions which are inevitably connected with any historical enquiry; thus, although I have tried to keep in mind the precept formulated by Gadamer whereby we should constantly strive not to superimpose hastily our expectations on the past, I cannot altogether avoid the possible contamination of an *a priori* intention, namely, the desire to shelter Shakespeare, the intellectual of his time, from the too easily pronounced charge of being a cham-pion of the *status quo*. As regards the construction or reconstruction of contexts, this has been carried out bearing in mind that the rela-tionship one intends to establish between texts, events or problems of a different nature should be immediately intelligible; and since the phenomenon I am considering is anything but marginal, I have tried to connect it with what I believe to be the most influential contemporary texts that have some relevance to the topics discussed:

the chronicles and other source materials, treatises on historiography, war treatises, the libels and tracts on the abuses of the theatre and defences of plays and players, the contemporary works in which such social, political and institutional realities as law, justice, vagrancy, witchcraft and so on are discussed; and those public statements that have seemed to me to be connected to the issues discussed; to these one obviously has to add the corpus of contemporary non-Shakespearean historical dramas, a most instructive although hardly entertaining reading. A context for discussion, evoked here and there, is that provided by the debate that has shaped the ideas of history and of history-writing in our century and that has given explicit formulation to issues that are presumably present pre-theoretically in the historiographical practice of all times. Obviously, what critical afterlife I have been able to tackle and thought fit to converse with, is acknowledged in the text and in the notes.[22]

All this, I am well aware, does not amount to a guarantee regarding the reconstruction of the author as historical subject and of the various cultural impulses which contributed to his formation. However, as Carlo Ginzburg argues, historical knowledge is always indirect, presumptive, circumstantial and based on a conjectural paradigm whose rigour is ineluctably flexible and where intuition, although it does not guarantee objective reconstruction, plays a decisive role;[23] and, indeed, there are ways in which Shakespeare's historical texts speak for themselves and to some extent for their author, although more through suggestion than through direct evidence. To our intuition they suggest, in the first place, that, although no reading of the history plays can demonstrate a subversive attitude in their author, the opposite stance finds even less support in the texts. Besides, if hypotheses about the author's opinions on the historical events, past as well as contemporary, are bound to remain a matter of speculation, the texts, on the contrary, are explicit in revealing their author's methods and procedures.

A study of the way in which he manipulated his historical sources, for instance, may help to settle, again on an intuitive basis, the much-debated issue of whether or not it was Shakespeare who invented the historical genre in drama. The answer we give to this question depends of course on the meaning we assign to the word *invention*. When we say that he invented a genre, we obviously do not mean that he did not use sources – dramatic or other; but we cannot base our arguments on chronological priority either. Even if the chronological priority of non-Shakespearean texts were to be convincingly demonstrated, in fact, this would not be sufficient on its own to indicate the prior *invention* of a new genre, unless, that is, the novelty were thought to reside in the simple choice of national history as a subject-matter for plays.[24] Sources there were, of course, but they were such as might simply yield basic information about plots and characters rather than constitute a real model to imitate: with occasional exceptions, the design of the chronicles was loose, their narration of facts was paratactic and undramatic, stylistic inventiveness was lacking, their linguistic rendering was dull and uniform, their way of producing historical explanations was through accumulation and contiguity, their relationship to tradition conformist.[25] Moreover, nothing better than compliance with the official political theories could be expected from the chroniclers.

To some of these biases Shakespeare may have subscribed, others he may have disagreed with or simply disregarded; or, rather, he made his characters subscribe to them, disagree with them or disregard them; others, again, he may have added, as suggested either by his own opinions or by the kind of political perspective that he wanted his characters to assume. But, from the very start, he abandoned the normal undifferentiated, monologic, chronological, cumulative, unmarked presentation of events; on the contrary, in each of his plays he focused on specific political problems, substituting a causal for a moral concatenation of events. His main contribution to the historiography of his time consisted, therefore, in practising a problem-oriented, multivocal kind of historiography that probed into events in depth rather than in extension.[26] My claim, in the last analysis, is that some hints about Shakespeare's political attitude may be gleaned if one enquires into the representational and presentational modes that he elaborated for the staging of English history.

And so we again touch on the issue of meaning and the author, this time with a question which concerns the way in which these are inscribed in a dramatic text. As Raymond Williams observed, criticism often makes the mistake of isolating 'speeches by particular characters as Shakespeare's own essential beliefs';[27] certainly, in Shakespeare's case, this common error has been one of the main sources of the charge of antipopulism that has been pronounced against him. Indeed, the question of *whose* meaning it is that we encounter in a text – and in dramatic texts in particular – is a thorny problem, while we may be more confident about the separate issue of *what* meaning; in fact, even assuming the fundamental complexity and ambiguity of certain texts, we should acknowledge that the liberty of the act of reading has limits that, as Eco affirms, 'coincide with the rights of the text';[28] and that, as Holderness has remarked, 'all readings, whatever their ideological tendencies, must observe the disciplined frame of reference, must inhabit the constrained area of meaning given by the text, if they are to remain in any way committed to the text as a category'.[29]

Thus, albeit timidly, we have started to remove the inverted commas from both meaning and the author, for the effort not to bypass the *intentio operis* might be productive also as concerns the recovery of the traces that the author leaves in a text, namely, of the *intentio auctoris*, at least as concerns that part of a text's meaning that gives information about its arranger.[30] In some treatments, the issue of the indiscriminate liberty of reading is even presented as a moral dilemma and as determining the necessity to 'restrain a certain hermeneutic libertinage'.[31]

Seen in this perspective, Shakespeare the Author becomes a set of principles and choices about the way in which true stories of the past that concern the public life of his country, past as well as present, may be conveyed to a variegated audience in such a way as to reach all the sectors of the playhouse and be judged interesting, comprehensible and pleasurable. This person exists in his texts; and although he may appear unwilling to state his opinions, he is willing to reveal his methods of truth-representation and the secrets of his trade. All the historians of Shakespeare's time had precepts to suggest and views and convictions (almost invariably conformist) to air about how history-writing should be practised. Shakespeare (no inverted commas) read those works – in some cases we know for certain that he did, in others it seems at least possible – and the declarations of principles, intentions and methods that they contained. But he was a playwright, and had to find his own way of doing things. Ultimately, then, his historiographical method may derive from the way in which the necessities of the theatrical medium interact with his use and misuse of the sources of his plays.

My concern, in the following pages, will be to discern the way in which Shakespeare faced, and solved, the problem of transmitting the sense of an alien reality, of 'conveying lost life', while at the same time profiting from 'the inevitable pressures of contingency' (Greenblatt); in other words, I shall investigate his exploration of the possibilities (and limits) of historiography, his dramatic rendering of those possibilities and, ultimately, the kind of historiographical perspective that his practice might have contributed to creating if contemporary English historians had been ready to capture its novelty.

But to do this, we must first become familiar with the kind of attitude he found in contemporary historiography – with the opportunities it offered and the constraints it imposed.

Notes

1. S. Greenblatt, 'Murdering Peasants', in S. Greenblatt (ed.), *Representing the English Renaissance* (Berkeley: University of California Press, 1988), pp. 1–29, 11.

2. B. Hodgdon speaks of 'several different "Shakespeares", each an altered, provisional state of what First Folio's title page calls "The True Originall Copies"'. *The End Crowns All. Closure and Contradiction in Shakespeare's History* (Princeton: Princeton University Press, 1991), p. 3. The politics of refutation by quotation marks and its assumptions has been energetically challenged by Richard Levin. Among the words that Levin lists as having been encountered in quotation marks in recent criticism are 'author', 'intentions' and, of course, 'Shakespeare'; see 'The Poetics and Politics of Bardicide', *PMLA* CV (1990), 491–504.

3. A revaluation of biography is in books like the one edited by W. H. Epstein, *Contesting the Author* (West Lafayette: Purdue University Press, 1991). S. Burke starts a discussion of this issue recalling the way in which the discovery of Paul de Man's wartime collaborationist articles, a biographical element concerning one of the main deniers of biographism, ironically reinstated the traditional categories of author-centred criticism. After the discovery of those writings, Burke says, 'De Man's denial of biography, his ideas of autobiography as de-facement, have come to be seen not as disinterested theoretical statements, but as sinister and meticulous acts of self-protection.' *The Death and Return of the Author. Criticism and Subjectivity in Barthes, Foucault and Derrida* (Edinburgh: University of Edinburgh Press, 1992), p. 2.

4. *Shakespeare's Dramatic Transactions* (Durham: Duke University Press, 1990), p. XIII.

5. G. Holderness, 'Prologue: "The Histories" and History', p. 16.

6. *Will Power. Essays on Shakespearean Authority* (London: Harvester Wheatsheaf, 1993), p. 18

7. 'Biography and Intention', in Epstein (ed.), op. cit., pp. 9–16, 13, 14.

8. A. Patterson, *Shakespeare and the Popular Voice*, pp. 4–5.

9. L. Marcus, *Puzzling Shakespeare. Local Readings and Its Discontents* (Berkeley: University of California Press, 1988), pp. 41–2.

10. S. Greenblatt, 'The Circulation of Social Energy', in *Shakespearean Negotiations* (Oxford: Clarendon Press, 1988), pp. 1–20, 12.

11. Various attempts have been made to qualify the *from* and the *for* of literary expressions, starting from the late sixties. These all, however diverse, share an interest in the description of the mechanics of cultural formations, and the effort to combine what the formalists (Sklovskij, in particular) called 'the literary series' with the historical series. The Konstanz school, particularly H. R. Jauss, produced an esthetics of reception precisely as the interrelation of a 'from' and a 'for', namely, viewing literary products as responses to social demands. Rezeptionsästhetik had, therefore, the merit of formulating the problem of meaning in relational terms. The more prolific Tartu school (especially Juri M. Lotman) put forward a composite description of the mechanisms of culture starting from a semiotic (informational) standpoint, viewing cultural formations as '*nonhereditary memory of the community*, a memory expressing itself in a system of constraints and prescriptions' (Ju. M. Lotman and B. A. Uspenskij, 'O semioticeskom mekanizme kul'tury', in *Trudy po znakovym sistemam*, V [1971], 144–76; English transl., 'On the Semiotic Mechanism of Culture', *New Literary History* IX [1978], 211–32, p. 213).

12. 'Philology', C. Segre argues, 'asserts the function of the sender, not as an isolated subject, but as the member of a cultural community, as the expression and interpreter of cultural codes'. *Semiotica filologica* (Turin: Einaudi, 1979), p. 20. Here and elsewhere, translations from works not available in English are mine.

13. J.-L. Baudry, 'Ecriture, fiction, idéologie', in *Théorie d'ensemble* (Paris: Seuil, 1968), pp. 127–47. Baudry writes that 'le sujet, cause de l'écriture, s'évanouit et l'auteur, l' "écrivain", avec lui' (p. 136).

14. Palermo: Sellerio, 1980; English transl., *The Pragmatics of Literature* (Bloomington: Indiana University Press, 1987).

15. M. Pagnini, 'Saggio sulla enunciazione letteraria', in *Semiosi. Teoria ed ermeneutica del testo, letterario* (Bologna: Il Mulino, 1988), pp. 31–55, 39, 40. The essay was first published in 1986. C. Segre argued that the absence of the author is 'a brilliant *jeu d'esprit*'. 'Discorso', *Enciclopedia*, vol. IV (Turin: Einaudi, 1978), pp. 1056–84, 1081.

16. Stanley Fish bases his defence of the author's meaning on the distinction between sentence meaning and speaker's meaning which has long been familiar to pragmalinguistics, claiming that 'there is no such thing as a meaning that is specifiable *apart* from the contextual circumstances of its intentional production' ('Biography', p. 11).

17. S. Greenblatt (ed.), *The Power of Forms in the English Renaissance* (Norman: Pilgrim Books, 1982), p. 6. The claim formulated in 1968 by Wilbur Sanders and his critique of what we would now call 'old historicism' was not dissimilar. Sanders complains about 'the imposition of a static, schematic conception of the major epochs of our literature', and particularly about the fact that 'our conceptions of the Elizabethans has been codified for us into an "orthodoxy" ' *The Dramatist and the Received Idea* (Cambridge: Cambridge University Press, 1968), pp. 1–2.

18. J. Dollimore, 'Introduction. Shakespeare, Cultural Materialism and the New Historicism', in J. Dollimore and A. Sinfield (eds), *Political Shakespeare*, p. 6.
19. R. Bushnell, *Tragedies of Tyrants. Political Thought and Theater in the English Renaissance* (Ithaca: Cornell University Press, 1990), p. x.
20. 'Prologue: "The Histories" and History', p. 19. Holderness reaffirms this idea in *Shakespeare Recycled*.
21. G. Holderness, *Shakespeare Recycled*, p. 42.
22. As far as textual problems are concerned, somewhat regrettably I only occasionally pause to justify the choice of a particular reading. However, if I have decided to rely on current editions, it is not through lack of awareness of the importance of the text one uses for interpretation, but because I am convinced that dealing with textual problems is an activity which requires the highest specific competence. It is certainly to be hoped that 'criticism' will eventually become fully aware of textual issues and methods; but the traditional separation of the two activities is a very longstanding one and cannot suddenly be turned into a generalised double competence. In other words, as someone said, 'whereof one cannot speak, thereof one must be silent'.
23. 'Spie. Radici di un paradigma indiziario', in *Miti emblemi spie* (Turin: Einaudi, 1986 [1979]), pp. 158–209. English transl., 'Morelli, Freud and Sherlock Holmes', *History Workshop* IX (1980), 5–36 and in U. Eco and T. A. Sebeok (eds), *The Sign of Three* (Bloomington: Indiana University Press, 1983).
24. Equally insufficient are arguments discussing such formal features as genre peculiarities. The most conspicuous effort in the direction of genre definition to date is D. Scott Kastan's book *Shakespeare and the Shapes of Time* (Hanover: University Press of New England, 1982). Kastan directs the attention to the shaping of time in the history plays as a genre feature, arguing that the 'unique and determinate shape' that time assumes in those plays 'emerges organically from the playwright's sense of the shape of history itself' (p. 41). While, however, 'the recognition of the continual pressure of time' seems relevant in distinguishing the history plays from 'the merely episodic play . . . in which events [are] related sequentially rather than causally' (p. 55), it seems insufficient as a criterion for distinguishing history plays from any tightly constructed play. Years ago, I tried similar arguments (mainly causality, serialisation, and the connection of events) with results that now seem to me equally unsatisfactory (P. Pugliatti, 'The History Play as Genre', *Il confronto letterario* I [1984], 29–52).
25. There is a tendency to revaluate Holinshed's *Chronicles* – certainly Shakespeare's most important source – as less conformist in attitude and more varied in style than most of the Tudor chronicles. As regards Holinshed's attitude, I find this difficult to grasp, owing to its extreme eclecticism; while as regards the book's style, I fully agree with G. K. Hunter: 'In his dedication to Burghley Holinshed says that the reading of his volumes will "daunt the vicious" – I find that the reading daunts nearly everyone' ('Truth and Art in History Plays',

SS XLII [1990], 15–24, p. 18). Indeed, reading extensively from the English chronicles is an exhausting experience which leaves a distinct impression of conformity and endless repetition.

26. The same cannot be said of most contemporary political plays. A play like *The Life and Death of Jack Straw*, although dramatically efficacious, works in only one direction, that of convincing the audience of the courage of the young king and of the *unnaturalness* of the rebels and of their claims (the word *unnatural*, applied to the rebels and their action, occurs in the play an unnatural number of times). A different claim might be advanced for a later play like *The Chronicle History of Perkin Warbeck* by John Ford (1633), a more mature and complex analysis of rebellion.

27. 'Afterword', in Dollimore and Sinfield (eds), *Political Shakespeare*, pp. 231–9, 231. Tillyard touches upon the same issue (a common mistake in drama criticism): 'When . . . I say that *Richard III* is a very religious play, I want to be understood as speaking of the play and not of Shakespeare', op. cit., p. 104.

28. *I limiti dell'interpretazione* (Milan: Bompiani, 1990); English transl., *The Limits of Interpretation* (Bloomington: Indiana University Press, 1990), pp. 6–7. Curiously enough Eco, who gave currency to reader-response criticism with his book *Lector in fabula* (Milano: Bompiani, 1979); English transl., *The Role of the Reader* (Bloomington: Indiana University Press, 1979), has recently affirmed that 'in the course of the last decades, the rights of interpreters have been overstressed'. 'Interpretation and History', in S. Collini (ed.), *Interpretation and Overinterpretation* (Cambridge: Cambridge University Press, 1992), pp. 23–43, 23. The same issue was developed by Georg Gadamer in Part II of his *Wahrheit und Methode*, where he argues that meaning cannot be understood in an arbitrary way.

29. G. Holderness, *Shakespeare Recycled*, pp. 37–8. William Dodd argues for the presence, in a text, of strategies tending to channel the possible interpretations of virtual receivers. Against the idea of the utter relativity of meaning in texts, Dodd concludes that texts have a predetermined 'salience threshold' which 'controls the experience of the reader (and hence, potentially, of the spectator)'. '*Richard II*, i critici, Nahum Tate e la resistenza del testo', in A. Marzola (ed.), *L'altro Shakespeare* (Milano: Guerini, 1992), pp. 81–113, 104. For arguments against extreme theories of misreading, see M. Pagnini, 'La conoscenza del testo', in *Semiosi*, 77–100.

30. U. Eco, '*Intentio lectoris*. The State of the Art', in *The Limits of Interpretation*, 44–63. In a review article of Eco's *The Limits*, M. Pagnini argues for the necessity of establishing, in connection with texts, an *intentio temporis*. 'Argini contro la deriva', in *L'indice dei libri del mese* V (1990), 20–1, p. 20.

31. M. Pagnini, ibid.

2

The Tudor Historians' Dialogue with the Dead

The general purposes shared by sixteenth- and early-seventeenth-century English historians are explicitly formulated in almost all the dedications and introductions to the chronicles and, more extensively, in treatises on history-writing (these, however, were mostly written after the first decade of the seventeenth century). From these texts, a remarkably uniform catalogue of aims can be easily compiled. For Edward Halle,

> wryting is the keye to enduce vertue, and represse vice. Thus memorie maketh menne ded many a thousande yere still to live as though thei wer present: Thus fame triumpheth upon death, and renoune upon Oblivion, all by reason of writyng and historie.[1]

In particular, Halle's narrative aims to show

> what mischiefe hath insurged in realmes by intestine devision, what depopulacion hath ensued in countries by civill dissencion, what detestable murder hath been committed in citees by separate faccions, and what calamitee hath ensued in famous regions by domestical discord & unnaturall controversy.[2]

For Lanquet, the use of history is mainly that of providing *exempla* of both good and bad behaviour:

> Histories be a treasure, which ought never to be out of our handes, that therby beyng ayded, we maie the more commodiously handle suche busynesse and lyke chaunces in the commune weale, for as much as the causes often tymes chaunce almoste lyke.
>
> Furthermore there be examples founde in hystories, convenient for every man privately in his degree, as, magistrates ought to be obeyde, and that they never escaped unpunished, whiche have rebelled against theim. . . .[3]

Daniel's purpose, similar to Halle's, is

> to shewe the deformities of Civile Dissension, and the miserable
> events of Rebellions, Conspiracies, and bloudy Revengements,
> which followed (as in a circle) upon that breach of the due course
> of Succession, by the Usurpation of Hen. 4; and thereby to make
> the blessings of Peace, and the happinesse of an established
> Gouernment (in a direct Line) the better to appeare.[4]

Years later, in the long preface to *The History of the World*, Sir
Walter Raleigh reaffirmed the usual catalogue of aims and the same
view about the purpose of history. Its utility, he says, is that

> it hath made us acquainted with our dead Ancestors; and, out of
> the depth and darknesse of the earth, deliuered vs their memory
> and fame. In a word, wee may gather out of History a policy no
> lesse wise than eternall; by the comparison and application of
> other mens fore-passed miseries, with our owne like errours and
> ill deseruings.

for, he adds, 'the Sea of examples hath no bottom'.[5]

George Puttenham, otherwise cool and technical in his description of rhymes, metres and figures, dedicates to historical poetry
the most passionate passage of his treatise. Here is its opening:

> There is nothing in man of all the potential parts of his mind
> (reason and will except) more noble or more necessary to the
> actiue life then memory; because it maketh most to a sound
> iudgement and perfect worldly wisedome, examining and *compar-
> ing the times past with the present*, and by them both considering
> the time to come, concludeth with a stedfast resolution, what is
> the best course to be taken in all his actions and aduices in this
> world.[6]

(Puttenham is also concerned about the decorum that he considers appropriate to the lofty subject of history, as opposed to the
'meane matters' concerning 'meane men').[7]

The fragment from Hayward's dedication which follows plays on
different strings; indeed, had it been developed, it might have proved
far more interesting than the others; unfortunately, its author did
not expand the argument which he announced in this passage,

maybe owing to the fact that his main interest lay in narrating certain events rather than in dealing with general theoretical issues:

> it may seeme not impertinent to write of the stile of history, what beginning, what continuance, and what meane is to be used in all matter; what thinges are to bee suppressed, what lightly touched, and what to be treated at large; how credit may be won, and suspition avoyded; what is to be observed in the order of times, and descriptions of places, and other such circumstances of weight; what liberty a writer may use in framing speeches, and declaring the causes, counsailes, and eventes of thinges done; how farre he must bend himselfe to profit; and when and how he may play upon pleasure. But this were too large a field to enter into.[8]

How far the tone of Hayward's dedication to the reader differs from similar passages in other chronicles and historical poems is evident. Hayward's interests seem to be for a secular kind of historiography, where narrational technicalities and constructive principles ('what beginning', 'what things are to be suppressed, what lightly touched', 'what to be treated at large') appear to be consciously assumed as a means of conveying relevance and markedness through selection and perspective ('what is to be observed', 'circumstances of weight'). But Hayward's 'heresy' is apparent above all in the absence of moral props (in the same dedicatory letter, he uses the expression 'lively patterns' where others would have used the word 'example').[9] When interrogated about his book on a charge of sedition, Hayward 'defended himself on the ground that his book was not meant to apply to the present.'[10] The passage quoted, however, sounds ironic, for the sequel of the story shows that Hayward was obviously unable to 'touch lightly' the thorny issue of the deposition of Richard II and thereby avoid 'suspition'.[11]

No text can better describe what I believe were Shakespeare's tensions; no catalogue provides a better survey of relevant procedures, revealing through what is presented as just a list of technical issues an overall attitude made up of pragmatic and worldly concerns and stressing the importance of the 'liberties' that can be taken in framing, narratively as well as conceptually, the historical tales.

Generally speaking, however, history-telling was evidently an exercise of conformist political ethics, since the reading of history was meant to engender wise rule in the princes and political obedience in their subjects; the corpus of written histories, in fact, represents a kind of civil utopia which, through a mixture of medieval Christian providentialism and of the classical doctrine of *exempla*, seems to aim at providing legitimation and strength for the ruling class as well as warding off all risks of disorder and subversion.

Turning our attention from aims to methods, I will now briefly discuss the procedures followed in the compiling of history books: the use, in other words, which historians made of the established historical tradition.

For the Tudor historian, history-writing was not the outcome of enquiry; rather, it almost implied the obligation not to enquire further once what was taken to be the acceptable tradition was established. Almost invariably, writing about history was considered a matter of re-writing and telling a matter of re-telling. Strategies were elaborated to present uncertain facts or to offer different versions of the same event. A good example of this latter procedure is Holinshed's report of Arthur's death in the story of King John. The chronicler is extremely cautious in relating this particular episode, and decides to rely on the authority of other sources, mentioning various possible causes (natural sickness, accidental drowning in the river Seine); finally, he mentions the possibility of murder but does so without committing himself, again relying on someone else's report (incidentally, he does the same in the passage in which he deals with the causes of the king's death): 'But some affirme, that king John secretelie caused him to be murthered and made awaie, so as it is not thoroughlie agreed upon, in what sort he finished his daies: but verelie king John was had in great suspicion, whether worthilie or not, the lord knoweth.'[12]

No chronicle is without a preliminary declaration regarding these major precepts and without a solemn undertaking to follow them carefully. These declarations served to testify to the truth-value of the stories told, and to endorse the book that contained them as a history book. Consequently, historical truth ended up being a side-effect of certain texts, established by their declarations of orthodoxy and of ethical engagement, but above all by their practice of re-production, and validated by frequent quotation of the chosen model. The guarantee of the text's reliability, therefore, was entrusted to openly declared intertextuality rather than to engagement in historical research.[13]

Obviously, censorship played a considerable role in establishing this kind of historiographical practice. History books were the most closely scrutinised publications (in 1599 a regulation prescribed that they had to be licensed directly by the Privy Council). What the authorities feared, in particular, as Hayward's case shows, was the way in which historians connected past events with the present, although they considered that the establishing of such connections was one of the obligations of historians.[14] The first thing that a historian had to do, therefore, was to declare in principle his full acceptance of the established precept that the tradition should not be interfered with.

As an example of the many declarations of conformity to the approved version of facts, let us repeat the following, penned by Daniel in the 'Dedicatory' of his *Civil Wares*:

> ... I have carefully followed that truth which is delivered in the Historie; without adding to, or subtracting from, the general receiv'd opinion of things as we finde them in our common Annalles: holding it an impietie, to violate what publike Testimonie we haue, without more evident proofe; or to introduce fictions of our owne imagination, in things of this nature.[15]

'More evident proofe', however, could hardly be produced, for research and perusal of state papers was not allowed, unless historians 'agreed not to pry'.[16] What may have been the effect of this compliance on the quality and reliability of historical texts is easily understood: 'the effects of conformity', Fussner writes, 'were in all likelihood far from salutary. The persistence of error in popular historical accounts may owe more to the censorship than can ever be proved.'[17]

What we find in Daniel's passage quoted above is a clear statement of the paradox that was the norm in Tudor historiography. The paradox is set out again by Daniel by means of a Latin motto (an extra element of validation, since by quoting Latin the author indirectly states his adherence to the classical tradition): 'Famae rerum standum est',[18] in other words, it is necessary to support, and stick to, the established version of the facts. Otherwise put, history (in the sense of *res gestae*) is memory as it has been imprinted in a corpus of texts validated by their being part of the approved social production (even, by their explicitly declaring to be so); it is the tradition as preserved in the Annals, a tradition of tales told and of 'receiv'd opinion'; it is *doxa*, common knowledge and belief that cannot and should not be altered, but should on the contrary be repeated and reproduced again and again. Paradoxically, then, not only did the *res gestae* coincide with the actual corpus of *historia rerum gestarum* (a basic contradiction of virtually all historiography), but also the perspective from which those facts have been told and evaluated, and therefore the very context and circumstances of their telling had to be preserved and perpetuated. In short, the facts are made to coincide with a corpus of texts that have already presented those facts in a certain way and *under certain conditions*. Once the first book of chronicles has been sanctioned as aptly re-producing those facts, subsequent accounts are sanctioned, provided that they comply with the prescribed practice of re-production of the text that first re-produced them.

Uniformity was a generalised requirement for acceptable histories. Brathwait illustrates the activity of comparing various histories as follows:

> There is another propriety in a History, which should be observed: and that is a Iudicious collation, or comparing of Histories one with another: the defect and want hereof, is the principall cause why so manie discordancies & mere oppositions in Histories arise.[19]

The sanction comes, obviously, from what is considered the authoritative text:

> Discursive Histories, are either true or feigned: If true, they comprehend in them a certaine ground, not onely fortified by a reasonable production, but also by the authority of such, whose Authentiquest labours claime to themselves, a kinde of Authority without further proofe.[20]

At most, the historian was invited to compare diverse versions when these existed. Such a historian is commendable

> who emploieth his time, wasteth his Oile, and macerates himselfe in the scrutinie of true Relations, by conferring Histories together, and with a iudicious approbation, or electing power, extract whatsoever may seeme most probable and authenticke. [21]

These precepts, when actually followed in texts, far from producing fresh hypotheses or different syntheses, tended to lead to the repetition of the same events narrated in the same way, which thus assumed a veneer of authoritative objectivity.[22]

Prescriptions were of course accompanied by restrictions. What the historian should not do is clearly stated in a passage by Edmund Bolton, when he warns the authors and translators of history books not to 'corrupt the Original, by the familiar Courses of Corruption, as Addition, Mutation, Mutilation, Subtraction, Distraction, or otherwise'.[23]

There is, as we can see, in the common judgement of historians and of those who licensed their works, a prototype, an *Original* that must be reproduced as faithfully as possible. The same idea of an authorised prototype, or sanctioned Original, is to be found also with regard to royal portraiture. In 1563, a proclamation established

> that some special commission painter might be permitted, by access to her majesty to take the natural representation of her majesty, whereof she has always been very unwilling, but also to prohibit all manner of other persons to draw, paint, grave, or portray her majesty's personage or visage for a time until, by some perfect patron and example, the same may be by others followed.[24]

The corruptions performed in the theatre to the detriment of historical truth were of many kinds. The so-called historical romances or comical histories established a genre that played around with historical characters, divesting their stories of the political burden of 'greater' history and imagining situations that constituted a relief from historical matter and provided 'a space of freedom from the event'.[25] Seemingly ineffectual from the historical and political point of view, those plays were also considered inoffensive towards the real persons represented, while they did not enter into collision with the historiographical tradition, which in fact they almost entirely ignored. Their overall effect, which was generally welcomed since it was obtained in a way that hardly touched on the political sphere, was to humanise the figures of power, playing, as it were, on the strings provided by the natural half of their body. Such plays hardly risked censorship, since the invented adventures, although presented in a romantic and popular tone, were not considered an offence to the dignity of the public characters. On the contrary, they were probably regarded as positive propaganda, for they had the commendable effect of bringing the distant king or prince nearer to the people's heart, by suggesting that they, too, albeit in their own way, suffered, loved, and enjoyed life just like other human beings and therefore could be appreciated also for their human side. In other words, although these texts never aimed at being accepted as properly historical, their choice of historical characters as protagonists was not irrelevant from the axiological point of view for, albeit half-covertly, it served to revive and enrich the myth of political power.

Thus, it seems that such prescriptions as those formulated by Bolton, as well as the restrictions of censorship, did not concern the utter disfiguring of, or disregard for, historical truth perpetrated in the historical romances. On the contrary, the tendency seems to have been to censure only such works (historical as well as theatrical) as aimed at telling the truth, in those cases where this was in some way in contrast with the generally accepted version of facts.

That Shakespeare's aims were thoroughly different from those of the writers of historical romances hardly needs arguing. Nor is there any doubt that, although he in fact corrupted the substance of the historical tradition, historical truth was a consciously pursued effect in his plays, or that these were received as history by the audience.[26] The choice of historical subjects, however, was neither neutral nor safe. Indeed, to go fishing for subjects in the established corpus of facts and political issues relating to national history was certainly a more demanding and more risky undertaking than simply ransacking the repertories of Italian novellas or even Plutarch's *Lives*. The risks involved were both theatrical and political. In the first place, the dramatist could not make indiscriminate alterations to the events narrated in the chronicles, since these were to a certain extent common knowledge, and therefore the audience expected to see them more or less accurately reproduced on the stage; and in the second place, the treatment of national political issues was more likely to attract the attention of the censor.

The often quoted Act V Chorus of *Henry V* shows Shakespeare's awareness that many members of his audience were familiar with the English chronicles ('Vouchsafe to those that have not read the story,/ That I may prompt them: and of such as have . . .', V. 0. 1–2), and that they therefore expected the truths that they were already familiar with from such reading to be reproduced on the stage. Naturally this offered the playwright all the advantages of playing against a familiar background, but at the same time it imposed certain constraints on him. On the one hand, he could rely on that knowledge and on the popularity of historical characters as a possible source of the particular pleasure which, as Aristotle suggested, is connected with the recognition of what is already known;[27] on the other hand, he was strictly limited by that knowledge: he could not significantly alter the substance of those events without jeopardising the truth-effect of his plays. Invention, therefore, had to be handled carefully in order to prevent the 'impiety' of truth-corruption compromising the impression of truth-reproduction that the plays were expected to produce.

But the need to respect the truth of the stories implied a close relationship with a well-established, almost sacrosanct and thus remarkably stagnant historiographical tradition. In the first and most obvious sense, this tradition was used by Shakespeare to substantiate the authenticity of what was presented on the stage. The names of the illustrious persons, their good and bad deeds, the way they lived and died, the places associated with their actions were there, clear and recognisable, and their function was to convince the audience that they were witnessing the true facts of history. Moreover, even the titles of the plays as they were advertised on the play-bills, bore the name of a king or of a dynasty, thereby showing that the author and the company complied with a fundamental tenet of Tudor historiography, namely, that histories are 'worthy to be called the bokes of great prynces and lordes'.[28]

However, reference to a source also involves a series of complex cross-cultural implications. To use a text as source, in fact, implies in the first place retrieval of the world that produced the source text, and it also means

> to acknowledge the existence and vitality of a text beyond the temporal span of its material appearance, it means to witness that a certain text has happily overcome the cultural obstacles of control, censorship and oblivion.[29]

Even in our case, the retrieval, however unrespectful, of the chronicles implied an acknowledgement of the social, cultural and political validity of the texts which were re-used; indeed, their communicative qualities and authority were thus activated again in the text that received the previous text. However, Shakespeare's homage to his Holinshed, Halle, Foxe or Grafton proved to be an exchange of favours, since the intertextual appeal to an approved historical source brought social, cultural, and political validation to the disreputable activities connected with the theatre. For the dramatist, in fact, to recall the institutional sources of historical knowledge in the

context of what was considered mere entertainment and often regarded as a politically dangerous activity, actually meant gaining
extra respectability for his own enterprise since his stories thus
appeared to be connected to the core of historical orthodoxy.[30]
   Looking at things from this point of view, we may attribute to
those elements that were *not* derived from a historical source a
function different from, and much more interesting than, the one
dictated by simple dramatic necessity of a technical kind; a function
that may, in some cases, be read as an instance of divergence or
even dissension from the official version of events. Once the basic
truth of the stories represented was reproduced on the basis of the
relevant intertextual reference, it became possible to introduce those
forms of corruption which did not interfere with truth; this created
the possibility of playing historically with what was either deeply
transformed truth or pure imagination and, on occasion, of marking axiologically the blank margins of the books of chronicles.

Notes

1. E. Halle, *The Union of the Two Noble and Illustre Famelies of Lancastre
    & Yorke* (London, 1548), 'Preface', p. ii.
2. Ibid., p. i.
3. T. Lanquet, *An Epitome of Chronicles* (London, 1559), p. ii. Lanquet's
    preface is entitled 'Of the use and profite of histories, and with what
    iudgement they oughte to bee redde'. Lanquet's *Chronicle* was
    'finished and continued' to the reign of Edward VI by Thomas Cooper.
4. S. Daniel, *The Civile Wares betweene the Howses of Lancaster and Yorke*,
    corrected and continued (London, 1609; first published 1595), 'The
    Epistle Dedicatorie' to the Countess Dowager of Pembroke, p. 2. It is
    interesting to note the explicit mention of the idea of a 'circle' as a
    conceptualisation of the course of history following the usurpation
    of Henry IV. The Epistle is not present in the first edition.
5. Sir Walter Raleigh, *The History of the World* (1614), ed. C. A. Partrides
    (London: Macmillan, 1971), pp. 48, 49. Raleigh believed that the same
    pattern showed itself in Jewish, French and English history.
6. G. Puttenham, *The Arte of English Poesie* (1589), ed. G. D. Willcock
    and A. Walker (Cambridge: Cambridge University Press, 1970 [1936]),
    p. 39; my emphasis.
7. Ibid., p. 152.
8. J. Hayward, *The Life and Raigne*, p. 64. Holinshed, too, presents his
    work by expanding on his method for collecting the events and as-
    certaining their truth, without mentioning any moral aim to his work:
    'My speech is plain, without any rhetoricall shew of eloquence, having

rather a regard to simple truth, than to decking words.' (*The Third Volume of Chronicles*, London, 1587, p. Aiii).

9. Op. cit., p. 62. After the failure of Essex's conspiracy and the suppression of his book in 1600, Hayward was imprisoned and he was released only after Elizabeth's death, in 1603. In the same year, he published *An Answer to the First Part of a Certain Conference, Concerning Succession* (Doleman/Parsons' *Conference about the next succession to the Crowne of England* had been published in 1594: see note 48 on p. 101), where he argues the Stuart case against the Jesuits' preference for the Spanish, and dedicated it to James I. As can be inferred from the dedication, Hayward's aim was to regain the royal favour, although without actually pleading guilty. On Hayward's case, see Campbell, op. cit., pp. 182–92, A. Patterson, *Censorship and Interpretation*, pp. 44–8; P. Rackin, *Stages of History* (London: Routledge, 1990), p. 236; L. Barroll, op. cit. Mervyn James discusses the contribution of Hayward's *Life and Raigne* 'to the reputation of the Essex circle as characterized by an atheistic political secularism' and remarks that 'as an exponent of Tacitean historical style, [Hayward] abandoned in his historical work the providentialist framework, and the stress on the moral exemplum which had been characteristic of earlier Tudor historiography.' (*Politics and Culture*, p. 420).

10. F. Smith Fussner, *The Historical Revolution. English Historical Writing and Thought 1580–1640* (London: Routledge, 1962), p. 39.

11. Hayward expresses a severe judgement of Richard: 'In this sort, the king bearing a heavy hand upon his subjects, and they againe a heavy heart against him, and being withall a prince weake in action, and not of valure sufficient to beare out his vices by might, the people at length resolved to revolt, and rather to runne into the hazard of a ruinous rebellion, then to endure safetie joyned with slaverie.' (*The Life and Raigne*, pp. 198–9). Hayward attributes Bolingbroke's return from exile to popular discontent and to the nobility's insistent pressures. This attitude, without any appeal to the contingent element of Hayward's connection with Essex, may be enough to explain the misgivings that the book raised.

12. *Chronicles*, 165.II.67–72. Richard Brathwait argues against the presentation of different versions of facts. He says he has observed many errors 'where divers Authors were cited, and their severall opinions marshalled on a row: but as in a battele, when the wings be broken, there insueth nought but universall confusion; so without reconcilement in the conclusion, he [the historian] leaves the Reader in suspence whose opinion to entertain; because not directed by the Author' (*The Schollers Medley: Or An Intermixt Discourse upon Historicall and Poeticall Relations*, London, 1614, p. 84). Brathwait's treatise was enlarged and reprinted in 1638 with the title *A Survey of History, Or, A Nursery for Gentry*.

13. The historian's debt to previous authors is almost always acknowledged in a list of sources which precedes the text. Halle explicitly declares the compilatory nature of his chronicle, naming the authors 'out of which this work was first gathered, and after compiled and

conjoined'. Sidney ironised about the historian, 'laden with old mouse-eaten records, authorizing himself (for the most part) upon other histories, whose greatest authorities are built upon the notable foundations of hearsay', *A Defense of Poesy*, 1595; my edn, *A Defense of Poetry*, ed. by J. A. van Dorsten (Oxford: Oxford University Press, 1966), p. 30.

14.   This last prescription, however, involved substantial risks. Since its central idea was that 'history repeats itself, the past is like the present, and the statesman may discover by reading history what is the proper course to be taken in the present', it follows that, if the historian's attitude was not orthodox, 'the argument of analogy [might be considered] treasonable' (Fussner, op. cit., p. 40).

15.   Op. cit., (1609 edn), p. A2^v.

16.   Fussner, op. cit., p. 41.

17.   Ibid., p. 39. Elsewhere in the same 'Dedicatory', Daniel is careful in dispelling the doubt that the poetic medium used in his work may have encouraged a 'poetic', contrary-to-fact vision of history, by carefully distinguishing between form and matter. In I.6.8 he declares: 'I versifie the troth; not Poetize.'

18.   Ibid., p. A2^v.

19.   Op. cit., p. 28.

20.   Ibid., p. 18.

21.   Ibid.

22.   Bacon's position requires at least to be mentioned. For Bacon, the task of the historian was 'to carry the mind in writing back into the past, and bring it into sympathy with antiquity; diligently to examine, freely and faithfully to report, and by the light of words to place as it were before the eyes, the revolutions of times, the characters of persons, the fluctuations of counsels, the causes and currents of actions, the bottoms of practices, and the secrets of governments' (*De augmentis scientiarum*, Book II, chapt. V, in *The Philosophical Works of Francis Bacon*, ed. John Robertson (New York: Books for Libraries Press, 1970), p. 432. However, although he in theory recognised the need for first-hand enquiry, when writing *The History of the Reign of King Henry the Seventh*, Bacon relied on existing sources (principally Polydore Virgil, Halle, Stow and Grafton) and, although he might have had access to the formidable manuscript collection of Sir Robert Cotton he never carried out research of his own.

23.   E. Bolton, *Hypercritica*, in J. E. Spingarn (ed.), *Critical Essays of the Seventeenth Century* (Oxford: Oxford University Press, 1908–9), 2 vols, vol. I, pp. 83–115, 94; my emphasis. The year in which Bolton's booklet was first published is uncertain (1618?).

24.   Quoted by D. S. Kastan from P. L. Hughes and J. F. Larkin (eds), *Tudor Royal Proclamations. The Later Tudors* (New Haven: Yale University Press, 1969), II, 240–1. Kastan comments on this prescription, remarking that an unregulated representation of the monarch might derogate majesty 'by subjecting it to the impudent gaze of its subjects'. ('Proud Majesty Made a Subject: Shakespeare and the Spectacle of Rule', *SQ* XXXVII [1986], 459–75, pp. 462–3). What the

proclamation established to be 'the natural representation of her majesty' was, of course, no more 'natural' than the sanctioned historical representations.

25. Holderness, *Shakespeare Recycled*, p. 19. On the historical romances, see Anne Barton, 'The King Disguised: Shakespeare's *Henry V* and the Comical History', in J. G. Price (ed.), *The Triple Bond* (University Park: Pennsylvania State University Press, 1975), pp. 92–117.

26. Here and elsewhere, by 'historical truth' I mean those circumstances and persons that were perceived as 'true' because recorded in texts explicitly presented as history books.

27. The very notion of mimesis, as the basis on which esthetic pleasure is constructed, rests on the idea of the recognition of what is known (see *Poetics*, 1448b). The connection between pleasure and recognition holds for all forms of poiesis; Aristotle, however, distinguishes certain general forms of recognition from the recognition of historical events. He says, for instance, that the myths that have been handed down by tradition cannot be altered (*Poetics*, 1453b) and that the repetition of historical names in tragedy makes credible what is only possible (1451b).

28. Walter Lynne, *The Thre Bokes of Cronicles* (London, 1550), p. iii. Lynne's is a translation from a Latin version of Johann Carion's *Chronica* (Wittenberg, 1532), that the translator dedicated to Edward VI. In Lynne's version, the introduction is entitled 'The use of readynge hystoryes'.

29. R. Zacchi, 'La citazione ovvero la memoria trasparente', *Quaderni di filologia germanica della Facoltà di Lettere e Filosofia dell' Università di Bologna*, IV (1988), 17–33, p. 22.

30. Extended to include Bakhtin's and Voloshinov's concept of dialogism, the field of intertextuality has been especially fruitful in suggesting new perspectives as concerns the study of sources. The practice of reuse, C. Segre suggests, varies in quantity as well as in quality; and these variations illustrate in the last analysis the user's attitude to the source text: the user may be a simple imitator, but also one who 'plays on estrangement as regards strongly implied epochal structures or, on the contrary, one who plays on the uniformity of themes and forms, reconstituting them for a different cultural context', *Teatro e romanzo* (Turin: Einaudi, 1984), p. 110. A microanalysis of source manipulation in Shakespeare's historical and Roman plays has been conducted in A. Serpieri *et al.*, *Nel laboratorio di Shakespeare* (Parma: Pratiche, 1988), 4 vols. The analysis of transformations produced in this work concerns such categories as fabula, plot, time, space, voice, perspective and discourse (see vol. I for a theoretical assessment of the phenomena considered).

3

Perspectivism

Methinks I see these things with parted eye,
When everything seems double.
A Midsummer Night's Dream, IV.i.188–9

The idea of duplicity in Shakespeare and the perception of the contradictory impulses which composed 'that extraordinary fluid compound we call Elizabethan culture'[1] started to be clearly formulated and systematically elaborated in the mid-sixties. This was a reaction against the already 'old' historicism of Tillyard and Campbell and the schematic picture of an orthodox Elizabethan mind which their books had created and which had been absorbed to the point of almost inducing 'complete apathy about these dull, conformist people'.[2] It started from Rossiter's seminal lecture on 'Ambivalence' in Shakespeare's history plays and from the first edition of his book *Angel with Horns*,[3] and may be considered as a historically-oriented offshoot of ideas that had been given currency by the first wave of new critics. In his lecture, Rossiter defined ambivalence as the procedure whereby 'two opposed value-judgements are subsumed as both valid' and spoke of 'two-eyedness' and of 'a constant doubleness' in Shakespeare's vision of history; he saw 'Shakespeare's intuitive way of thinking about history as characteristically dialectical' and its intellectual origin in 'a thoroughly English empiricism which recognizes the coextancy and juxtaposition of opposites'.[4]

The Problem of Order by Ernest Talbert was published in 1962.[5] The keynote of Talbert's book is again ambivalence. In his exemplary analysis of *Richard II*, Talbert showed the coexistence and competition, in Shakespeare's play (but also in his historical sources), of the antithetical meanings of the Lancastrian and the Yorkist perspectives. With Talbert's book, the dismantling of Tillyard's description of a comparatively uniform world picture received a decisive impulse and specific trends which had been established by Tillyard's approach started to be challenged in a number of culturally-oriented works.

Elton's *King Lear and the Gods* inaugurated a series of works which questioned the uniformity and tenacity of the idea of providence in the Elizabethan culture;[6] in their different ways, all these works discuss the idea of ambivalence and duplicity, which, in works like those of Madeleine Doran, Joel Altman or Rosalie Colie, is presented as an example of reasoning *in utramque partem*, a kind of reasoning which formed an essential part of the curriculum of Elizabethan grammar schools.[7] Doran discusses the technique of the scholastic debate, where two aspects of a question are argued with equal conviction, as something which profoundly affected the structure of Elizabethan drama. She found, however, that this sort of reasoning produced structural defects in the drama of Shakespeare's contemporaries and a 'failure of direction' which engendered 'confusions'. Understandably, then, she mentions Shakespeare's history plays, as suffering 'from the same double direction', and in particular the Yorkist-Lancastrian tetralogy, whose weakness in her opinion is that 'the rival claims of the two factions are equally well argued'.[8] The connection of Colie's book with our problem is less direct, since it rests on the fact that 'duplicity' or 'doubleness' is one of the ways in which paradoxy may manifest itself. One of the basic features of paradox as a way of reasoning, however, is the reconciling of contradictory statements. A further important critical contribution to the discussion of Shakespeare's ambivalences came with Norman Rabkin's book *Shakespeare and the Common Understanding*. Rabkin evokes the principle of 'complementarity' in physics and of the coexistence of opposites as purposefully designed esthetic construction.[9] Directly inspired by Rabkin's book is Grudin's *Mighty Opposites*, where the source of the intellectual play on paradox and contrariety, a pattern of thought to which Shakespeare 'could consciously and meaningfully appeal', is seen in the influence which such works as those of Paracelsus, Castiglione and Giordano Bruno exerted in England.[10]

The paradigm of duplicity and the idea of Shakespeare's purposeful ambivalence has then long been established; and it appears to be tenacious and capable of further refinement, as is shown by the fact that it has recently been revived in the work of differently oriented scholars.[11] It should be noticed that both in the works of the sixties and seventies and in recent discussions, the intellectual disposition to argue *in utramque partem* ('the moral cultivation of ambivalence', as Wilbur Sanders calls it) is seen, more or less explicitly, as an anti-authoritarian tendency in that – following Bacon's terminology – it showed a preference for the 'Probation' mode of

reasoning as against the 'Magistral'.[12] It was Robert Grudin, however, who first stated explicitly the radical potentialities of contrariety and its connections with a non-Christian view of history. The
rationale of contrariety, Grudin says, 'announces a radical morality
in which the value of innocence is wholly refuted, and worldly
wisdom becomes the basis for just action'.[13]

It is to this same paradigm of duplicity and contrariety that we
should probably connect Hattaway's definition of Shakespeare's perspectivism in the *Henry VI* sequence as 'a dramatic cross-examination'
of issues seen 'from differing points of view, embodied in different
dramatic styles', already quoted. Here, again, one finds implicitly
evoked the intellectual exercise of arguing *in utramque partem*, and
the complexity of vision which that exercise produced.[14]

The theatrical implications of this kind of mental disposition are
alluded to by Joel Altman. 'What happens', he says, 'when academic
exercises become public entertainments . . . ? Do they retain the ethical neutrality which they enjoyed in the schools . . . or must they
become responsible to the doxa of the audiences they have come
out to entertain?'[15] And perhaps, one should also ask, is exercising
one's mind on purely academic questions the same thing as dealing
with problems involving moral choices?[16] And finally, what happens
when the subject-matter is history – national history – and the issues
presented by public entertainments are clearly political and often
overtly topical? Indeed, to raise problems like the legitimacy or
opportunity of the deposition and killing of a sovereign, to question
assumptions like the divine right of kings, to dismantle the rhetoric
of war-values, to raise doubts as to the source of disorder, to challenge the very doctrine of order and degree, was certainly not the
same as debating whether the owl or the nightingale should win, or
as deciding whether Lucres should marry Gaius Flaminius or Publius
Cornelius as in the *jeu parti* of *Fulgens and Lucres*; it was even less
neutral than setting out the good reasons Shylock had to hate the
Christians.

Indeed, this logical and rhetorical training, which was designed
to develop the pupils' ability in the art of holding contrary arguments may have appeared innocuous and merely technical to the
pedagogists in charge of grammar-school curricula; in reality, by
encouraging the cross-examination of moral issues from a multiplicity of viewpoints, it may have contributed to producing that
attitude of 'probation' which results in a distrust of 'received ideas'
and which, when transferred from the schoolroom to practical life,

may have become a source of divulgement of unorthodox views. We may expect, at the very least, that when engaged in historiographical work, the 'probing' mind tends to see all the possible sides of an issue, to give equal weight to contrasting moral and political problems, while refraining from suggesting final solutions.

The ambivalence or polyvalence which distinguishes Shakespeare's plays, and which appeared as a structural defect to Madeleine Doran, has been recently qualified by Paul Dean in historiographical terms as a way of dealing with the problem of historical causation which, Dean argues, is surprisingly similar to the suggestions made by certain modern theorists of historiography. In particular, Dean detects in Shakespeare's plays – and above all in the histories – a tendency to replace the exposition and explanation of causes by the fullest possible narrative; and therefore an attempt, similar to that suggested by Hempel and Gardiner, to construct historical narratives 'as the expansion of a skeleton outline into a narrative whose fullness is its own justification, whose detailed particularity obviates the need for any external causal mechanism'.[17] 'Detailed' and 'full', as applied to Shakespeare's historical narratives, are obviously meant as a correlative of what narrative fullness may become when translated into dramatic form. In reality, when we read or watch one of these plays, the impression we get is not one of *completeness* but that of a *polyphony* which signals the dialogic and conflictual nature of historical issues.

Boris Uspenskij has argued that multi-perspectivism in historical narratives is a way to show and illustrate the non-monologic nature of history. According to the Russian scholar, the variety of possible interpretations of historical events mirrors the complexity of the historical process. Often, he argues, the different interpretations of a historical fact are not to be seen as contradictory, but as merging into one another:

> if a historical event can produce different explanations, one can think that this is due to the fact that diverse impulses converge in it which have all led to the same outcome (creating, so to speak, an effect of resonance or of reciprocal strengthening). Thus, the very possibility of offering different explanations may mirror the real, objective, non-accidental nature of the event.[18]

The concepts that seem to constitute a pertinent background against which the idea of multi-perspectivism can be discussed are, again, those elaborated by Bakhtin and Voloshinov in the field of related notions bearing on what Todorov has termed 'the dialogic principle', which comprises such concepts as heteroglossia, plurilinguism, dialogism, pluristylism and polyphony.[19] Bakhtin's treatment of the dialogic imagination characterises polyphony, plurilinguism and dialogism as the social dialogue of different languages and points of view. Polyphony, he holds, is built culturally into the language that we use; language, in fact, is a culturally saturated tool, intrinsically dialogic and even potentially conflictual. However, certain texts – those that Bakhtin defines as 'monologic' – tend to neutralise the conflictual and controversial potential of language, while others exploit or even enhance this potential, for instance by playing with various styles and genre conventions, but also by presenting conflicting perspectives and evaluations.

But what does polyphony suggest in terms of the mental attitude that it presumably implies in the representation of history? Does it signal a pessimistic or sceptical approach which involves regarding the events as inevitably random and incomprehensible or is it rather evidence of a serious attempt to communicate the turbulence and complexity of historical processes? Generally speaking, readings focusing on Shakespeare's polyphony tend to connect it with the effort to come to terms with the problem of historical interpretation. Heinemann elaborates on the 'raw material' and 'unvarnished representations' that Brecht discerns in Shakespeare (Brecht even speaks of 'illogicality') and adds that 'this material is not tidied up or harmonized in accordance with a preconceived idea, and can therefore preserve some of the complexity, irregularity and contradictory movement of history itself';[20] Serpieri, in turn, ties down Shakespeare's polyphonic treatment of history by connecting it to the emergence of a clash between the semantic, or symbolic, world model, which is typical of medieval culture, and the syntagmatic model 'that was to mark the rationalistic and sceptical laicism of the new bourgeois culture and of the "new science"'. According to Serpieri, from the point of view of historical perception, this clash illustrates the contrast between 'cyclical and linear time, and therefore between the idea of history as dominated by an immanent pattern and one that sees historical patterns as imposed by human actions'.[21]

Illogicality, irregularity, complexity, contrariety, complementarity, polyphony, doubleness, ambivalence, even *discoherence*:[22] we are used to absorbing contradictions and discrepancies when reading Shakespeare; indeed, conflicts and antitheses do not concern solely his function as negotiator of historical explanations (and after all, drama – at least in its Western manifestations – *is* conflict and anti-thesis).[23] My claim, therefore, would seem to be reduced to virtually nothing: that is, to acknowledging – albeit maybe from a different standpoint – the point that has frequently been made about the openness of issues in Shakespeare's plays, and therefore to explicitly extending to the history plays something that is in any case obvious, namely, that Shakespeare could not but feel about politics the same way he seems to have felt about other human predicaments. But, as John Hayward remarked, history and politics are different matters: the conflicts, contradictions, disharmony, confusion and illogicality that might be safely predicated of life in general acquired danger-ous meanings when attributed to political issues. Indeed, showing disorder and disharmony in things historical constituted a radical overturning of the stagnant idea of history as dominated by a deter-ministic pattern, which was the norm among contemporary histor-ians. The practice was not without risks for, ultimately, the validation of various gestalts carried historical narratives to the verge of sub-version, for it sanctioned that eminently transgressive practice that was '*Amphibologia*, . . . *the ambiguous*, or figure of sence incertaine', that 'vicious speach' occurring 'when we speake or write doubt-fully and that the sence may be taken two wayes', which Puttenham treats as a most subversive figure, connecting it to the speeches of famous rebels like Jack Straw, Jack Cade and Captain Ket.[24]

But perspectivism and polyphony are also features characteristic of problem-oriented, rather than simply sequential, forms of historiography. Indeed, even though each of Shakespeare's plays bears in its title the name of a king or of an illustrious family, the story enacted is only a fragment of that reign: that part, obviously, which on the one hand appeared to provide the most interesting dramatic material and on the other served to illustrate the particu-lar political problem or problems that it seemed relevant to present on each occasion.[25]

The conceptual alternative between a general sequential history of kings and reigns and a history illustrating political issues seems to have emerged in England only around the second decade of the seventeenth century. In a less clear form, however, the issue is pre-sent by the middle of the sixteenth century, as when Ascham dis-cusses the alternative between 'the order of persons' and the order of 'time and matter' as different methods which cannot coexist in the narration of historical events.[26]

Later theoreticians have framed the alternative more clearly. Bolton seems to be aware of the fact that the narrative method of the chronicles or of the annals produced unmarked historical information, and that a different kind of narration, one that related particular, circumscribed events presenting a hierarchy of problems rather than a sequel of facts was possible and, within limits, desirable. However, he concluded his discussion of this (apparently) technical problem by claiming that sequential narratives are easier to follow. Here is how Bolton illustrates the alternative:

> For the penning whereof [of our Histories], whether it be best to do it by Distinction into several Actions, without intermixture of coincident Matter, or by Lifes, and Reigns of Princes, that is, by the Order of Times, and Sequences of Events, may worthily seem questionable: because the first way is absolutely best for presenting to the Mind the whole State of every particular great Business, tho' the other is best for Narration, as that in which the natural Method of the doing is observed according to the Time of the doing, with the Intermixture synchronical, or contemporary accidents.

Bolton goes on with a few examples that explain his meaning of 'History by Actions':

> To pen our History by Actions is to describe some eminently main Affair. For example, the *Norman Conquest*, and the effects of that Tyranny till the Common-weal freed it self; the Interposal of K. *Stephen*: the famous Controversies about Church-mens Privileges, between the King and *Canterbury*: which were in a manner original and fundamental to all the incredible Changes which have followed in the Rule, and Policy of our Country. . . .[27]

The list of examples continues for a while. What I think should be underlined, however, is that Bolton is evidently connecting what he calls 'the manner of writing by actions' to a problem-oriented kind of historiography, or at least that he is acknowledging that to tell a story by actions implies a historiographical attitude that gives prominence to causation (he mentions, in fact, 'the effects' of a given event, and qualifies another one as 'original and fundamental to' others). Conversely, he qualifies 'the other Way of penning our History by Races, Lives, and Reigns' simply as 'an orderly and distinct Explication of principal Matters as they happen'd under those several Monarchs'.[28]

The English historians of the previous century, however, seem not even to have considered the possibility of anything other than sequential and cumulative narratives; indeed, a new historiography and a different political understanding of the events, more conscious of the heterogeneous 'converging impulses' of historical processes, would have required an inquisitive disposition which was alien to the tasks (and the limits) that Tudor historians took on themselves; as Holderness suggests, in order for new significance to be assigned to old materials, these 'had to be incorporated into new theoretical models, new modes of conceptual analysis, new techniques of investigation and new methods of sociological definition'.[29]

Shakespeare read the chronicle materials and re-enacted them 'by actions' and problems rather than 'by lives'. Even his reproduction of certain instances of indecision in his chronicle sources (such as those discussed by Talbert in *The Problem of Order*) is to be considered meaningful. Where in Holinshed indecision signals eclecticism in information-gathering, in Shakespeare it assumes the form of problematisation, it becomes *polyvalence*. Often, in fact, the 'truths' or the opinions that these texts seem to present are doubted, questioned or challenged by the appearance of a different and sometimes contrary truth or opinion: which is the perspective from which the events are viewed in *Richard II*? Does the text side with the usurper or with the deposed king? In *1 Henry IV*, are our sympathies directed unassailably towards the prince? And if this is the text's (and the author's) intention, why is Hal's rival depicted as noble and courageous, why is the seriousness of his enterprise appreciated, and his failure presented as a danger; why are so many reasons given to justify his rebellion, why are the ladies introduced in the touching private scenes if the audience is supposed to side with Hal and with the king's order? Why, in short, should the playwright undermine our sympathy for Hal? And, if Henry V is intended to be perceived as the perfect Christian prince, why do so many voices, more or less directly and overtly, condemn his military venture and denounce the violence of the war so convincingly? Certainly, dramatic instinct played a relevant role in the rejection of one-sided interpretations; just as certainly, however, the cross-examination of historical issues, and the invitation implicitly extended to the audience to re-evaluate them was an entirely new feature of historical presentation, and one that could by no means have been derived from contemporary chronicles.

But we should also consider the fact that the dramatist's responsibility was even heavier than the historian's, for the dramatist addressed a large and varied audience, which did not coincide with
the public that read history books, or indeed any books at all. This
meant that for a large part of the audience the past of their country
was not what was set out in written narratives but rather what was
presented on the stage, and what the stage presented was often
much less conformist than what they could read in the chronicles:
not only on account of the 'amphibology' of certain plays, but also
because of their realistic stance and their sceptical attitude towards
the idea of a history dominated by providence. As has been argued,
in fact, in Shakespeare's plays second causes tend to prevail over
the workings of providence as the first cause of human actions;
indeed, whenever first causes are mentioned, they seem to reflect
just one of the many perspectives that make up a 'problematically
multivocal' context or alternatively the characteristic thought of
certain characters (those who are depicted as believing in the action
of providence, like the saintly and impotent Henry VI), a perspective that Shakespeare could hardly dismiss since he was reflecting
on a medieval world.[30]

Besides, the kind of time-vision that Shakespeare's histories seem
to construct renders extremely problematic a providential reading
of historical events. The cyclical vision of time in the Christian tradition probably derived from the reflections expressed by the phi-
losopher who speaks in Ecclesiastes: 'What has been is what will
be, and what has been done is what will be done; and there is
nothing new under the sun. Is there a thing of which it is said, "See,
this is new"? It has been already, in the ages before us.'[31] In the
wake of Tillyard's book, Shakespeare's histories have long been
thought to embrace a cyclical vision of time. According to this view,
Shakespeare's two tetralogies were seen as following a pattern of
sin–punishment–redemption originally derived from Halle, in which
the repetition of the same design is used to celebrate the Tudor
myth, and therefore as presenting a vision of time not unlike that
of Ecclesiastes, a vision both cyclical and eschatological, describing
a circular and recursive pattern in historical events; a course that,
revolving upon itself, tends to return to certain relevant points which
are regarded as salient and from which the events are bound to
start again (the event which functions as a starting-point repeated
in time is the initial sin of the killing of a legitimate king, and its
consequence is the punishment which takes the form of a repetition

of the same event involving the second or third generation). This kind of structure, which tends to show that 'everything has been already', was used, according to the Tillyardian view, to glorify the Tudor dynasty and to present a moral lesson (the inescapable chaos following the killing of the king) based on the conservative doctrine of order and degree, which culminates in the glorification of the Tudors and the appearance of Richmond as liberator (although it should be remarked that Richmond, too, obtained power by killing a king).

Historiographical theories of recursiveness have an anthropological parallel in archaic thought, that views events as modelled on the recursiveness of natural cycles. The conservative character of those doctrines consists in the fact that, by claiming that events repeat themselves, they provide a sort of reassurance against the new and the unknown, which are always closely associated with a linear vision of time and always somewhat disquieting or even frightening because unforeseeable. And indeed, certain important events do repeat themselves in the sequence of Shakespeare's plays, and they lead each time to analogous effects of disorder. However, the recursive design is a pattern that Shakespeare could hardly ignore since it was simply there, set out before his eyes in the sequence of recorded facts. What on the contrary I believe is not present in his plays is any clear interpretation of the repetition of those facts in the form of *exempla* or their presentation as in any way necessary. At least, it should be affirmed that in Shakespeare's historical vision 'the narrowly Tudor-political or "moral" approach will most oversimplify, and thin, the true Shakespearean vintage'.[32] But above all, although certain events are indeed re-enacted in the plays, their repetition occurs under markedly changed political conditions. If we consider the plays in their chronological sequence, when we come to *Henry VI* after the experience of *Henry V* we feel that the king's deposition and killing could not be – and in fact is not – *repeated* in the strict sense. Although the historical laws that led to the end of Richard II may still obtain, the framework in which they operate has changed radically: what is no longer present is the sense of inevitability that permeates Richard's story. In spite of the prophetic tone that pervades the *Henry VI* sequence, nothing similar to doom or destiny, nothing intensely ritual and strange is connected with the events that mark the struggle between Lancaster and York, where the events seem rather to be determined by the randomness of disorderly human volition and by the extremes of human ambition.[33] Historical laws, in short, as well as events and their causes, do not operate in Shakespeare outside historical time; the pastness of what took place at the end of the fourteenth century has not the same flavour as the pastness of what took place sixty years later.

It is also in this sense that Shakespeare might be said to have invented a genre: he may not have been the first to bring English history before the audience of a public playhouse, but he was certainly the first to treat it in the manner of a mature historian rather than in the manner of a worshipper of historical, political and religious myths. Although no personal stance of dissension as regards the official political perspective can actually be demonstrated, it may certainly be argued that no historian of his time questioned the Yorkist, Lancastrian and Tudor myths as deeply and as dangerously: any more traumatic, radical and open criticism was simply unimaginable under the prevailing circumstances, especially considering the medium by which a playwright disclosed his allegations. Commenting on what may have been a general policy of playwrights, Larry Champion observes that plays on national history needed to be shaped 'into a pattern that provided for the lower and middle classes a sense of temporary social release within a framework which the aristocracy would construe, at best, as a panegyric for monarchism or, at worst, as nothing seriously in violation of the constraints of orthodox politics'.[34] The balance was indeed delicate, for among the people who watched those performances there probably were 'many descendants of the Knights and Earls who made up the *dramatis personae*'.[35] More explicit dissension in the age of Elizabeth was mostly anonymous and secretly circulated; it lived privately and hid in corners, in a way that public performances could not; and in the end, in most cases, it met with repression. The fact that the deposition scene in *Richard II* was never printed during Elizabeth's lifetime may be considered as evidence that political plays could indeed be cut down to size and indicates what would have happened had there been a more boldly expressed display of dissension.[36]

However, if we are to believe that historical narratives were closely scrutinised by the censor, we may well ask ourselves how such an unorthodox view could find its way on to the stage. There are, indeed, scholars, like Richard Dutton, who have expressed scepticism as to the efficiency of censorship in those years;[37] others, like Janet Clare, argue both against the tendency 'to dismiss censorship as lenient and posing no serious threat' and against viewing it 'as consistently repressive and menacing'. Her view is that under both Elizabeth and James I the system was 'dynamic and unstable';[38] while Paul Yachnin has recently argued that in those years there was a tendency, on the part of the authorities, to underestimate the real power of the theatre to influence public opinion. Yachnin says that the idea that the theatre had the power to influence audiences 'diminished considerably during the late Elizabethan and entire Jacobean period', when theatre was viewed as 'irrelevant to the system of power'. By so arguing, however, he does not intend to 'imply that the theater was without real historical consequences'.[39] But, however lenient it could on occasions be, the system of censorship was certainly concerned to make a display of efficiency. It is possible, therefore, that Shakespeare's departures from, and criticisms of, the official tradition were allowed theatrical life thanks to the fact that they could be understood as defending more than one perspective. In an imaginary trial centred on those texts, the orthodox perspective could be supported with weighty arguments if the defendant – as was the case in Flaubert's trial – was sufficiently well versed in managing the issue of polyvalence in highly sophisticated literary products: that polyvalence which, in this case, is also to be read as an effort at historical criticism.

This effort is recognised by Holderness when he affirms that Shakespeare's historical plays contributed in a significant way to the discovery of new principles and procedures for the reconstruction of past events and that, therefore, they can be considered 'as major initiatives of Renaissance historical thought'.[40] Indeed, it is precisely from the point of view of the methods of truth-reconstruction that, within the comparatively anaemic debate on historiography that took place in England, Shakespeare's voice was profoundly innovative. His main contribution to the progress of historical exegesis becomes clearer when we see the kind of relationship that he established with the sources of historical knowledge in the context of the intertextual practice of contemporary historians described in Chapter 2. In the first place, by perceiving that when recounting the facts of history it is possible to accommodate a multiplicity of viewpoints as well as revise choices that have been made by others, Shakespeare severely questioned the conformist and passive kind of relationship that contemporary chroniclers entertained with the tradition; by introducing invented, marginal elements, he viewed history as, to some extent, a set of retrospective possibilities; by showing awareness of how the past, apparently crystallised in unchanging documents and monuments, may turn out, from the distant vantage-point of the historian, to be unstable and multiform, he was inaugurating a perspective which is usually associated with more mature forms of historiography than those practised by professional historians in Renaissance England: a perspective that views the reconstruction of historical events as a matter of one's outlook on a world of problems rather than as unconditional belief in, or even worship of, a world of facts.

In the last analysis, therefore, Shakespeare's critical attitude is above all revealed by the way in which, while apparently closely reproducing the 'true facts' of history as they were narrated in the Tudor chronicles, he was in fact reacting to his source materials. Source manipulation and sheer invention may be read as a distinctly critical gesture, in that they show the need to question the official historiographical tradition. Indeed, as Gary Taylor has observed, 'Resemblances to the chronicles establish Shakespeare's use of them; but, as always, his departures from his sources most illuminate his intentions.'[41]

However, the treatment of Shakespeare's manipulation of historical sources as an exclusively literary operation has encouraged the idea that those alterations were without political significance. On the contrary, as I will argue in the following chapter, 'fained history' was generally reputed to be politically dangerous, as is shown by the fact that contemporary attacks on the theatre as a subversive activity always made some special mention of the staging of national history.

Notes

1. W. Sanders, op. cit., p. 146.
2. Ibid., p. 2.
3. 'Ambivalence: the Dialectic of History' is the text of a lecture delivered at Stratford in 1951 and printed in *Talking of Shakespeare*, ed. J. Garrett (London: Hodder & Stoughton, 1954), pp. 149–71; now in *Angel with Horns*.
4. *Angel with Horns*, pp. 51, 62. Rossiter constructed his argument essentially examining the effects of dramatic irony in the *Henry IV* plays; he affirmed that '*comic* history was [Shakespeare's] true genre' and considered on the contrary *Henry V* as 'one-eyed' and as a play where 'allness is gone' (p. 58). A recent discussion of 'why a Shakespeare

play can evoke such a wide range of different and sometime dia-
metrically opposed interpretations' is in Peter Wolfensperger's
Shakespeare: Impartial and Partial (Tübingen: Francke Verlag, 1994);
the sentence quoted is on p. 13. Although the book concentrates on
an analysis of *The Comedy of Errors* and *Much Ado*, the text which
Wolfensperger uses to exemplify polyvalence in the 'Introduction' is
Henry V.

5. E. Talbert, *The Problem of Order* (Chapel Hill: University of California
Press, 1962).

6. G. R. Elton, *King Lear and the Gods* (San Marino: The Huntington
Library, 1966; repr. Lexington: University of Kentucky Press, 1988).
For a reexamination of the idea of providence see W. Sanders, op.
cit., the important contribution of H. A. Kelly, *Divine Providence in the
England of Shakespeare's Histories* (Cambridge, Mass.: Harvard University Press, 1970) and J. B. Altman, *The Tudor Play of Mind* (Berkeley
and Los Angeles: University of California Press, 1978). Sanders' idea
that in Tudor England 'the most important attack on providentialism
came from the historians' (p. 115) cannot, I think, be agreed upon.
While this is true in the case of books which appeared on the continent (the obvious examples quoted by Sanders are Machiavelli and
Bodin), no explicit challenge to the providential idea of history was
formulated by Tudor historians. Sanders in fact only quotes a passage from Bolton's *Hypercritica*, a book which was not published
until the second decade of the seventeenth century.

7. M. Doran, *Endeavors of Art* (Madison: University of Wisconsin Press,
1954); R. Colie, *Paradoxia epidemica* (Princeton: Princeton University
Press, 1966); J. B. Altman, op. cit. Paul Dean says that the ability to
argue *in utramque partem* 'was taught to Shakespeare's generation
above all by Erasmus's *De copia*, which is often seen merely as a
manual on style but which' Dean believes 'to be implicitly also a
work of historiography', 'Shakespeare's Causes', *CE* XXXVI (1989),
25–35, p. 26. Dean discusses this aspect of Erasmus's work also in
'Tudor Humanism and the Roman Past', *Renaissance Quarterly* XLI
(1988), 84–111.

8. Op. cit., p. 319.

9. N. Rabkin, *Shakespeare and the Common Understanding* (New York:
The Free Press and London: Collier-Macmillan, 1967).

10. R. Grudin, *Mighty Opposites. Shakespeare and Renaissance Contrariety*
(Berkeley and Los Angeles: University of California Press, 1979), p.
14. For a discussion of the first and second generation of scholars
who reacted against Tillyard's vision, see R. Headlam Wells, 'The
fortunes of Tillyard', *English Studies* LXVI (1985), 389–99.

11. Independently from the elaborations discussed here, the issue of
ambivalence has recently been treated on the basis of Puttenham's
treatment of the figure which he calls *Amphibologia*. (See S. Mullaney,
'Lying Like Truth: Riddle, Representation and Treason in Renaissance England', *ELH* XLVII [1980], 32–47; and C. Belsey, 'Love in
Venice', *SS* XLIV [1992], 41–53.) A. Serpieri uses the word 'polyphony'
in the title of one of his essays. In the case of Shakespeare and the

Elizabethans, Serpieri argues for a culturally necessitated polyphony, brought into being by the dissolution of the comparatively monolithic medieval symbolic cosmos. In this essay, Serpieri discusses at length *Richard III, Richard II, 1 Henry IV, Henry V* and *Hamlet*. 'Polifonia shakespeareana', in *Retorica e immaginario* (Parma: Pratiche, 1986), pp. 109–92.

12. Altman (op. cit.) established two dramatic paradigms which he calls Demonstrative and Explorative and which, in his opinion, correspond respectively to Bacon's 'Magistral' and 'Probation' modes of arguing. See also, for a discussion of the two modes, S. Fish, *Self-consuming Artifacts* (Berkeley: University of California Press, 1972), pp. 78–155.

13. The remark occurs in Grudin's discussion of Castiglione's *Il Cortegiano*, op. cit., p. 21; but see also pp. 17–18, 34 and *passim*.

14. I wish to point out that 'perspectivism', in the sense of perceptual and representational relativity, is a recognised historiographical category. See K. H. Whiteside, 'Perspectivism and Historical Objectivity: Maurice Merleau-Ponty's covered debate with Raymond Aron', *H&T* XXV (1986), 132–51. In this article, Whiteside examines Merleau-Ponty's unpublished papers and illustrates his 'private' dissent from Aron's refutation of scientistic rationalism and of positivism as regards historical objectivity which is the subject of his *Introduction à la philosophie de l'histoire. Essai sur les limites de l'objectivité historique* (Paris: Gallimard, 1938). Merleau-Ponty considered Aron's arguing for the impossibility of objectivity in historiography as the sign of a sceptical conservatism and responded to Aron's scepticism via the optimism of his *Phénoménologie de la perception* (Paris: Gallimard, 1945).

15. Op. cit., p. 4.

16. Doran lists a few of the questions which were argued from opposed standpoints in the '*jeu parti*': 'Who might be expected to make the most beautiful songs, the unhappy lover or the favored lover? Which is preferable for a lover, the death or the marriage of his beloved? Of two lovers, which is the least unhappy, the one who loses his sight, or the one who loses his hearing? Of two husbands, which is the more to be pitied, the one who has his suspicions, or the one who has his proofs? Who is the more to blame, the lover who boasts of the favors he has received from his lady, or the one who boasts without having received them?' Doran adds, however, that 'the same habit of mind was put to quite serious uses' (op. cit., p. 311).

17. 'Shakespeare's Causes', p. 33.

18. B. A. Uspenskij, 'Storia e semiotica. La percezione del tempo come problema semiotico', in *Storia e semiotica* (Milan: Bompiani, 1988), pp. 9–36, 9–10.

19. M. Bakhtin, 'Slovo v romane', in *Voprosy literatury i estetiki* (Moscow: Izdatel'stvo 'Chudožestvennaja Literatura', 1975; English transl., *The Dialogic Imagination*, ed. H. Holquist (Austin: University of Texas Press, 1981); see especially, 'Discourse in the novel', pp. 258–422. See also T. Todorov, *Michail Bakhtine: Le principe dialogique* (Paris: Seuil, 1981); English transl., *Mikhail Bakhtin: The Dialogic Principle* (Manchester: Manchester University Press, 1984). In the third Book of *The Arte of*

English Poesie ('Of Ornament'), Puttenham treats among the 'figures sententious' what he calls 'Dialogismus, or the right reasoner'. In Puttenham's system, *dialogismus* concerns the mimesis of different social discourses according to the condition of persons and it has obviously to do with point of view and evaluation, although it is discussed as an ornamental procedure. When reporting speeches, Puttenham says, a writer should imitate the style which is proper to the social condition of the speaker; but he seems also to imply a social conversational rule, namely that one should adapt one's discourse to one's interlocutor. The passage deserves a lengthy quote: 'We are sometimes occasioned in our tale to report some speech from another mans mouth, as what a king said to his priuy counsell or subiect, a captaine to his souldier, a souldiar to his captaine, a man to a woman, and contrariwise: in which report we must alwaies geue to euery person his fit and naturall, & that which best becommeth him. For that speech becommeth a king which doth not a carter, and a young man that doeth not an old' (op. cit., p. 235). The notion corresponds to the dialogic procedure that Bakhtin terms 'stylization', 'forms of verbal masquerade, "not talking straight"' ('Discourse in the novel', p. 275). Bakhtin connects the reproduction of a particular discursive style to the expression of a point of view or world-vision.

20. M. Heinemann, 'How Brecht read Shakespeare', in Dollimore and Sinfield (eds), pp. 202–30, 206–7.

21. 'Shakespeare: le storie, la storia', *Annali-Anglistica* XXX (1987), 1–14, p. 12. The distinction between semantic and syntagmatic cultural models is illustrated by Lotman in an essay entitled 'Il problema del segno e del sistema segnico nella tipologia della cultura russa prima del XX secolo', in Ju. M. Lotman and B. A. Uspenskij (eds), *Ricerche semiotiche* (Turin: Einaudi, 1973), pp. 40–63. (I have not come across an English translation of this essay.)

22. The term *discoherence* is used by Dollimore in its seventeenth-century meaning to qualify the readings of materialist criticism. *Discoherence* is defined as 'incongruity verging on contradiction'; a 'meaning-full', 'always readable' kind of contradiction, however, that, while rejecting 'idealist concepts of coherence, does not thereby subscribe to the (residually idealist) notion that all is ultimately incoherent, random, arbitrary or whatever'. *Radical Tragedy* (London: Harvester Wheatsheaf, 1989 [1984]), p. xxii.

23. 'Drama consistently dwells upon conflict and debate', Grudin said, 'but few dramatists have tested the potential of contraries as profoundly as Shakespeare, or employed them in such a wide variety of ways.' (op. cit., p. 3) On Shakespeare's role as cultural and even economic negotiator, see T. B. Leinwand: 'For every argument enlisting him among the subversives or antiprovidentialists of the period we find an argument for the patriarchal bard or for the keeper of the great chain. Yet it seems clear that he was in many ways an interhierarchical figure: capitalist and artist, bourgeois and artisan, shareholder and actor, urban and provincial. He is perhaps less this or

that than a stage for contestation and intermixing.' ('Negotiation and New Historicism', *PMLA* CV [1990], 477–90, p. 487).

24. *The Arte,* p. 260.

25. Even the initial and final demarcations of the fabula may be employed in a text to construct a paradigm and to encompass a world of problems. While plays usually exploit this possibility, in the chronicles beginning and end are more or less arbitrary. On the framing of literary texts, see Ju. M. Lotman, *Struktura chudozestvennogo teksta* (Moscow: Iskusstvo, 1970); English transl., *The Structure of the Artistic Text* (Ann Arbor: The University of Michigan Press, 1977), pp. 209–17; on the categories of beginning and end in historical drama, see G. Martella, 'Inizio e fine nel dramma storico', in F. Marucci and A. Bruttini (eds), *La performance nel testo* (Siena: Ticci, 1986), pp. 113–19.

26. R. Ascham, *A Report and Discourse written by Roger Ascham, of the Affaires and State of Germany* (1570, written in 1553), in *English Works of Roger Ascham,* ed. W. A. Wright (Cambridge: Cambridge University Press, 1904), p. 168.

27. *Hypercritica,* pp. 102–3. The alternative seems to foreshadow that between general and particular histories which has been widely discussed by theorists of historiography in recent times. On the contradictions implied by general histories, mostly owing to the non-homogeneous structure of the historical universe, see S. Kracauer, *History. The Last Things Before the Last* (Oxford: Oxford University Press, 1969), particularly chapters VII and VIII.

28. *Hypercritica,* p. 103. Bolton's attitude to the providentialism of Christian historians should be mentioned: 'while', he argues, 'for their ease they shuffled up the reasons of events, in briefly referring all causes immediately to the Will of God, have generally neglected to inform their Readers in the ordinary means of Carriage in human Affairs, and thereby singularly maimed their Narrations' (pp. 84–5).

29. *Shakespeare Recycled,* p. 7.

30. Cox argues that 'historical empiricism is emergent in Shakespeare'; and contends that 'Shakespeare's secular history not only looks forward to the Enlightenment but also backward to the residual political realism of Augustine.' (op. cit., p. xii) Kastan says that the open-ended structure of the histories 'stands as dramatic challenge to the providential assumptions of most Tudor historiography'. (*Shakespeare and the Shapes of Time,* p. 57) Elsewhere he affirms that 'nothing in the plays encourages us to recognize a divine potter molding the character and fate of his creatures of clay' ('"To Set a Form Upon that Indigest": Shakespeare's Fictions of History', *Comparative Drama* XVII [1983], 1–16, p. 3). Hattaway argues that 'If there is a grand design, it is only dimly glimpsed, for the emphasis of Shakespeare, if not always of his characters, rests firmly upon efficient and not final causes' ('Introduction' to *The Second Part of King Henry VI,* p. 1). Evidence of a vast area of disbelief in providence in Elizabethan England was first produced by Elton (op. cit.).

31. Eccl., 1:9–10.

32. Rossiter, *Angel with Horns,* p. 52.

33. Hattaway says that spectators or readers coming to *3 Henry VI* after the experience of the first two parts will not find a redemptive or tragic conclusion, but rather 'a relentless demonstration of political degradation as the turbulent warlords who rule England destroy what is left of the commonweal'. 'Introduction' to *The Third Part of King Henry VI* (Cambridge: Cambridge University Press, 1993), p. 1.

34. Op. cit., p. 131.

35. P. Thompson, *Shakespeare's Professional Career* (Cambridge: Cambridge University Press, 1992), p. 28.

36. There is no evidence, however, that the scene was not staged. Recently, Janet Clare has argued for both printing and staging censorship in 'The censorship of the deposition scene in *Richard II*', *Review of English Studies*, New Series, XLI (1990), 89–95. Stephen Greenblatt remarked that although 'modern historical scholarship has assured Elizabeth that she had nothing to worry about', for '*Richard II* is not at all subversive but rather a hymn to Tudor order, in 1601 neither Queen Elizabeth nor the Earl of Essex were so sure: after all, someone on the eve of rebellion thought the play sufficiently seditious to warrant squandering two pounds on the players, and the Queen understood the performance as a threat' (*The Power of Forms*, p. 4). The allusion is to the well-known fact that a play on Richard II (almost certainly Shakespeare's) was staged on the eve of Essex's rebellion, as a means of encouraging people to join the revolt.

37. *Mastering the Revels* (Iowa City: University of Iowa Press, 1991).

38. *Art Made Tongue-tied by Authority* (Manchester: Manchester University Press, 1990), p. ix.

39. 'The Powerless Theatre', *ELR* XXI (1991), 49–74, pp. 50, 51.

40. *Shakespeare's History* (Dublin: Gill and Macmillan, 1985), p. 31.

41. G. Taylor, 'Introduction' to *Henry V* (Oxford: Oxford University Press, 1984), p. 31.

4

The Contribution of the Theatrical Medium

... in open presence
Thomas Nashe

Theatre as a medium is a specially suitable channel for conveying an impression of truth. In many ways, therefore, writing for the theatre helped Shakespeare to authenticate his historical fictions. In performance, historical plays provide a peculiar historical experience, entirely different from the one provided by the reading of history books, since in the theatrical situation *éleos* and *phòbos*, pity and fear, are things that happen in the here and now, and are simultaneously and collectively experienced. The theatrical medium, then, while imposing restrictions, allows opportunities that are unknown to the narrational medium: while a narrator will have to state and argue the truth of the facts reported, a dramatist can rely on the reality effect of the performance to induce belief in the truth of what is represented.[1]

Generally speaking, therefore, the dramatist has a better chance of inducing belief in the reality and truth of a story than the historian. This is in part what Nashe meant when he compared the 'worm-eaten books' of chronicles to the live re-enactment of things past on the stage. But there is more to this than what Nashe was affirming in defence of historical drama. One of the genre assumptions of theatre, in fact, is that of possessing the same truth status as we attribute to history in the sense of *res gestae* without the mediation of the *historia rerum gestarum*, because the representation of an event on the stage coincides with the event; in the theatrical situation, in fact, what is represented on the stage is by itself both *memorable* and *true*, two qualities that the theatrical event shares with a certain conceptualisation of historical events.[2] It is, then, the representation itself that sanctions the event and that furthers its claim to be kept in the audience's memory. What the staging of an event produces

60

is, therefore, a strong, though implicit, sanction of the truth of the acts performed before our eyes.

The difference in perception between reading a story and watching a staged play also resides in the more concrete, and therefore more direct, way in which the theatre enables us to apprehend time and time sequences. In the theatrical situation, the illusion of dominating the events derives in part from our tendency to associate time with space: when we watch a play, unlike what happens when we read a tale, we feel that time is not *somewhere else*; rather, we perceive it as accessible because it develops *in praesentia*, even though unity of time is not respected. In other words, a staged play produces a restricted spatial experience where the category of time is almost literally 'seen', in the same way that the objects are seen in the restricted and controllable space of the stage. What, therefore, in written narratives is a temporal 'elsewhere' of which we only know that it was but not *where* it was, is apprehended empirically and simultaneously within the limited compass of the stage.[3]

In his *Apology for Actors* Heywood, too, insisted on the incomparable reality effect of theatrical representations, and in particular on their suitability to induce behaviour, especially when they show historical characters and events. After remarking that 'Oratory is a kind of a speaking picture', that 'Painting likewise, is a dumbe oratory', that 'A Description is only a shadow receiued by the eare but not perceiued by the eye', that 'so liuely portrature is meerely a forme seene by the eye, but can neither shew action, passion, motion, or any other gesture', he contrasts these with theatrical representations, saying that 'to see a souldier shap'd like a souldier, walke, speake, act like a souldier: to see a *Hector* all besmered in blood, trampling upon the bulkes of Kinges. A *Troylus* returning from the field in the sight of his father Priam . . . Oh these were sights to make an *Alexander*.'[4]

Shakespeare was certainly aware of these potentialities of the theatrical medium, although there are moments when he felt the need to stress them, in order to enhance belief in the truth of the world represented. In the Prologue to *Henry VIII* (whose subtitle bears the promise that *All Is True*), the authenticity of the story that is going to develop before the eyes of the spectators is repeatedly stressed, and culminates with an invitation to the audience to enter the world of the play with full confidence:

> think ye see
> The very persons of our noble story
> As they were living; think you see them great,
> And followed with the general throng and sweat
> Of thousand friends . . . .
>   (*Henry VIII*, I.0.25–9)

Even the Choruses of *Henry V* (particularly the Chorus to Act I)
do not seem so much to express distrust in the *effet de réel* of the
staged events as in the stage's aptness to feign distant realities. The
stage, the Chorus seems to say, has the same constraints that reality
has: in the theatrical situation the audience cannot be taken to different, distant places as a reader of historical narratives can. Obviously,
the Chorus is also complaining about the inadequacies of the
'wooden O' to represent grandeur (the physical grandeur of 'the
vasty fields of France' as well as the political grandeur of the 'two
mighty monarchies'). In other words, the Chorus seems precisely to
complain about the supreme physicality and reality of the theatrical
situation.[5]

Besides, the activity of memory – which is the first condition for
the survival of historical deeds – is unmediated in the staged event:
what is presented in performance has a tangibility that can be neither
doubted nor invalidated. The audience is, therefore, called on to
play an important role: thanks to the simultaneity and immediacy
of the events represented, the spectators attain the status of eye-
witnesses, and of course eye-witnesses have always been considered the most dependable among historiographical sources.

But, although the author – by definition voiceless in a playscript
– simply pretends to 'show' and although the responsibility for
opinions may seem to rest solely with the characters, a number of
axiological options are connected with the dramatic medium and
these enable the dramatist to suggest opinions and evaluations.[6]
The indirect procedures by which playwrights may insinuate their
voice while disguising or concealing their responsibility has obvious
degrees of manifestation; and Shakespeare, as we know, rarely committed himself to sharply defined and limpid viewpoints; rather, he
manipulated the audience's reactions by exploiting such indirect
procedures: montage, selection, cutting and foregrounding, temporal
dislocation and the arrangement of sequences are all tools which he
used to create the equivalent of the historiographical categories of explanation and causality, to highlight discrepancies and disharmonies,

to imply social and political friction or simply to shake established readings.

A few instances of such indirect forms of explanation and evaluation may be briefly mentioned.

Various estrangement effects appear in the *Henry IV* plays. Act II of *2 Henry IV* is almost entirely devoted to the comic plot. This, however, is wrenched from its comic track by the intrusion of disturbingly serious themes (justice, in the Hostess's plea against Falstaff and the subsequent appearance of the Lord Chief Justice, the prince's weariness and the sudden summons to war); it is as if the easy side of Hal's and Falstaff's Eastcheap life were beginning to dissolve under the external pressure of serious events. But most of all, the sheer technical problem of giving the prince and Poins time to move from Hal's habitation (in sc. ii) to the Eastcheap tavern (in sc. iv), allows the playwright to present the strikingly discrepant situation of a private conversation (sc. iii) between Northumberland, his wife and Lady Percy, Hotspur's young widow. The disharmony between the two situations is made particularly evident by the contrast between the prince's own thoughtlessness and the valour of Hotspur's solitary enterprise as recalled by his wife. Even after death, Harry Percy has a lesson to teach Hal, who seems still unable to learn it.[7]

In certain cases, strategies of sequencing and temporal compression may deeply affect our reading of a text's stance. Let us consider, for instance, the discrepancy arising in the interpretation of Bolingbroke's motives from the fact that Northumberland announces his return from exile in the same scene in which Richard, after Gaunt's death, has disinherited him. (*Richard II*, II.i). The serious gap which the condensation of events opens in our construction of the usurper's motivations casts an ambiguous light on Bolingbroke's decision to return from France and renders suspicious the reasons he will later give for his return.[8]

That the opening scene of *Henry V* casts a shadow on the transparency of Canterbury's favourable response to Henry's project to conquer the French crown needs no arguing. But the darkest shadow on Henry's conduct is cast by the sequencing of scenes vi and vii in Act IV. Henry's order that 'every soldier kill his prisoner' (vi.37) is in fact given just before the killing of the baggage-train boys by the French is made known in a dialogue between Fluellen and Gower (vii.1–11). Although Gower says that the order was given in response to the boys' slaughter – 'wherefore the king most worthily hath caused every soldier to cut his prisoner's throat' (9–10) – we know that the order was given simply on hearing that 'The French have reinforc'd their scatter'd men' (vi.36), and before the slaughter of the baggage boys was made known to Henry. The status of witness that the audience assumes by the mere fact of being in the playhouse *while these things happen*, allows strategic sequencing and other dramatic procedures designed to influence audience opinion to assume the status of direct evidence: the spectators can, in a way, bear witness to what actually happened; they can report, in this case, that Henry gave that order before he knew of the boys' slaughter.[9]

Not least among the factors which account for the exceptional impact that history acquires on the stage is the particular social make-up of the audience in contemporary public theatres. If the Elizabethan playhouses were, as seems to be the prevailing opinion, attended by an extremely heterogeneous social aggregate,[10] then the reception of plays produced a complex and variegated 'popular' response that involved an almost complete cross-section of contemporary society;[11] thus, national history was presented to people who acknowledged it as their shared collective memory, witnessed in its re-enactment by a public that was representative of the whole variegated metropolitan society of London and thus subjected to a collective and immediate – although differentiated – response. The impact and influence of history presented on the stage was, therefore, indubitably greater than that exerted by the 'worm-eaten books'. In turn, the playwright that staged events from the common past assumed an enormous responsibility: the visual and aural memory of a performance leave strange marks, that have the power of cancelling the graphic signs of the book, superimposing on them, as in a palimpsest, a new vision.

When Stephen Gosson penned his attack on the abuses of the theatre, he denounced precisely the risks of collective attendance. After listing a few plays (including his *Catiline*) that he judged 'tollerable at sometyme' and that appeared to him generally laudable especially because they show 'howe seditious estates . . . & rebellious commons in their owne snares are ouerthrown' and others where 'the rewarde of traytors' and 'the necessary gouernment of learned men' is depicted, he expresses his fears about collective popular attendance. Although the plays he mentions are 'the best playes and most to be liked', he adds that they are not 'fit for every mans dyet: neither ought they commonly to be shewen' (the meaning of the word *commonly* is made clear in the margin caption:

'Playes are not to be made common').[12] Gosson is here echoing a preoccupation expressed by the authorities on many occasions. Even as early as 16 May 1559, in fact, restrictions on the abuses of public performances were issued by Elizabeth. These prescribed that 'matters of religion or of the gouernance of the state of the common weale' should only be played before an audience of 'graue and discrete persons', to the exclusion of commoners.[13]

Indeed, both Gosson and the official restriction of 1559 imply that the treatment of historical and political topics in theatres was seen as a danger to the state's political stability. (It is superfluous to quote Elizabeth's anxiety about the play on the deposition of Richard II being shown '40tie times in open streetes and houses').[14]

Stephen Orgel discusses the intrinsic subversiveness of the theatrical 'miming of greatness' and makes suggestive points to explain the anxieties produced by the dangers of representing politics in a public playhouse. His conclusion on this point is that 'Theatrical pageantry, the miming of greatness, is highly charged because it employs precisely the same methods the crown was using to assert and validate its authority. To mime the monarch was a potentially revolutionary act – as both Essex and Elizabeth were well aware.' Orgel also quotes a remark of Sir Henry Wotton, who attended the first performance of Shakespeare's *Henry VIII* and found that the play made 'greatness familiar, if not ridiculous'; a remark which confirms that 'to mime nobility on the stage was to diminish it'.[15] A more radical opinion on the dangers of representing greatness is expressed by Kastan: 'In setting English kings before an audience of commoners, the theatre nourished the cultural conditions that eventually permitted the nation to bring its King to trial, not because the theatre approvingly represented subversive acts, but rather because representation became itself subversive.'[16]

Besides, theatrical activities, although comparatively marginalised, had an ambiguous status as regarded their potential influence. As argued by Mullaney, 'In a certain sense outcast, the popular stage also possessed, by virtue of its situation, a power to shock and scandalize'.[17] However, the playwright's responsibilities were not only strictly political, for they also involved his ability to create an impression of truth while at the same time leaving scope for invention. As I have already remarked, in the case of Shakespeare's histories, the overall authenticity of the stories was guaranteed by the presence of the basic events recounted in the chronicles, whose function was to convince the audience that 'all was true'; with this sound basis, the introduction of invented elements which *might have existed* immediately beyond the threshold of history was not felt to be falsification, provided that they did not collide with the events of true history. Therefore, while not undermining the general effect of historicity, invention opened up a free area where things might be safely imagined to have happened and opinions and evaluations might be safely expressed or conveyed implicitly. In other words, what was perceived as the *fabula vera* made it possible to play around historically with the *res fictae*, while invention was in turn allowed to generate truth or, at least, verisimilitude.[18]

Notes

1. Two different notions are implied in this statement, as two different effects may inhere to drama in performance. What I mean by 'true' is connected with the knowledge that the events represented have actually happened, or have a counterpart, in the real world. On the other hand, the reality effect of the theatrical experience is connected with the realism or lifelike quality of certain representations and also with the impression that what happens on the stage is actually happening, simultaneously with its perception. Bacon defined what he calls 'Poesy representative' (as distinct from the Narrative and the Allusive) as 'a visible History', and 'an image of actions as if they were present, as history is of actions in nature as they are, (that is) past' (*The Advancement of Learning*, in *The Philosophical Works of Francis Bacon*, p. 88).

2. The category of what is *memorable* is here used to refer to a particular kind of historical conceptualisation, as distinct from the conceptualisation of history as *exemplum*. The Greeks used the term *apomnemòneuma* for those events which exceeded the occasional or routine quality of everyday experience and therefore deserved to be recorded and kept in the conscience of a given social community. 'Unlike the *exemplum*', Jauss says, 'which allows us to draw a moral lesson from an action in the past and to give it a univocal formulation, in what is *memorable* the meaning of the historical experience is complex, sometimes even paradoxical and unfathomable.' Jauss proceeds to argue that what is memorable is a-teleologic, and 'does not provide a criterion for the reading of future actions, but provides an experience of the ineludible contingency of historical life'. *Ästhetische Erfahrung und literarische Hermeneutik* (Frankfurt: Suhrkamp, 1982). There is an English translation of the 1977 edition (Munich: Wilhelm Fink Verlag) of Jauss's book, *Aesthetic Experience and Literary Hermeneutics* (Minneapolis: University of Minnesota Press, 1982), which does not contain the chapter entitled 'Die kommunicative Funktion

der Fiktive' from which the passage is taken. Here and elsewhere, therefore, I quote from the Italian translation of the 1982 edition quoted above, *Esperienza estetica ed ermeneutica letteraria* (Bologna: Il Mulino, 1987), 2 vols, vol. I, pp. 404–5.

3. Uspenskij discusses the tendency to apprehend time in terms of space as an attempt to construct a more direct and empirical cognition of an eminently abstract category (op. cit., pp. 27–9). He quotes Augustine: 'If the future and the past are, I want to know where they are' (*Confessions*, XI, 18.23).

4. T. Heywood, *An Apology for Actors*, ed. R. H. Perkinson (New York: Scholars' Facsimiles and Reprints, 1941), B3ᵛ, B4. Heywood's *Apology* was published posthumously in 1612.

5. See the lines addressed to Fletcher by Thomas Palmer prefacing the 1647 Beaumont and Fletcher Folio: 'How didst thou sway the Theatre! make us feele / The Players wounds were true, and their swords, steele! / Nay, stranger yet, how often did I know / When the spectators ran to save their blow? / Frozen with griefe we could not stir away / Untill the Epilogue told us 'twas a Play'.

6. W. N. Dodd discusses a strategy of attention control that he terms 'alignment', by which the spectators are placed in a reception position which aligns them with one of the characters and makes them apprehend things with or alongside him or her. 'Positioning' and 'packaging' are, according to Dodd, strategies of attention control underlining a cause–effect relationship between two different events or emotions by exploiting the scene as a cognitive unit. 'Shakespeare's Control of Audience Reaction', in K. Elam (ed.), *Shakespeare Today: Directions and Methods of Research* (Florence: La Casa Usher, 1984), pp. 134–49.

7. Elton discusses sequencing as one of the instruments producing contrariety and remarks that the *liaison des scènes* may by itself carry meaning (op. cit., p. 329).

8. Discussing this point, Dodd stresses the spectator's position (as against both the ordinary reader's and the analytic reader's) and argues that what the audience perceives is an *impression* of cause–effect; in other words, the spectators' immediate reaction develops at the plot level and does not involve a reconstruction of the fabula, the level where the discrepancy is located ('*Richard II* . . .', pp. 87–96).

9. In the present debate concerning performance criticism *vs* text criticism, this particular privilege of the audience has not, to my knowledge, been discussed.

10. But see the opinion of A. Jennalie Cook, *The Privileged Playgoers of Shakespeare's London, 1576–1642* (Princeton: Princeton University Press, 1981).

11. I use 'popular' in the sense defined by M. Hattaway, namely as a function of the plays' 'appeal to the whole spectrum of Elizabethan society', in *The Elizabethan Popular Theatre* (London: Routledge, 1982), p. 1.

12. S. Gosson, *The School of Abuse*, in A. F. Kinney (ed.), *Markets of Bawdry. The Dramatic Criticism of Stephen Gosson* (Salzburg: Institut für Englische Sprache und Literatur, Universität Salzburg, 1974), p. 97.

In his defence of plays, Nashe affirmed, against this argument, that spending the afternoon in a public playhouse keeps people from sloth and crime (op. cit., pp. 211–12). The preoccupations of the authorities as concerns collective attendance may be explained by Kastan's remark that 'in the theatre images of authority become subject to the approval of an audience' ('Proud Majesty . . .', 466–7).

13. Chambers, *The Elizabethan Stage* (Oxford: Clarendon Press, 1923), vol. IV, p. 263. The restriction concerned 'all maner Interludes', 'either openly or privately' performed. The first recorded inns, hostels and taverns where public performances were held were active about 1557.

14. Elizabeth seems to have mentioned this in a conversation with William Lambarde. See Chambers, op. cit., vol. II, p. 206, n. 4.

15. 'Making Greatness Familiar', in S. Greenblatt (ed.), *The Power of Forms*, pp. 41–8, 47.

16. 'Proud Majesty . . .', pp. 460–1. A similar argument had been previously proposed by Franco Moretti in his essay ' "A Huge Eclipse": Tragic Form and the Deconsecration of Sovereignty', in S. Greenblatt (ed.), *The Power of Forms*, pp. 7–40.

17. *The Place of the Stage. Licence, Play and Power in Renaissance England* (Chicago: University of Chicago Press, 1988), p. 30.

18. The issue of invention is touched upon, again, by Holderness. Discussing the *Henry IV* plays as 'less firmly attached to the solid *mimesis* of literary historiography' than *Richard II*, and as displaying 'an infinitely greater liberty of invented incident', Holderness argues that 'The principal effect of this expanded form . . . is its enlarged capacity for the juxtaposition of contradictions' ('Prologue: "The Histories" and History', p. 42).

5

The Fictionalisation of History and the Issue of Verisimilitude

Not truth, but things like truth
George Chapman

The 'fictionalization of history' has been in recent times a much-debated issue for theorists of historiography. Hayden White, in particular, argues that, when told by the historian, the meaningless and arbitrary sequences that reach our experience in the form of *res factae* need to be given coherence and conclusiveness in the form of *res fictae* if historical narratives are to capture and communicate a specific social reality and to attribute a certain meaning to it.[1]

In the Renaissance, the concept which was best fit to describe these issues was that of *verisimilitude*, Aristotle's *eikòs*. The word indicates what is *similar, convenient, apt, relevant,* and also *natural*. In connection with other terms which belong to the same semantic field, Aristotle uses it to distinguish what is truth-like and pertains to poetry from what is true and pertains to history.[2] However, the fact that in his *Poetics* Aristotle assigned the simple statement of fact to the historian and the search for verisimilitude to the poet was taken at its face-value throughout the Renaissance and long after. Indeed, commentators failed to see that Aristotle's formulation was perhaps of greater importance to the historian than to the poet, since it implied that what is simply true is not always truth-like. In fact, Aristotle established at the same time a connection and a distinction between verisimilitude and truth, saying that there are true facts that are suitable for being recounted by the poet because, independently from their being true, they appear possible and verisimilar.

The notion of verisimilitude in connection with history and poetry appears in all those Renaissance writings where the Aristotelian theory is expounded or summarised, usually with little that is new even as far as interpretation and commentary are concerned. Rather

69

than report these, I will quote a playwright's point of view, for the poet's intuition, it seems to me, completes Aristotle's reasoning, assigning to what is verisimilar ('things like truth') a distinct role in historical narratives. In the 'Epistle Dedicatory' of *Bussy D'Ambois*, addressed to Sir Thomas Howard, George Chapman highlights the oxymoronic and mixed quality of fictionalised truth, to which he gives the name of 'natural fictions':

> And for the authentical truth of either person or action, who (worth the respecting) will expect it in a poem, whose subject is not truth, but things like truth? Poor envious souls they are that cavil at truth's want in these natural fictions: material instruction, elegant and sententious excitation to virtue, and deflection from her contrary, being the soul, limbs, and limits of an authentic tragedy.[3]

Richard Brathwait's treatment of more or less the same issue as far as history books are concerned raises a few questions. Brathwait divides histories into four categories: Feigned, Morall, Physicall and Mixed. What appears uncommon – and contrary to both Aristotelian and Tudor prescriptions – is that verisimilitude is not evoked, as one might expect, in connection with Feigned Histories, but rather in connection with the Mixt type, a form that is described as 'mixt' because it draws from various domains of knowledge rather than because it is corrupted by fictitious elements. Brathwait prescribes that Mixt Histories should possess three qualities ('truth', 'an explanation in discovering, not onely the sequence of things, but also the cause and reasons drawing to the conclusions' and 'Judgment in distinguishing things by approving the best, disallowing the contrary'); and when expanding on the first quality (truth), he says that

> For the first, stories should be true, or *at least resemble truth*, because by so much, they are more pleasing, by how much they resemble truth the neerer; and so much more gracefully, by how much more *probable and doubtfull*. We have many histories (even of this kinde) mixed, that comprehend in them nothing lesse than truth: yet by their smooth carriage, and their proper circumstances with such aptnesse drained and disposed, they have been taken for truth, and registered amongst works of more serious consequence.[4]

The passage seems to justify, and even express appreciation for, the presence, in true histories, of things that 'resemble truth' or that are 'probable and doubtfull', as elements which contribute to enhancing the reader's pleasure. It is not clear, however, whether Brathwait is here speaking of procedures ('with such aptnesse drained and disposed') or of invented elements ('things probable and doubtfull'). In any case, it may surely be said that, however unclear the treatment of the *eikòs* may be in these texts, verisimilitude is considered as a link between poetry and history and that at least some Renaissance writers seem to be aware of the communicative function of fictitious elements or at least of fictional procedures in histories. While in general terms we may conclude that this awareness seems to reduce the distance between poetry and history, it remains uncertain what value contemporary texts attribute to verisimilitude: in particular, it seems that these texts fail to make a clear distinction between subject-matter and narrative procedures.[5] However, the suggestion that the use of fictional elements (either in content or in presentation) may enhance the reader's pleasure is present in almost all treatments of the subject. And the many warnings against the 'impiety' of truth-corruption which were addressed to historians may indicate that at least some of them were already discovering one of the principles elaborated by certain theories of historiography, namely that written accounts of history should constantly strive to render truth verisimilar; that no truth can be validated simply by virtue of having had a counterpart in the real world (a counterpart that is indeed never actually retrievable as fact); that, in short, truth is a method and to some extent a textual effect, and that strategies, which are largely fictional, must be invented to render it truth-like, that is to say, as coherent and convincing in a way life never is. For, as Dumas *père* put it, 'life is not interesting, but history is'.[6]

   In other words, the misleading search for 'things as things were' and the illusion of objectivity which came to the annals and to the chronicles from a notion of truth as correspondence in which the text was seen as a reproduction of the world is slowly giving way to a more problematic notion of truth as *internal coherence of the system*, where objectivity is replaced by the completeness and cohesion of plots and problems.[7] Such a notion of truth not only implied the exploitation of fictional procedures but also, especially in the practice of what Bacon called 'poesy representative', the introduction of invented elements. Shakespeare's mixing up of truth and falsehood, therefore, was not by itself a transgression: as Puttenham and others conceded, poets historical were in fact allowed to invent. However, the introduction of invented materials in historical texts

may produce a number of different effects. It may serve as a means
to de-historicise history, namely, as a reprieve from the weight of
serious historical matter – as is the case with the historical romances,
whose principal aim seems to be that of fostering populistic myths
as regards the king's natural body; on the contrary, it may serve as
a means to re-orient, at least in part, the historical picture by exercising, so to speak, an external pressure on some of its parts. This
last, it seems to me, is the function which can be attributed to the
introduction of invented characters and incidents in Shakespeare's
historical texts. It might even be said that their weight is inversely
proportional to their numbers and their social status: indeed, precisely because they appear only sparsely and marginally, they do
not endanger the truth of the historical events in which they take
part and from which they, in turn, absorb the status of history.
Their presence, therefore, produces a peculiar exchange of validation moves between what is true and what is verisimilar, between
the prescriptions of historiography and the necessities of poetry:
while half-truths and lies get a strong sanction from being placed
alongside what is recognised as true, true events, in turn, gain in
verisimilitude from being mingled with invented incidents. Furthermore, the inclusion of invented characters in historical plots allows
the conflation of heterogeneous components and points of view;
and the orchestration of diversity in discourses, genres, conventions
and languages highlights discrepancies and conflicts of interest,
introducing differences (social, linguistic, and other) as relevant data
of historical experience and thus foregrounding the concurring systems of a multiplicity of 'histories'.

'The use of this Fained History', Bacon said, 'hath beene to give
some shadow of satisfaction to the mind of man in those points
wherein the nature of things doth deny it, the world being in proportion inferior to the soule.'[8] Holding the mirror up to history,
Shakespeare must have realised that history as fact is insufficient,
inferior to, and less verisimilar than, history as possibility.

Notes

1. White's most conspicuous contribution is his book *Metahistory* (Baltimore: Johns Hopkins University Press, 1973). In a concise form, his idea of 'emplotment' as an explanatory tool is the following: 'By emplotment I mean simply the encodation of the facts contained in the chronicle as components of specific kinds of plot-structures, in precisely the way that Frye has suggested is the case with "fictions" in general. . . . The events are made into a story by the suppression or subordination of certain of them and the highlighting of others, by characterization, motific repetition, variation of tone and point of view, alternative descriptive strategies, and the like – in short, all the techniques that we would normally expect to find in the emplotment of a novel or a play.' 'Historical Text as Literary Artifact', in R. H. Kanary and H. Kozicki (eds), *The Writing of History. Literary Form and Historical Understanding* (Madison: University of Wisconsin Press, 1978), pp. 41–62, 46, 47) History as a literary genre is also treated in P. Veyne, *Comment on écrit l'histoire* (Paris: Seuil, 1971) and H. R. Jauss, *Ästhetische Erfahrung*. See also E. Scarano and D. Diamanti (eds), *La scrittura della storia* (Pisa: T.E.P., 1991).

2. In Aristotle's *Poetics*, the field comprises at least five different concepts: *ta genòmena* (the facts), *ta dunatà* (things that are possible), *to eikòs* (what is verisimilar), *to anankàion* (what is necessary) and *to pithanòn* (what is credible). One of the passages in the *Poetics* where all these terms appear is 1451b.

3. *The Revenge of Bussy D'Ambois*, ed. R. J. Lordi (Institut für Englische Sprache und Literatur: Universität Salzburg, 1977), p. 41.

4. Op. cit., p. 67; my emphasis.

5. As far as procedures are concerned, treatments of the subject generally mention the order and disposition of the events narrated, while as regards the introduction of imaginary elements it is suggested that the historian is only allowed to reconstruct speeches or dialogues. Hayward's passage ('what liberty a writer may use in framing speeches') is worth recalling.

6. The cognitive function of fictional strategies in historical narratives, Jauss argues, has been ignored owing to the biased opinion that the *res factae* are separable, in content as well as in form, from the *res fictae*. Fictionalisation in history, Jauss says, does not simply mean to use fictional instruments in historical narratives. Rather, it should be recognised that 'the *res factae* are not a primum' and that no event is simply raw fact: therefore, some kind of fictionalisation is inherent in the historical experience, because the content of a historical event 'is conditioned from the start by the perspective from which it is perceived or reconstructed, but also by the mode of its exposition or interpretation' (*Ästhetische Erfahrung*, p. 374, Italian transl.). A similar claim is made by P. Nora, 'L'évènement monstre', *Communications* XVIII (1972), 162–72.

7. G. G. Droysen argues that 'objectivity is a quality of what lacks thought' and that 'facts would be dumb in the absence of a narrator that gives

them voice' (*Historik. Vorlesungen über Enzyklopedie und Methodologie der Geschichte*, Munich, 1967, par. 91). The passage is quoted by H. R. Jauss (*Ästhetische Erfahrung*, p. 383, Italian transl.).

8.   *The Advancement of Learning*, p. 88.

Part II
Cross-Examining Political Issues

6

The Scribbled Form of Authority in *King John*

Lily Campbell opens her discussion of *King John* by quoting the Bastard's final speech and a parallel passage from Holinshed on the disruptive effects of treason and rebellion. The fragment records an event far removed from the story of John, since it concerns what was argued in 1581 during the trial for treason of Edward Campion:

> *This little Lland*, God having so bountifullie bestowed his blessings upon it, that *except it proove false within it selfe, no treason whatsoever can prevaile against it*. . . . Secret rebellion must be stirred here *at home* among our selves, the harts of the people must be obdurated against God and their prince; so that when *a foren power* shall on a sudden invade this realme, the subiects thus seduced must ioine with these *in armes*, and so shall the pope atteine the sum of his wish.[1]

The Bastard's words, in the closing lines of *King John*, are:

This England never did, nor never shall,
Lie at the proud foot of a conqueror,
But when it first did help to wound itself.
Now these her princes are come *home* again
Come the three corners of the world *in arms*
And we shalle shock them! Nought shall make us rue
If England to itself do rest but true.
                    (V.vii.112–18; my italics)

Holinshed's passage is so near to these lines that it might be used as an argument against those – like Dover Wilson – who have argued that the sole source of *King John* was *The Troublesome Raigne;*[2] indeed, the play's relationship with tradition, together with its projection of the story of John on to the contemporary political arena, are the main themes to which criticism has directed attention. In discussions of both these themes, which are frequently treated together, *King John* has suffered from the fact that the search for parallels with *TR* has mainly been aimed at showing the chronological priority of one of the two plays. Similarities have, therefore, often been thought to be more relevant than dissimilarities, and the only important point which has been made in the comparison is the evaluation of *King John* as less radically anti-papist than the anonymous play.[3] As far as the use of historical sources is concerned, proposals range from the idea that Shakespeare's sole source was *TR*, of which *King John* becomes a revision, and whose departures from historical truth we therefore find reproduced in Shakespeare's play; to the idea that Holinshed was the play's source (and to the suggestion that *King John* may have preceded *TR*), supported by quotations of similar passages in the play and in the chronicle. As regards the play's general attitude, we go from Campbell's idea that in *King John*, as in the other history plays, Shakespeare mirrors the prevailing opinions of the political establishment of his time, to the recent claim that the play subverts Tudor ideology.[4]

But the real critical impasse regarding this play concerns the way we should evaluate contemporary allusions. Although all critics agree that these are present in *King John* perhaps more pervasively than in any other of the histories, one encounters both the opinion that they were clear and deliberate, and therefore meant to be picked up by the audience, and the opposite opinion that they appear merely as latent hints; in other words, as connotations whose potential dangerousness was neither perceived by the audience nor even perhaps consciously intended by the author.[5] In other words, while the presence of dangerous parallels is generally admitted, their subversive potential has often been denied. Campbell's treatment of this point is particularly puzzling. She mentions four outstanding political issues which she sees represented in the play and whose risky implications she seems willing enough to admit, for she views them as rehearsing delicate political problems which tormented Elizabeth: '1) the right of Elizabeth to the throne; 2) the right of the pope to deprive a ruler of his crown; 3) the right of subjects to rebel; and 4) the right of a king to be answerable for his sins to God alone'.[6] She then goes on to find other dangerous parallels: in particular, she stresses the fact that the relationship between John and Hubert regarding the blinding of Arthur, with Hubert subsequently becoming the scapegoat, recalls the relationship between Elizabeth and her secretary Davison, who was among those who pressed the

Queen to sign Mary's death warrant and thereafter suffered her displeasure. Arguing that 'the aspect of the problem of regicide which interested Shakespeare in *King John* was the aspect presented by the problem of the refugee queen, Mary of Scotland', Campbell even affirms – rightly, I think – that the Bastard 'might well have been speaking of Elizabethan England when he spoke his elegiac lines over Arthur'[7] (the lines quoted are those in IV.iii.143–7, in which the Bastard complains that 'From forth this morsel of dead royalty, / The life, the right and truth of all this realm / Is fled to heaven', closing with the allusion to 'the unowed interest of proud-swelling state'). Campbell also sees a connection between the conflict of power versus right, which she recognises as fundamental in the play, and the uncertain right of Elizabeth herself, and expresses the opinion that the words pronounced by Elinor ('Your strong possession much more than your right': I.i.40), 'having no historical authority, were, in fact, put there to echo the situation of Elizabeth rather than John'.[8] (Incidentally, the right of the historical John was not considered to be uncertain.) Regarding the last of the problems she raises, namely, the divine right of a king to be judged by God alone, Campbell further remarks that Elizabeth's problem was harder than those occasioned by rebellion, since it concerned the question of 'whether a king may judge another king'. The moral import of this problem, she notes, is to be seen in the (unhistorical) way in which 'Shakespeare portrays John's sore repentance and his furious reproaching of Hubert when he believes him to have executed the royal command'.[9]

However, after reviving the Hubert-Davison parallel again, with more sound historical evidence, Campbell closes her discussion of the play on the harmless – and frankly uninteresting – question of who is its hero, the Bastard or John. She wisely concludes by stating the opinion that history plays were suited to representing not heroes but political conflicts, and she summarises those of *King John* but entirely neglects the one for which she has convincingly and punctiliously argued: regicide. In short, notwithstanding the soundness of the arguments she uses to throw light on a series of highly dangerous contemporary allusions, Campbell does not give up her idea of Shakespeare as mirroring the policy of the Elizabethan regime, although one cannot help feeling that the idea is less convincingly argued for here than elsewhere in her book.

Not dissimilar is Bullough's attitude when he says that parallels 'were probably intentional, but we must beware of making them too close' and adds that 'It would have been highly dangerous to remind the audience that Elizabeth had wished to have her rival quietly assassinated rather than formally executed, especially since the dramatic parallel would have made the Queen a murderess in fact as King John was only in intention.' Bullough, too, mentions the Hubert–Davison parallel, recalling the ways in which, by imprisonment and heavy fining, Davison had been made a scapegoat; but then he affirms that 'To have recalled that affair (which reflected no great credit on the Queen) in 1590, when Essex and others were vainly trying to obtain for Davison the Secretaryship left vacant by Walsingham's death, would have been most inopportune.' After which, ignoring his own last argument, he emphasises the close similarity, although the use he makes of it is to argue that 'the parallel tells against an early date for the play'.[10]

The relevant question, it seems to me, is not whether *King John* exhibits parallels with contemporary political issues, for these have been most convincingly pointed out; nor whether such allusions are in fact dangerous or not: some of them – those concerning regicide, illegitimacy and bastardy – evidently are. It is rather to whom and to what extent they were actually apparent. Obviously, any answer to the question of how open these allusions were and of whether they were immediately comprehended by the audience would be pure speculation, since it would presuppose that we had a clear idea of how well-informed and politically aware the persons that attended public performances were. Indeed, the theatre audience comprised all kinds of persons, from the naive to the politically aware, and all kinds of allusion were, therefore, exposed to detection. The only possible way of dealing with this issue is by saying that anything that is in a text is liable to be perceived and that, therefore, dangerous allusions represent, to say the least, a dangerous subversion potential, even though they are protected by the shield of indirectness. So, once again, in *King John*, Shakespeare was running close to the threshold of disobedience, balancing risky political allusions with mild applause and mitigating blame with moderate consensus; once again, the fact that more than one reading was possible may have been crucial in allowing this play to make it on to the stage.[11]

In different, or rather complementary ways, duplicity has been recognised as a fundamental feature of *King John*. Vaughan has spoken of a 'dual perspective', underlining what she believes to be the deliberate oscillation, in the play, between a medieval and a

Renaissance political context; and John R. Elliot concentrates on the way in which Shakespeare exploits two different traditions about John: the medieval one, frankly hostile, and the sixteenth-century one that elevated John to the position of a protestant proto-martyr.[12] Indeed, nowhere else in the corpus of the histories is the fluctuation between historical reconstruction and contemporary political commentary more pronounced; nowhere else does intertextuality and source-corruption play a more significant role as political commentary. For *King John* is 'Shakespeare's most unhistorical play',[13] but it is also the play in which Shakespeare is most interested in contemporary political implications (it has been argued that the play mirrors not only specific political problems but also 'the uncertainties of an epoch in which the sacred right of sovereign power was perilously shaken').[14]

Let us now go back to Holinshed's report of Campion's trial in connection with the closing lines of the play. The similarities between the two passages cannot be mere chance: moreover, they lead one to suggest that, while writing *King John*, Shakespeare was reading Holinshed not only to gather information about the story of John, but also to see what parallels could be drawn between that story and contemporary politics; and that, in his search for such parallels, he came as near to his own time as possible, and even picked up suggestions from a trial held as late as 1581. Apart from providing more evidence for Holinshed as a source of the play, therefore, they may suffice to confirm that, while writing *King John*, Shakespeare was looking for parallels with contemporary events in his favourite chronicle. Obviously, he cannot have omitted to read at the same time the story of the king about whom he was then writing. If Holinshed was his only source, then, it is evident that the story of John as it was narrated by the chronicler did not satisfy him, that he wanted both to modify it and update it in the way we know, and that in order to do so he also read extensively from the story of Elizabeth. On the other hand, if he also read and used *TR*, he used it as a repertory of contemporary allusions rather than of real facts, for the reading of Holinshed had shown him what the historical truth about John was thought to have been and in what ways the anonymous play had altered it. In other words, if – as is probable – he read both, he knew perfectly well what was true and what was false, and thus actually decided to use the lies of *TR*, while he also picked up anachronistic elements and suggestions from a different point in his historical source.

Whether *TR* was one of his sources or not, therefore, the intertextual situation remains complex and such as to reveal a certain intellectual tension and to suggest that certain significant decisions had to be taken. For the allusions to contemporary politics derive precisely from the play's departures from historical truth. Illegitimacy, bastardy, the conflict between possession and right, the way in which the theme of regicide is alluded to, the treatment of rebellion, all served to update the story, and did so by stressing issues which could not fail to be familiar to the contemporary audience. On the other hand, there is significant manipulation also of what may have been the one non-historical source: in *King John*, in fact, both the anti-papist protestant propaganda and the anti-French rhetoric are played down while, unlike *TR*, Shakespeare's play depicts the scenario of a confused world from which God has departed.

The political significance of such source manipulation and of the contemporary allusions that this served to highlight has been aptly summarised by Honigmann. I quote the passage in full as a complete catalogue of the relevant issues which connect Shakespeare's story of John to that of Elizabeth. These I will take for granted in the development of my argument:

An English sovereign, said to be a usurper (I.i.40), and perhaps a bastard (II.i.130), defies the pope (III.i.73), becomes 'supreme head' (III.i.81), is excommunicated (III.i.99), imprisons his rival (IV.i.), who was barred from the crown by a will (II.i.192); the pope promises his murder canonization (III.i.103), invites another king to invade England (III.i.181), the English sovereign darkly urges the murder of the rival 'pretender' (III.ii), then needs a scapegoat (IV.ii.208), a foreign invasion is attempted (IV.ii.110), the invaders intending to kill the Englishmen who help them (V.iv.10), their navy is providentially wrecked off the English coast (V.v.12), English unity being finally achieved through the failure of invasion (V.vii.115) ... That Shakespeare found *some* of these facts in the chronicles does not detract from the overwhelming effect of the parallel, which is entirely due to the selection of incidents relevant to a particular purpose.[15]

To discuss those parallels, many of which have been known since 1874,[16] would be superfluous, as would a discussion of the parallels between the story of John and that of Henry VIII (these mainly affect the apologetic, Protestant side of the play). Nevertheless, a few issues – the theme of *possession* versus *right* and the related topic of rebellion – seem to me to allow scope for further discussion. Starting from Vaughan's thesis that in *King John* Shakespeare 'played against the inherited text' subverting the ideology of both the chronicle and *TR*,[17] I will discuss the way in which the interplay of power, right and authority is elaborated in *King John*.

The conflict between power and right – or possession and right – is usually discussed on the basis of an exchange between Elinor and John in I.i. Against Arthur's claim which, as Chatillon's embassy communicates, is supported by the French king, John sets his 'strong possession' and his 'right', a statement that Elinor corrects, reminding her son that his right is in fact much less certain than his strong possession (I.i.39–40). Critical discussions of this point usually take for granted John's 'strong possession' and partly reject his 'right' (the weakness of the sovereign's right and the comparative strength of his/her power is the first of the parallels that the text establishes with Elizabeth's situation). But, as I will try to show, the text has more to say on this point: in fact, the alternative posited is not simply that between possession and right; it is, rather, a more uncertain and subtle one, where a third factor – authority or lack of authority – is introduced in such a way as to act against both. The main question, then, is not simply John's acquiring or affirming a right by vanquishing his opponents; it is, rather, his authority which is repeatedly contested, and without which neither right nor possession can be assured. Even in the words of Chatillon ('The borrow'd majesty, of England here', I.i.4), John's essential weakness is held to reside not in his usurpation of a title, but in his borrowing 'majesty', namely, the dignity of sovereignty.

Historically speaking, the question of right was most uncertain and debatable in the twelfth and thirteenth centuries. Peter Saccio says that 'of the six kings since the Conquest, only one (Richard I himself) had gained the throne without dispute', and adds that 'The real or supposed wishes of the dying king, the preferences of the leading magnates, the strength and celerity of the various heirs, and sheer luck were all potentially powerful elements in the highly fluid situation created by a demise of the crown.'[18] These are some of the elements that could contribute to winning power and thus initiate *de facto* possession of it. However, once won, power must be maintained and its maintenance – especially in a dubious and fluid situation regarding legitimacy – depends both on the way it has been won and on the outward signs that accompany it, which should be such as to indicate that it is beyond doubt in the right hands.[19]

The assurance of power, in other words, comes both from *a right to right* and from *a title to possession*. The right to right, when it is not established by means of a legal contract, rests on a series of concurring factors (more or less those mentioned by Saccio) which, however, do not imply personal merit; the title to possession, instead, is sanctioned by the social acknowledgement of the monarch's authority which is the key factor in establishing consensus. Power and authority, in other words, are not synonyms, nor does the presence of one necessarily imply the presence of the other. Even divine sanction ratifies power but not necessarily authority, which rests more on the natural side of the monarch's body (that both power and authority may be disputed implies, in the final analysis, the liberty to question the divine right of kings). Power is *potestas*, namely, 'the capacity to actually put one's own will into effect, thus the legitimate fulfilment of one's will'; authority, from *augere*, means 'to beget something or somebody, to be the source and origin, author and artificer', to augment, amplify, develop something, to allow something to grow.[20] It is this last set of capacities that, when recognised, lends a person authority and therefore guarantees the enjoyment of power; and since authority is 'an extra quality which inheres in power when this is legitimised by consensus',[21] there can be no unaccepted or unacknowledged authority. Moreover, the acknowledgement of authority depends in part on the way in which the symbolic act of conquering power has been carried out. When, in an uncertain situation concerning right, power is gained by means of a heroic enterprise or through political wiliness, the requirement that there be a right to right is less binding, since in such a case the uncertain right is counterbalanced by the fact that the possessor is assigned the additional authority deriving from charisma (*chàris* is an extra gift of some sort which is socially recognised as such). It is this additional authority that, when legitimised by consensus, allows the maintenance of power.

Manipulating historical truth, Shakespeare depicts John as one who lacks both right and authority (the historical John seems to have had an almost undisputed right and a certain amount of charisma).[22] To affirm his right to right, Shakespeare's John could rely – like Elizabeth – on a will (the historical sources tell us only that Richard named John as his successor on his deathbed) which, however, in the play is considered insufficient; to support his claim to power, on the other hand, he only had the even weaker assurance of *de facto* possession. Furthermore, unlike his brother, John cannot rely on a heroic enterprise which might signal him as the undisputed leader;[23] his conquest of the crown, in fact, was not marked by either strength or wiliness or even wickedness. Indeed, the apparently sterile critical dispute about who is the hero of the play, often solved by assigning this role to the Bastard, derives from the fact that it would be impossible to attribute to Shakespeare's John the authority which derives from charisma. Lacking the extra gifts which produce acknowledgement of one's power through general consensus, John is even deprived of a right to possession;[24] while the Bastard acts as a supporter of John's weak title and in some way makes up for his lack of charisma.

The scene where John's weakness becomes apparent is II.i. The reason why the citizens of Angiers are not willing to recognise his right is that they do not acknowledge his authority; no such dispute, in fact, would arise if John's authority were not open to dispute. The Citizen, in fact, refuses the legal terms in which the dispute is couched by the French king ('Whose *title* they admit, Arthur's or John's', 200; my emphasis) and turns it into an issue of valour: right is not an abstract principle, but something that should be *proven* physically and won in the field: 'He that *proves* the king,/ To him will we prove loyal' (270–1; my emphasis). In lieu of valour and authority, John can only allege the weak principle that *in aequali iure melior est conditio possidentis*: 'Doth not the crown of England prove the king?' (273); but both he and the Bastard know that possession does not in itself constitute a title to hold power when consensus is not granted. John's question is not followed by an answer, but by an attempt on his part to strengthen his own argument by producing *witnesses*: 'And if not that, I bring you witnesses,/ Twice fifteen thousand hearts of England's breed –' ('Bastards and else' is Philip's comment), 'To verify our title with their lives' (274–7). The trial by combat is in fact suggested by John himself.

'Directly or indirectly,' Rackin says, 'the trials represent efforts to clarify the relationship between power and authority and answer the riddle of legitimacy.'[25] In the case of John, however, it seems that neither his claims to legitimacy nor God's judgement are able to settle the controversy. The trial by combat proves inane (either God is unwilling to take sides or he is absent), and the Citizen is compelled to repeat his argument again and again:

Both are alike, and both alike we like.
One must prove greatest: while they weigh so even
We hold our town for neither, yet for both.
                    (II.i.331–3; my emphasis)

A further effort by John, based this time not on legitimacy but on
an attempt to assert his own authority, produces a pure tautology.
Once more, France has asked the Citizen to recognise the King of
England in Arthur, whose right he is supporting ('Know him in us,
that here hold up his right', 364); the following statement by John
and the Citizen's answer, constitute some of the most ambiguous
and controversial lines of the play:

K. *John*. In us, that are our own great deputy,
        And bear possession of our person here,
        Lord of our presence, Angiers, and of you.
Cit. A greater pow'r than denies all this,
        And till it be undoubted, we do lock
        Our former scruple in our strong-barred gates,
        King'd of our fears, until our fears, resolv'd,
        Be by some certain kinred purg'd and deposed.[26]
                    (365–72)

John is here simply recalling that, unlike Arthur, he does not
need a 'deputy' or vicar to assert his possession (or his right); he is
in the position of being his own 'great deputy' and of pleading for
himself simply because he is in possession of the crown.[27] For the
following two lines I assume Beaurline's explanation as 'having
exclusive control over myself, and (unlike Arthur) capable of managing my own affairs, domains and subjects'. John also seems to
allude to the issue of the king's two bodies, especially in the distinction he makes between *person* and *presence*: however, if these are the
key words which are used, in John's speech, to evoke the king's
double nature, it seems to me that, while John is attributing to
himself full mastery of his body physical (*person*), he is limiting his
political power to the outward show of regality (*presence* is on the
one hand the mere fact that one is present and on the other one's
outward appearance; that here what is meant is the outward show
of regality will be apparent in the Bastard's speech that follows the
Citizen's).[28]
The Citizen's answer is immediately connected to John's (limited)

claim, in that it evokes a higher authority than that represented by
the outward appearance of regality: We, the Citizen says, are dominated by a power which is more compelling than *de facto* kingship,
namely, our uncertainty (*scruple*) about who is to be recognised as
worthy to be our ruler; and until they are dispelled, we will keep
our uncertainties locked inside the gates of our town. If one adopts
the emendation of line 371 (see note 26), the passage reads: 'in the
meantime, we shall be ruled by our fears, and only yield the power
to the man who shall be able to depose, or dispel, them',[29] the man
who has the authority, or the *chàris*, to do it – the one who *proves
greatest*.

John's (and France's) authority emerges abased from this exchange.
That both kings are being exposed to the censure of the common
people, and that they are therefore being lessened in their might,
is apparent to the Bastard, who compares the situation to that of
attending a theatrical performance. Not only should the recognition
of authority come from below, but when this is withheld – again
from below – kingship is flouted:

> *Bast.* By heaven, these scroyles of Angiers flout you, kings,
> And stand securely on their battlements,
> As in a theatre, whence they gape and point
> At your industrious scenes and acts of death.
>
> (II.i.373–6)[30]

The attempt to solve the problem by means of political agreements proves to be ephemeral. From these agreements, John emerges
stripped even of those signs of power that take the form of material
possession: neither his right nor his authority are going to be proved
beyond dispute. At this point, the transition to rebellion appears an
inevitable political consequence.

Discussions of the theme of rebellion in *King John* usually start
with the open act of political disobedience on the part of Salisbury,
Pembroke and Bigot when, on hearing of Arthur's death, they abandon John to join the French Dauphin. But, however crucial, their
abandonment of John and their final return to the fold follow the
usual script of Christian and Tudor ethics (although in this case the
rebels are drawn back to their king less by sincere regret and remorse
than by the fear of the Dauphin's intention to kill them). What
appears much more interesting, because much less conventional,
is the intricately knotted story of Hubert's disobedience, especially

if one considers that Shakespeare's treatment of the episode goes against the received tradition (not only against the tradition of his historical and dramatic sources, but also against Christian tradition, as exemplified by the Biblical story of Abraham). Let us briefly compare three versions of the episode: Holinshed, *TR* and Shakespeare's play, keeping in the background the text of Genesis 22:1–19.

It seems to me that the relevant stages of the story are: 1) the king's command; 2) its non-execution and the reasons given for the failure to execute it; 3) the king's reaction.

On the first point, Holinshed partly justifies John's decision to have Arthur blinded with the questionable argument that Arthur's supporters, the Britons, were in revolt and wanted to set the young prince free: the king, Holinshed reports, was consequently convinced that 'so long as Arthur liued, there would be no quiet in those parts'.[31] As regards John's order, Holinshed is rather cautious:

> *it was reported*, that king John *through persuasion of his councellors*, appointed certeine persons to go unto Falais, where Arthur was kept in prison, under the charge of Hubert de Burgh, and there to put out the young gentlemans eyes.[32]

The Executioners refrain from blinding Arthur, 'through such resistance as he made . . . and such lamentable words as he uttered'.[33] Hubert de Burgh's decision not to execute the king's order is then justified on the grounds that John would regret having given the order to blind Arthur, and that he would therefore be obliged to Hubert for not executing it:

> not doubting but rather to haue thanks than displeasure at the kings hands, for deliuering him of such infamie as would haue redounded unto his highnesse, if the yoong gentleman had beene so cruellie dealt withall. For he considered, that king John had resolved upon this point onelie in his heat and furie . . . and that afterwards, upon better advisement, he would both repent himselfe so to have commanded, and give them small thanke that should see it put in execution.[34]

As for the king's reaction on hearing that his order had not been carried out, Holinshed affirms that

he was nothing displeased for that his commandement was not
executed, sith there were diuers of his capteins which uttered in
plaine words, that he should not find knights to keepe his castels,
if he dealt so cruellie with his nephue.[35]

Thus, Holinshed's treatment seems to rely on explanations based
on political expediency both for Hubert's disobedience (Hubert
imagines that he will receive little thanks if he blinds Arthur) and
for John's reaction ('nothing displeased') on hearing that Hubert
has not carried out his order (in fact, Arthur's subjects are by no
means pacified by the rumour of his death); therefore, there is no
hint in the chronicle that Hubert was made a scapegoat for not
obeying the king's order.

TR proceeds as follows: in scene ix of Part One, Arthur, who has
been taken prisoner, is entrusted by John to the care of Hubert:

> *Hubert de Burgh* take *Arthur* here to thee,
> Be he thy prisoner: *Hubert* keep him safe
> For on his life doth hang thy Soveraignes crowne,
> But in his death consists thy Soveraignes blisse:
> Then *Hubert*, as thou shortly hearst from me,
> So use the prisoner I have given in charge.
>   (1118–23)[36]

The order to blind (or kill) Arthur is therefore given *in absentia*.
What we see next (scene xii) is Hubert with 'three men', claiming
to have shown them 'what warrant I have for this attempt' (1314–
15). Once again, John's order is not communicated to Arthur by
Hubert; rather, the prince is invited to 'peruse' the king's written
warrant (whose contents are: '*Hubert* these are to commaund thee,
as thou tendrest our quiet in minde and the estate of our person,
that presently upon the receipt of our commaund, thou put out the
eyes of *Arthur Plantaginet*': 1363–6). But what are more interesting
are the contents of Arthur's peroration and Hubert's reasons for
refraining from executing John's order. What Arthur reminds Hubert
of is that the king's order is contrary to God's command ('Subscribe
not *Hubert*, give not Gods part away', 1383; 'Yet God commands,
whose power reacheth further,/ That no commaund should stand
in force to murther', 1393–4). Arthur's final peroration, which contains a curse on his tormentors, convinces Hubert that there is a
higher authority than the king's:

My King commaunds, that warrant sets me free:
But God forbids, and he commaundeth Kings.
That great Commaunder counterchecks my charge,
He stayes my hand, he maketh soft my heart.
                                                    (1435–8)

The episode is significantly different in *King John*. In the first place,
the king's command is emphasised by being shown to the audience:

K. *John*. . . .
        Good Hubert, Hubert, Hubert, throw thine eye
        On yon young boy; I'll tell thee what, my friend,
        He is a very serpent in my way;
        And wheresoe'er this foot of mine doth tread,
        He lies before me: dost thou understand me?
        Thou art his keeper.
Hub.   And I'll keep him so
        That he shall not offend your majesty.
K. *John*. Death.
Hub.   My lord?
K. *John*.   A grave.
Hub.   He shall not live.
K. *John*.   Enough.
                                              (III.ii.69–76)[37]

The first moments of IV.i., when Hubert is in front of the young
prince, about to carry out the king's order, are charged with dramatic irony. Arthur perceives his executioner's inner torment and has
words of affection for him:

Arth. Are you sick, Hubert? you look pale to-day.
        In sooth, I would you were a little sick,
        That I might sit all night and watch with you:
        I warrant I love you more than you do me.
                                                    (28–31)

Hubert is moved by the boy's words ('His words do take possession of my bosom', 32), and although John's order is still absolute
for him, the boy's peroration at the end wins him over. The reasons
why Shakespeare's Hubert desists from blinding Arthur, however,
have nothing to do with God's superior command; it is the boy's

'innocent prate' (25) and shame for the inhuman act that he is on the point of committing that moves the executioner, not God's forbiddance as in *TR*. Nor does Arthur himself invoke arguments of a moral nature; rather, he declares, 'I will not struggle, I will stand stone-still' (76) and 'I will sit as quiet as a lamb' (79). Hubert's decision comes exclusively from pity and affection for the boy: he is prompted neither by political considerations, as in Holinshed, nor by the conflict between John's will and the superior will of God as in *TR*.

It is impossible not to be reminded of the story of Abraham and Isaac, the prototypical case of Christian obedience, and not to read the two dramatic versions of the John–Hubert–Arthur episode in the light of that story.[38]

In the Christian tradition, Abraham embodies the primary myth of non-resistance and the prototype of obedience to a superior order, however unjust this is recognised to be. Abraham's choice, although presented primarily as an ethical dilemma, has distinct political implications that were familiar to Shakespeare's contemporaries through the doctrine of non-resistance and the arguments which the Christian tradition had elaborated authoritatively although by no means uncontroversially.[39] The two stories do indeed have significant parallels: a command from a superior authority, obedient compliance, the preparations for executing the command (the stories coincide even in a number of details: the two servants that are left behind while preparations are made, Isaac's suspicions when he does not see the victim for the sacrifice, which parallel Arthur's suspicions on seeing Hubert's sadness); where the stories differ is in the agent that restrains the executioner's hand: with Abraham, as with Hubert in *TR*, it is God's command (and in Holinshed political expediency) or the recognition that God would be displeased if the order were executed – while in *King John* it is simple pity. In Shakespeare's play, it is not a superior force – either religious or political – which prevents the king's command being executed; rather, it is the subject's affection and pity for the victim (precisely what was denied to Abraham); while in *TR*, as in the Abraham story, there is a last-moment summons in the shape of God's will, in *King John* Hubert is left alone with his moral dilemma, and decides against the king's order. In Shakespeare's version, therefore, the king's authority is overturned neither by a supreme will nor out of political considerations, but merely as a result of an independent and arbitrary decision on the part of the subject: Hubert's resistance is a case of pure disobedience. Moreover, although his disobedience is quite independent of God's voice or of any angelic visitation, by disobeying Shakespeare's Hubert *does the right thing*. F. Cordero comments on the implications of 'wylful obedience' that the story of Abraham can assume in concrete situations:

> In similar circumstances, others have had a worse destiny [than Abraham]. Rudolf Höss, commander at Auschwitz and by nature a gentle soul, suffers as a result of being ordered to undertake a programme of extermination; but since this is a command from the Führer, he suppresses all the feelings and impulses which are contrary to discipline; when he looks back on the matter in a more detached fashion, with the benefit of his discussions with Eichmann, he understands the meaning of that *faiblesse*; he was betraying the Führer within himself: perfect obedience requires a soul permeated with faith.[40]

Cordero also recalls Kierkegaard's rewriting of Abraham's story in a passage of the *Diaries*. In Kierkegaard's version, Abraham does not hear God's last-minute countermand and kills Isaac. In this case, Abraham is mistaken because, just as in the case of John, God no longer wants the victim to be killed. But even the Biblical story has a flaw. Although Abraham heard God's countermand, how could he know that this did not come from the devil? Would not perfect obedience in fact mean that he was obliged to carry out *the first command* in any case? Cordero's comment is that, in the end, 'it is only a matter of chance. Rudolf Höss, too, is a knight of the faith, but he does the wrong thing.'[41]

As for Hubert, while in Holinshed's version he is convinced that he is doing the right thing and that he will even be rewarded by John for not obeying him, in *TR* he is much less assured, and in *King John* he is definitely convinced that he will displease the king by disobeying him. This simple observation leads us to conclude that Shakespeare's version is the one that most openly sanctions the kind of decision which is dictated only by the subject's 'wylful disobedience', that is, by his own free evaluation of the command he has been given: this is, in short, the version that most straight-forwardly sanctions rebellion; by the same token, Shakespeare's is also the version that most openly questions the sovereign's authority, by questioning the unquestionable charm of the superior command.

We know that Elizabeth was torn between the political necessity of having Mary executed and a feeling of uncertainty that was perhaps in part humane pity but above all fear of the possible reaction of Mary's friends; indeed, after signing her cousin's death warrant, she asked Sir Amyas Paulet, who had Mary in his custody, to kill her secretly. Although she wanted Mary dead and considered her death necessary from the political point of view, she was obviously most unwilling to be thought responsible for it and, curiously enough, with regard to an anointed sovereign, assassination seemed to be more acceptable than execution. But, not unlike the Hubert of *King John*, Paulet refused on personal moral grounds: 'God forbid that I should make so foul a shipwreck of my conscience', he seems to have answered.[42] Elizabeth reacted harshly, for she perceived that even her most faithful subjects were inclined to let the blame for Mary's death, and the risks of what might follow, fall upon her. She may also have been irritated at seeing her own authority disregarded. She thus 'blamed the niceness of those precise fellows . . . who in words would do great things for her surety, but in deed perform nothing'.[43] The Davison story completes the picture. In the event, signing the death warrant was all that Elizabeth was willing to do; and it fell to Davison to dispatch it, interpreting the Queen's undecipherable will, and become a scapegoat for having contributed to the execution. In the case of Elizabeth, then, much more so than in that of John, there was no escape for the subject, for both disregarding the sovereign's authority and acting in accordance with it would have produced a negative reaction on her part. Davison knew, in fact, that his situation was hopeless, and that both obedience and disobedience would cause displeasure and vengeance. Unlike God with Abraham, moreover, Elizabeth did not restrain Davison's hand, while we may imagine that, unlike John, she would not exactly have rejoiced had Davison not carried out the task. She had reacted badly to Paulet's refusal to obey, thereby revealing symptoms of anxiety and maybe even of fear. Davison, for his part, had no choice but to act on the warrant. And he had to pay for his obedience (in that circumstance, however, what obedience amounted to was unclear).[44]

But the sovereign's position was no less hopeless than the subject's. Elizabeth was convinced that it was necessary to act, although she had more than one reason for hesitating so long to sign the warrant and for refraining from commanding to have it dispatched. Are we to imagine it was affection that restrained her? Was it a sense of tragedy from which she recoiled? Or were there rather more subtle, deep and unutterable anxieties concerning authority and majesty

that were tearing her mind and soul apart? Whatever the exact
truth of the matter, it is fairly clear that Elizabeth was much more
intensely conscious of the risks that she was running in terms of
authority, popularity and ultimately power than John was.

Commenting on Elizabeth's assumed moral dilemma and on the
fact that she 'did not want to kill a king', Campbell rightly argues
that the queen, 'deep in her heart' agreed with the truth etched in
Mary's Latin epitaph, which, understandably enough, was soon
removed from her tomb. The fragment, in Camden's English translation, runs as follows:

> and by one and the same wicked sentence is both Mary Queene
> of Scotts doomed to a naturall death, and all surviving Kings,
> being made as common people, are subjected to a civill death. A
> new and unexampled kinde of tombe is heere extant, wherein the
> living are included with the dead: for know that with the sacred
> herse of Saint Mary here lieth violate and prostrate the majesty of
> all Kings & Princes. . . .[45]

Indeed, the Bastard's speech over Arthur's dead body seems to
me to deploy similar arguments, and to produce a conclusive comment on the story of John that could also be applied to the story of
Elizabeth, as well as showing Shakespeare's use of sources different
from *TR*:

> I am amaz'd, methinks, and lose my way
> Among the thorns and dangers of this world.
> How easy dost thou take all England up
> From forth this morsel of dead royalty!
> The life, the right, and truth of all this realm
> Is fled to heaven; and England now is left
> To tug and scamble, and to part by th' teeth
> The unow'd interest of proud swelling state.
> Now for the the bare-pick'd bone of majesty
> Doth dogged war bristle his angry crest
> And snarleth in the gentle eyes of peace:
> Now powers from home and discontents at home
> Meet in one line; and vast confusion waits,
> As doth a raven on a sick-fall'n beast,
> The imminent decay of wrested pomp.
>
> (IV.iii. 140–54)

The dead body of Arthur – that 'morsel of dead royalty' – is, in the Bastard's evaluation of the event, the site where all England lies prostrate; in just the same way, in Mary's tomb 'the living are included with the dead' in the person of 'all surviving kings'. In both cases, the death of the rival pretender has prostrated 'the majesty of all kings and princes', debasing authority and bringing confusion to the whole land.

The surprising aspect of the Bastard's speech is that it clearly implies an acknowledgement of Arthur's right: if 'the life, the right, and truth of all this realm / Is fled to heaven' with Arthur's death, then, according to the Bastard, right and truth belong to the person who has just lost his life. This reading, which seems to me the most plausible, is usually either admitted only as a secondary possibility or dismissed altogether. Honigmann, for instance, says that 'Faulconbridge does not necessarily recognize Arthur's claims here: he says that sovereignty has departed, since Arthur's death will cause revolt from John'; but right and truth, it seems to me, refer to the dispute that runs through the whole play rather than to the condition of sovereignty in general. Beaurline, although admitting that the Bastard is here alluding to 'the death of the rightful heir', does not take the argument to the logical consequences that seem to me to be clearly alluded to in at least two other passages from the speech, namely, 'the unow'd interest of proud swelling state' and 'the imminent decay of wrested pomp'. As regards these expressions, Honigmann reads *unowed* as either '(a) unow'd title or right; (b) the accruing interest of power of the nobles unowed to a king'; Beaurline reads 'of uncertain ownership, nor owed to anyone (since there is no rightful king)'; as for the 'wrested pomp', Honigmann says that 'some think that Faulconbridge now "wavers in his allegiance", recognizing John's authority as *wrested* (usurped from Arthur)', but suggests that the Bastard is here foretelling the chaos which 'awaits the imminent general dissolution consequent upon the wresting of power from John'.[46]

And yet the Bastard's speech is a central point in the play; on its interpretation, a great deal, therefore, depends both in terms of the dynamics of meaning within the text itself and in terms of the connections that the text establishes with the contemporary situation. Besides, the presence of a topical allusion is rendered more evident in the mention of 'powers from home and discontents at home', another expression that editors tend to force into improbable meanings.[47]

The execution of Mary took place in 1587; the following year saw the victory over the Spanish which seemed to the general public, if not to the Queen and her counsellors, overwhelming. But things had by no means been settled, either internally or externally. Troubles with the Puritan faction and Roman Catholic discontent shook the Church of England, the menace of Spain and France was ever-present, the defence of the Netherlands continued to absorb more money than was reasonable and to take more lives than was acceptable, while the Queen's succession had become a troublesome issue, which there seemed little hope of solving. 'Powers from home and discontents at home', therefore, appears to be an accurate description of the political situation in the years following the execution of Mary, when *King John* was composed and shown in a public playhouse.

Shakespeare's John had deluded himself that he would reinforce his grip on power by eliminating his rival; but the Bastard, who proves once more to be the political conscience of the play, knows that Arthur's death has in fact only served to debase the king's authority even further. Until the last scene of the play, John is denied both right – which remains uncertain notwithstanding Arthur's death – and might – which has been irremediably shaken because of his rival's elimination.

The final scenes of the play may give the impression of hastening towards an easy solution. Indeed we may be surprised by the fact that immediately after John's death strong intimations of future stability seem to settle all the troubles of John's 'scribbled' and 'confounded' royalty. In a situation where right is suddenly seen as undisputed, the prospect of Prince Henry's coronation seems in fact to offer the opportunity of resolving all problems.

On the Elizabethan political scene such reassuring prospects were lacking: indeed, no one could have pronounced a euphoric, albeit dubitative, prophecy such as the one proffered by the Bastard in the closing lines of *King John*. Ought we to consider the conclusion of the play as a warning and an admonition? If this is the case, then the haste of the final scenes and the somewhat unconvincing sudden smoothing over of all the problems that tormented John's reign may be accounted for by the urgent need to exert further pressure for a solution to the hotly debated problem of Elizabeth's succession.

But *what* succession?

Marie Axton argues that *King John* and *TR* hold radically different theories and support different claims in the debate about succession and considers *King John* as 'a searching and skeptical reply to the anonymous author's jingoistic play which excluded all foreign claimants to the English crown'.[48] According to Axton, Shakespeare's play, quite to the contrary, tends to admit foreign claims, albeit somewhat indirectly. Indeed, to argue that Shakespeare's play deploys arguments in favour of the Stuarts would be taking things too far. Axton's discussion of *King John*, which corroborates my reading of the play, closes in fact with a question ('who is England?') that the play leaves unanswered: 'During John's troubled reign the two bodies of the monarch had been disjoined; with the death of Arthur one fled like Astraea to heaven. The crown was clearly unable to protect the vulnerable child to whom it should have miraculously descended. Who, then, is England?'[49]

Axton concludes her argument by remarking that the rhetoric of the Bastard's final speech avoids answering the crucial question, while 'there had been no such doubt in *The Troublesome Raigne* where the crown had defined the king.'[50]

It is in keeping with this lack of a definite answer that Shakespeare's John should die desperate, feeling 'a hell' within himself (V.vii.46) and deeming himself a 'module of confounded royalty' (58). Unlike what happens in *TR*, where John is comforted in his last moments by the return of the rebel barons and by the assurance that Prince Henry will soon be crowned, Shakespeare's John dies without hope: the last words he hears are the news that the Bastard somewhat ungenerously gives him about the armed approach of the Dolphin in a situation which appears hopeless for the English ('For in a night the best part of my power', the Bastard tells him, '. . . . Were in the Washes all unwarily / Devoured by the unexpected flood', V.vii.61–4). Only after John's death are the comforting words of peace from the Dauphin and those concerning Henry's coronation uttered. John is the only character in the play to whom no knowledge of the future is allowed. He will never know what all the others – even the audience – seem to know: that Henry was born 'to set a form upon that indigest'.[51]

Notes

1. *Chronicle*, 1323.II.33–46, italics mine. The passage is quoted by Campbell, op. cit., p. 126.
2. J. Dover Wilson, 'Introduction' to *King John* (Cambridge: Cambridge University Press, 1936), p. xxiv. *The Troublesome Raigne of John King of England* (henceforth *TR*) was published anonymously in 1591. Which of the two plays was source for the other is still in dispute.
3. Tillyard says that 'Shakespeare's play is but mildly Protestant in tone and shows no extreme hostility to the French' (op. cit., p. 215).
4. See V. Vaughan, '*King John*: A Study in Subversion and Containment', in D. Curren Aquino (ed.), '*King John*': *New Perspectives* (Newark: University of Delaware Press, 1989), pp. 62–75, and the following works by P. Rackin, 'Anti-Historians: Women's Role in Shakespeare's Histories', *Theatre Journal* XXXVII (1985), 329–44; 'Patriarchal History and Female Subversion in *King John*', in Curren Aquino (ed.), pp. 76–90; *Stages of History*, passim.
5. See, respectively, E. A. J. Honigmann (ed.), *King John* (London: Methuen, 1954) and G. Bullough, *Narrative and Dramatic Sources of Shakespeare*, vol. IV (London: Routledge, 1962), mainly pp. 1–2. But see the opinion of R. Simpson, who says that 'it is only wonderful that allusions so plain should have been tolerated'. 'The Politics of Shakespeare's History Plays', *The New Shakespeare Society Transactions* (1874), 396–441, p. 400. (To *King John* are devoted pp. 397–406).
6. Op. cit., p. 150.
7. Ibid., p. 164.
8. Ibid., p. 145.
9. Ibid., pp. 160, 161.
10. Op. cit., pp. 1–2.
11. A. R. Braunmuller argues that the play 'both claims and denies the censor's authority'. '*King John* and historiography', *Journal of English Literary History* LCV (1988), 309–32, p. 320.
12. V. Vaughan, op. cit.; J. R. Elliot, 'Shakespeare and the Double Image of King John', *Shakespeare Studies* I (1965), 64–84.
13. Honigmann, op. cit., p. xxxi.
14. D. Montini, '*King John*: anatomia della regalità', in M. Tempera (ed.), '*King John*' *dal testo alla scena* (Bologna: CLUEB, 1994), pp. 71–90, 71.
15. Op. cit., p. xxix. Honigmann, however, attributes the play's departures from historical truth to dramatic requirements (ibid., pp. xxxi and xxxiii).
16. R. Simpson (op. cit.) shows that all the points in which Shakespeare modifies the sources contain allusions to contemporary politics, and in particular to the controversy about succession.
17. Op. cit., p. 63.
18. P. Saccio, *Shakespeare's English Kings* (Oxford: Oxford University Press, 1977), p. 190. On the issue of the title to the crown in Shakespeare's histories and its legal and political implications, see G. W. Keeton, *Shakespeare's Legal and Political Background* (London: Pitman, 1967), pp. 248–63.

19. B. H. Traister discusses John's failure to embody majesty in 'The King's One Body: Unceremonial Kingship in *King John*', in Curren-Aquino (ed.), pp. 91–8.

20. G. Trentin, 'Potere/Autorità', *Enciclopedia*, vol. 10 (Turin: Einaudi, 1980), pp. 1041–53, 1043, 1044.

21. J. Gil, 'Potere', *Enciclopedia*, vol. 10 (Torino: Einaudi, 1980), pp. 996–1040, 1010. Elizabeth endeavoured to overcome the uncertainties of her right by playing on her 'extra gifts' as a way of gaining consensus.

22. Tillyard says that Shakespeare 'goes against Holinshed in quite denying John a princely heart' (op. cit., p. 215).

23. Richard's charisma came from the fact that he 'robb'd the lion of his heart/ And fought the holy wars in Palestine' (II.i.3–4).

24. Rackin speaks of a conflict between 'strong possession' and 'right', and equates these to 'power' and 'authority' respectively (*Stages of History*, p. 53). My assumption, on the contrary, is that 'right' and 'authority' cannot be considered as synonyms.

25. *Stages of History*, p. 54. On the legal technicalities connected with the trial by battle and Shakespeare's treatment of them, see Keeton, op. cit., pp. 211–22.

26. In this case, I adopt the reading suggested by L. A. Beaurline (ed.), *King John* (Cambridge: Cambridge University Press, 1990). The Arden editor, Honigmann, assimilates the Citizen to Hubert (see, for motivations of the editor's choice, p. xxxvi) and reads 'Kings of our fear'. The fusion of the two characters in some editions depends on the fact that from line 325 onwards, F assigns all the character's speech headings to 'Hubert'. As most of the play's editors have done, Beaurline reads 'Citizen', following J. P. Collier's explanation that 'Possibly the actor of the part of Hubert also personated the citizen . . . and this may have led to the insertion of his name in the MS' (op. cit., p. 189).

27. I do not agree with Beaurline's expansion of John's claim as being 'the pre-eminent deputy, second only to God'.

28. Beaurline discusses the double nature starting from a different opposition, namely, 'our person' as meaning the body natural and 'Lord of "Angiers, and of you"' as representing the body politic. On this explanation, John's assertion of his political power would appear to be more assured, but the difference between *person* and *presence* remains unexplained.

29. The F reading, 'Kings of our fears', seems less convincing: if the Citizen is suggesting that they are going to master their fears, then it is they, not their fears, that would be 'deposed' by 'some certain king'.

30. Kingship is by its very nature exposed to the censure of the subjects. In various contexts, this has quite aptly evoked the theatrical analogy. The fact that power, when shown in a theatre, risks to 'make greatness familiar', is alluded to by James I in his *Basilikon Doron*: 'It is a true old saying, That a King is as one set on a skaffold, whose smallest actions & gestures al the people gazingly do behold: and therefore although a King be neuer so precise in the dischargeing of his office,

the people who seeth but the outwarde parte, will euer judge of the substance by the circumstances & according to the outwarde appearance (if his behauiour be light or dissolute) will conceiue praeoccupied conceits of the Kings inward intention' (ΒΑΣΙΛΙΚΟΝ ΔΩΡΟΝ, A Scholar Press Facsimile, Menton, 1969, pp. 121–2). For a comment of this passage, see Orgel, 'Making greatness familiar'.

31. *Chronicles*, 165.I.73–4.
32. Ibid., II.1–5, my emphasis. The allusion to the counsellors' persuasion may have triggered the parallel with the Elizabeth–Davison story.
33. Ibid., 6–11.
34. Ibid., 12–31.
35. Ibid., 49–53.
36. My reference text is the one reproduced by Bullough (op. cit., pp. 72–151), based in turn on a facsimile ed. by C. Praetorius (1888).
37. Both plays manifest a discrepancy on this point: while John's verbal order is to kill Arthur, the written warrant states that he should be blinded.
38. I am not suggesting that what we have is a conscious rewriting of the Biblical episode, but rather that there is an obvious evocation of one of the founding myths of Christianity, a myth which had also been transmitted by means of theatrical representations. Roberta Mullini has suggested to me that the very rhythm of the episode in *King John* – the pauses and the postponement of the act – recalls the way in which the theatrical versions of the Biblical story (the Brome version in particular) represent it.
39. Aquinas, in *De regimine principum*, argues that tyranny is to be tolerated, for fear of worse evils. However, in his *Summa Theologiae*, he admits that laws may exist which appear unjust although issued by a legally credited authority. That owing to the divine origin of authority absolute obedience to the sovereign is necessary, is also argued in St Paul's Epistle to the Romans.
40. 'Diritto', *Enciclopedia*, vol. IV (Turin: Einaudi, 1978), pp. 895–1003, 913. The passage is suggested by R. Höss, *Kommandant in Auschwitz* (Stuttgart: Deutsche-Verlags-Anstalt, 1946).
41. Ibid., p. 915.
42. Neale, op. cit., p. 279.
43. *Calendar of State Papers relating to Scotland and Mary Queen of Scots*, IX, 292; quoted by Anne Somerset, *Elizabeth I* (London: Fontana, 1992), p. 438.
44. In his *Annales rerum anglicarum et hibernicarum regnante Elizabetha* (London, 1615), Camden gives a different account of the episode. I quote the passage from the first edition of the English translation: 'She deliuered a writing to *Dauison* one of her Secretaryes, signed with her owne hand, that a warrant under the great seale of *England* should be in readinesse if any danger should growe in the fearfull time; and commanded him to acquaint no man therewith. But the next daie, while feare dreaded euer her owne designes, her minde changed, and she commanded Dauison by *William Kellegrey* that the warrant should not be drawen. *Dauison* came presently to the Queene,

and told her that it was drawne and under seale already. She being somewhat moued, blamed him for making such hast. He notwith-standing acquainted the Councell both with the warrant and the whole matter, and easily perswaded them being apt to beleeue what they desided, that the Queene had commanded it should be executed.' Quoted from the English translation: *The Historie of the Life and Reigne of the Most Renowned and Victorious Princesse Elizabeth, Late Queene of England* (London, 1630), Book III, p. 109.

45. Ibid., p. 114. The epitaph also says that Mary was 'by barbarous and tyrannous cruelty extinct.' (ibid.)

46. Beaurline's comment on this point is ambiguous: 'imminent . . . pomp. This and 142–5 show what the Bastard thinks of John's claims to the throne and of his prospects.'

47. Distorting the meaning of the sentence, Honigmann glosses 'from home / at home' as 'out of their element' and 'in their element', while he prefers a non-military reading for the 'meet in one line' that follows.

48. *The Queen's Two Bodies. Drama and the Elizabethan Succession* (London: Royal Historical Society, 1977), p. 108. Seen in this perspective, *TR* may be considered as one of the statements in the debate which set defenders of foreign claimants (principally the Stuarts), and there-fore of a contractual theory of sovereignty, against supporters of succession by genealogy. Arguments in favour of foreign succession had been circulated, mainly in support of Mary, since the late sixties; see the pamphlet written by John Leslie, Bishop of Ross, entitled *A Defence of the Honour of the Right Highe, Mightye and Noble Princesse Marie, Quene of Scotlande and Dowager of France* (London, 1569), where Leslie produced the example of Arthur, who was born in Brittany. Years later (1580), Leslie repeated the arguments in favour of Mary in a pamphlet in Latin, *De titulo et iure serenissimae principis Mariae Scotorum Reginae, quo Regni Angliae successionem sibi iuste vendicat, libellus* (Rheims, 1580) which he later translated into English as *A Treatise Towching the Right, Title, and Interest of the Most Excellent Princesse Marie, Queene of Scotland, and of the Most Noble King James, her Graces Sonne, to the Succession of the Croune of England* (Rheims, 1584). Leslie tried to give the widest possible circulation to this latter treatise by translating it into French (Rouen, 1587) and Spanish (Rouen? 1587?). The contractual theory was soon to have a determined supporter in Doleman (the Jesuit Robert Parsons) in favour of the Infanta of Spain (*Conference*). Incidentally, Blanche and Lewis, who appear in the two plays, were the Infanta's forebears.

49. Op. cit., p. 110.

50. Ibid., p. 111.

51. Holinshed comments on the sudden recovery of England under Henry III and on how soon it was 'from a troubled fourme reduced to a flourishing and prosperous degree: chiefelie by the diligent heed and carefull provision of the king himselfe' (*Chronicles*, 203.II.21–3). Shake-speare's expression 'scribbled form' (V.vii.32), which echoes Holinshed's 'troubled fourme', is a further piece of evidence for Holinshed as a source of the play.

7

Time, Space and the Instability of History in the *Henry IV* Sequence

THE GENERAL FRAME: RUMOUR, OR THE FALSIFICATIONS OF HISTORIOGRAPHY

The issue of the 'structural problem' of the *Henry IV* plays seems still to attract the attention of critics. In a recent article, Paul Yachnin has taken up the subject once again, remarking that those critics who have argued for the unity of the two plays have normally not developed 'the idea of sequence into an interpretive approach'.[1] Starting from what are considered discrepancies in the sequence (Hal's two reformations being the main one), Yachnin adopts an interpretative model which, far from viewing change as an element producing discontinuity, '*includes* change as the central condition of the production of meaning'[2] and in the second play shows a revisionist attitude which, he holds, works as a critique and even as an undoing of the first.

Yachnin's model is interesting in the first place because it rejects the assumption, which has been fundamental to virtually all discussions of the 'structural problem', that we should 'render Shakespeare's meaning full, stable, and permanent'; and in the second place because it pertinently discusses the 'structural problem' in close connection with the kind of historical vision that the sequence presents. In particular, Yachnin argues that the two plays 'develop Shakespeare's critique of Renaissance historiography, and enact the revisionist, open-ended nature of historical change', 'persistently altering the basic shape of history, and so depriving history of basic shape altogether'.[3]

However, although I agree with Yachnin's general claims, I prefer to consider the second play as a development of certain equivocal elements which are present in the first rather than, like Yachnin, as an outright contradiction of its meanings; I will therefore discuss 'change' and 'open-endedness' from a different set of premises. In particular, I see destabilisation in the progressive corruption of the value system which the first play presents. Apparently neatly defined and delimited and mutually contrasted, the three axiologies which determine the conflicts of the sequence – rule, misrule and rebellion – are in reality blurred right from the start, and they get more and more disfigured as the action progresses: basically, the space of rule is corrupted by being occupied by an illegitimate king;[4] the popular nature of the sphere of misrule is contaminated and deflected from 'low' style by the presence in it, and belonging to it, of the heir apparent (in the sphere of misrule, we may say, the disruption of the *norm* is accompanied by a corruption of the *form*); while the sphere of rebellion tends to present itself as a space of legitimation, for it supports the restoration of someone who is presented as the legitimate heir of Richard II. These discrepancies vitiate the plays' alleged system of values and therefore compromise the possibility of clear moral and political discriminations.

More generally, the sequence puts forward the idea that instability of meaning is a problem which also affects historiography: there are, as we shall see, more or less explicit suggestions that transmission may corrupt historical truth and that knowledge of past events is in any case problematic; but even more problematic is the business of foreseeing and planning future developments for, principally in the sphere of rule, the course of (historical) events does not develop according to either projects or expectations. Time corrupts, infects, contaminates and disfigures, and future developments often bring the frustration of expectations. Thus, both historical knowledge and political project are presented as uncertain predicaments, and historical time tends to be reduced – again, mainly in the sphere of rule – to the mere consciousness of the present.

The whole structure of meaning is developed progressively and cumulatively, although this is brought about in the two plays by means of different strategies. As regards the 'structural problem', then, my idea is that the second play strengthens and clarifies certain premises of the first; that what have been considered discrepancies cease to be problematic if we acknowledge the fact that the framework of the sequence is one of instability rather than one of coherence or consistency; and that this framework is precisely the means by which the sequence questions the pattern of coherence which is at the basis of all providential views of history. Nevertheless, while it is undoubtedly true that Part Two integrates Part One, I would not go so far as to affirm that Part One would be incomplete without Part Two.[5] Simply, as Harold Jenkins argued, *Henry IV* 'is both one play and two', and if 'The two parts are complementary, they are also independent and even incompatible.'[6]

My presentation of the framework described will start from a reading of the *incipit* of the two plays where I consider many of the premises of future developments to be laid. As a start, I will go back to Yachnin's article and pick up a few of the points he makes, which, I believe, call for some comment.

Yachnin quotes, as one of the moments in the sequence in which 'the meaning of actions and words is changed and destabilized by subsequent actions and words',[7] Henry's speech which opens the first play. However, he reads the speech as expressing in the first part the king's intention to go on a crusade and as disclaiming this same intention in the second. In particular, he interprets Henry's meaning in ll. 28–30 ('But this our purpose is now twelve month old/ And bootless 'tis to tell you we will go;/ Therefor we meet not now') as 'his statement . . . that a crusade is out of question at this time'. Yachnin's reading of the speech as 'Henry's actorly performance of zeal', then, triggers a series of metatheatrical comments about 'the actorly nature', in the play, 'of characters' actions and words' as intended 'to crystallize their own meanings in the face of the fluidity of meaning'; 'actorly', then, is equated with 'non-stable' and 'changeable', as opposed to a not altogether clear *authentic*, meaning.[8] These assumptions, I believe, and in particular the unclear relationship obtaining between the notions evoked (revisionist attitude, actorly performance, instability, authentic meaning), obscure Yachnin's arguments; besides, I believe that Henry's opening speech in the first play may be read in a light which might better support Yachnin's main claims about the representation of history as unpredictable and open-ended, albeit on the basis of a different set of arguments.

Let us bear in mind, in the first place, that the speech is the statement which opens the sequence and that, therefore, it is through that speech that the spectators – and the readers – are introduced into the world of the play; and in the second place that the occasion is official and ceremonial and that it involves onstage witnesses of a certain importance who are listening to a public statement from the king. The speech has, therefore, a decisive function in establishing the text's historiographical perspective.

Whether Henry is here putting up an 'actorly performance' or not (an attitude which, besides, does not seem to be suggested by the text, either explicitly or implicitly) is, I believe, hardly important. What is crucial, instead, is his recognition – and both the onstage and offstage audience's recognition – of the inanity of his own purposes and of the unreliability of (historical) predictions. (Henry had expressed the same purpose to go on a crusade, in an almost prophetic tone, when, so to speak, we last saw him, in the lines with which he closes *Richard II*.)

It seems clear to me that in the first part of his speech Henry is expressing his purpose with perfect assurance ('As far as to the sepulchre of Christ/ . . . Forthwith a power of English shall we levy', 19–22) and that in the last part he is simply reminding the nobles – and the audience – that the project is long rife and that its execution is beyond doubt. At the same time, he stresses his conviction with a negation of the necessity of the reminder ('But this our purpose now is twelve month old,/ And bootless 'tis to tell you we will go', 28–9); the sentence which follows ('Therefor we meet not now', 30) means precisely that the decision has been taken, and that the present meeting is not meant to establish *whether* to go or not. Instead, the king's purpose *now* is simply to hear what suggestions the Council has made 'in forwarding this dear expedience' (33). Besides, Henry does not seem to depend on the Council's opinion; on the contrary, he is merely expecting them to 'decree' what support or marginal advice they can supply *in forwarding* the enterprise.

It is, in all evidence, Westmoreland's speech which introduces a new and unexpected element which disrupts the fulfilment of Henry's purpose. This, moreover, is characteristically unexpected for, as Westmoreland explains, it was determined by a sudden interruption of the Council's meeting with the irruption of the post from Wales. None of the 'heavy news' (37) that the post has brought to the Council has as yet been disclosed to Henry, who is informed of them at the same time as the audience and is *therefore* forced to abandon his 'twelve month old' project: the decision to abandon the expedition is therefore dictated by an external destabilising factor which gives an unexpected turn to what the king appeared to envisage as the predictable chain of (historical) events. The spectacle of the king's failure is displayed before our eyes.

But the sequence stages an even more explicit and crucial instance of destabilisation. It is again an opening, again the audience's first contact with a dramatic world: *Enter Rumour, painted full of tongues.*

Directly addressing the audience, Rumour opens his speech imposing attention:

> Open your ears; for which of you will stop
> The vent of hearing when loud Rumour speaks?
>
> (2 *Henry IV, Induction*, 1–2)

Rumour proceeds to communicate – albeit somewhat indirectly – the news of Henry's victory at Shrewsbury and of Hal's killing of Hotspur, but he then goes on to say that he has been spreading news to the contrary. It might seem reasonable to suppose that the *Induction* was intended as a device to sum up the main events of Part One, or at least as a reminder of the outcome of the battle of Shrewsbury. However, it deserves attention for it is unique in the whole corpus of histories (why, in the first place, did Shakespeare not feel that a similar link was needed to connect the events of the *Henry VI* plays?), with perhaps the sole exception of Gloucester's soliloquy which opens *Richard III* (this, however, focuses much more on future events than on past ones).

Yet, by the time we get into the first scene of the play we feel that Rumour's speech was by no means necessary as a means of setting out past events. The play might in fact easily have started around line 30 with Travers arriving and informing Northumberland of the disaster at Shrewsbury. No clumsiness in the exposition would have followed, for no information already possessed by the characters would have been transmitted. But quite apart from that, the *Induction* triggers a rather peculiar scene in which the audience's attention is strongly directed towards the workings of the mechanism of newsspreading. This involves three onstage 'messengers' (Lord Bardolph, Travers and Morton), two offstage 'gentlemen' who in turn communicated the news, good to Bardolph and bad to Travers; it makes it impossible the first two messengers (Lord Bardolph and Travers) to be eye-witnesses – which is rather unusual – and the questions from Northumberland to Bardolph, 'How is this deriv'd?/ Saw you the field? Came you from Shrewsbury?' (23–4), which sound slightly odd, since it is conventionally agreed that messengers are considered to be reliable. Obviously, the mechanism of the *Induction* was not meant to create suspense in the audience, for it is precisely from the *Induction* that the spectators know what the truth is (but, do they really *know*?); nor does Northumberland's grief at his son's death deserve the emotional enhancement which may come from the strain of absorbing subsequently contrary truths (we, again, *know* from Rumour that the sickness which he alleged as an impediment to his taking part in the battle was *crafty*).

In other words, the device is not technically necessary; on the contrary, its inclusion renders necessary an overelaboration of the first scene which is not easy to justify in terms of dramatic logic. But, apart from its uniqueness, this particular *Induction* may seem rather surprising as an introduction to a historical play because it is eminently and overtly destabilising.[9] What Rumour in the final analysis seems to communicate to the audience is a reflection on the instability of meaning in historiography: past events, when they are reported, are subjected to distortions; 'rumour' stands, therefore, for one of the possible factors which contribute to the falsifications of historiography, of its 'continual slanders' (6), others being 'surmises, jealousies, conjectures' (16). The implication is clear: what has already been told about this story – in the first play of the sequence – may have suffered from falsification, and may therefore stand in need of revision.

A different reading of the *Induction* is possible, one which once again focuses on instability, change and uncertainty but which treats these as an unavoidable part of the pursuit of historical awareness and thus as inherent in historiographical practice. By spreading false news, Rumour is in fact suggesting that witnesses need to be evaluated on the basis of their proximity to the events ('Saw you the field? Came you from Shrewsbury?'), and of their reliability ('A gentleman well bred, and of good name', 26; 'A gentleman almost forspent with speed', 37; 'some hilding fellow that had stol'n/ The horse he rode on', 57–8); in short, he is prompting research. Naturally, research may lead us to change and revise our account of events, and change and revision are, as Yachnin says, the central conditions of the production of meaning in the *Henry IV* plays.

In the following pages, I aim to show that the moral and political system of values is not only presented right from the start as unstable, but also gets progressively more and more distorted and corrupt. This is achieved by means of different but concurring strategies in the two plays: in Part One it is time – both as a topic of discourse and as an element in the plot's development – which is used to compare and contrast the three axiologies mentioned above; while in Part Two the corruption of those same axiologies is brought out mainly through space manipulation and in particular through the trespassing implicit in the action of border-crossing.

As I have suggested, the various spaces of the plays – roughly, what is commonly identified with the double plot plus the rebels' space (to which is assigned an independent semantic space in both plays) – adumbrate notions which are obviously not simply spatial, since they evoke the easily identifiable and highly charged political and moral models of *rule, misrule* and *rebellion*. My aim is to show that the sorts of political and moral evaluations that the plays apparently encourage are undermined by the way in which the various spatial configurations are organised and interconnected in time and by the way in which they are made to interfere with each other.[10] In particular, following certain suggestions by Lotman regarding the organisation of space, I am interested in developing the notion of *border*, holding that peculiar meanings may be connected – in a given text and in a given culture – with the ideas of keeping within or transgressing certain boundaries.[11]

In Part One, each of the three semantic spheres is presented as managing and, up to a point, controlling its own space and time; the separation between them is responsible for the comparatively neat differentiation of the political and moral issues which each of the spaces stands for: rule, rebellion and misrule each dominate certain relevant space–time loci which are mutually contrasted by means of sequential juxtapositions and of the contrasts produced by certain of their characteristics: night/day, north-west/south, inside/outside, moving/still, etc., are some of the ways in which the various axiological differences are made relevant and by which the various settings and their inhabitants are made to make sense. But the overall structure of meaning is constructed sequentially and is developed in time. While, in fact, the first play mainly establishes those axiologies and meanings and gives them a comparatively clear set of distinctive prerogatives, in the second we see their progressive disfigurement and finally their utter corruption: trespassings and interferences, in fact, are comparatively ineffectual in the first play, where they figure merely as hints and suggestions of what may in the end happen and as partial and temporary distortion of the prerogatives of each of the spaces; while in the second they are responsible for the blurring and final collapse of the issues for which each of the spaces stands. Besides, although the *dénouement* of the sequence is the triumph of the space of *rule*, the way this comes about involves an interesting exchange of prerogatives, for it is achieved by means of a double betrayal: the betrayal by John of Lancaster of the forces of rebellion and the betrayal by Hal of the forces of misrule.

This general frame is established in different ways in the two plays: while in the first it relies principally on time (the impression of simultaneity is the means by which the various spheres are both contrasted and interrelated), in the second it is constructed mainly by playing on the different spaces and on the various events which involve crossings of their boundaries, with violations which become more and more frequent and more and more fatal.

1 HENRY IV: TIME'S MASTERS AND TIME'S FOOLS

That time, in a number of aspects, is an extremely important component of *1 Henry IV* is evident throughout the text.[12] Indeed, nowhere else does Shakespeare emphasise the time component so punctiliously or underline its importance for almost all the characters in so many different circumstances. Scarcely a scene goes by without our attention being drawn to time or without some discussion of the meaning of time: thus, there are occasions where basic information about the time of day (or of night) is given, occasions where some future time is envisaged and looked forward to, occasions where it is stated that the time has come for some enterprise to be set in motion; finally there are occasions where alien times (and spaces) thrust themselves before us through the arrival of posts and through the delivery of letters. Allusions to and specifications of time tightly connect the sequences developing in the various spaces activated by the action; they help to create contrasts between diverging thoughts occurring at the same time to different characters while connecting and/or contrasting axiologies and attitudes by creating an impression of temporal contiguity or coexistence. Indeed, the play exploits this basic historical (and theatrical) component almost obsessively, although it suggests that there is profound difference between the various views of time (and therefore utter instability in any definition of historical time), a difference which is determined by the characters that inhabit the various times and by the way they manage and master – or are not able to master – time; this until the battle of Shrewsbury forces all to meet in one and the same time and space – a space which is alien to all and which is entrusted with the task of dispersing, albeit temporarily, Henry's rival axiologies.

Henry's time is indeed unquiet. The time which he mentions in the second line of the play, which he has planned to devote to the 'frighted peace' and to the crusade is, as we have seen, turned into a time of war by the news which arrives from Wales and Scotland. But it is in the second scene of the play that the temporal component is made thematically relevant. The very first words we hear from Falstaff at the opening of the scene concern time ('Now, Hal, what time of day is it, lad?', I.ii.1), and they are used in Hal's reply and in the subsequent five speech turns in a way that completely deautomatises the casual character of Falstaff's question. Hal does not answer it but replies elaborating on its absurdity and thus uses his speech to introduce Falstaff to the audience:

> *Prince.* . . . What a devil hast thou to do with the time of the day? Unless hours were cups of sack, and minutes capons, and clocks the tongues of bawds, and dials the signs of leaping-houses, and the blessed sun himself a fair hot wench in flame-coloured taffeta, I see no reason why thou shouldst be so superfluous to demand the time of the day.
>
> (I.ii.6–12)

Falstaff then further elaborates on Hal's cue in two subsequent speeches, establishing the first significant opposition of the play regarding time, namely, the night/day opposition:

> *Fal.* . . . we that take purses go by the moon and the seven stars, and not 'by Phoebus, he, that wand'ring knight so fair'. . . . Marry then sweet wag, when thou art king let not us that are squires of the night's body be called thieves of the day's beauty: let us be Diana's foresters, gentlemen of the shade, minions of the moon; and let men say we be men of good government, being governed as the sea is, by our noble and chaste mistress the moon, under whose countenance we steal.
>
> (13–15 and 23–9)[13]

Even Falstaff's space is inhabited by some kind of temporal prospect: there we find both short-term forward projections ('tomorrow morning, by four o'clock', 120–1, 'tonight', 125, 'tomorrow night', 126, 187, 'tomorrow', 156–7), which envisage in advance supper-time and the time appointed for the highway robbery, and a long-term one (the often repeated 'when thou art king', 16, 58, 60, 141–2), in which Falstaff foresees a better legitimation of his revels once Hal has assumed the role of king and maybe even an extension of his own kind of time to the space of rule. But the scene is sealed by Hal's mention of a different kind of time, which makes us perceive the groundlessness of Falstaff's expectations. In the closing line of his soliloquy, in which he reveals his project to forsake his present friends (one of the few projects in the sequence which are not destined to be frustrated), it is not by chance that Hal chooses time – Falstaff's transgressive time – as the present offence to be 'redeemed'.

Following what appears to be a neat expositional pattern, the third scene presents the face of rebellion, and with it yet another view of time. Hotspur's time is forward-projected and characterised by impatience. Once the plot is sketched and the rebellious enterprise is agreed between him, Northumberland and Worcester, Hotspur produces an explicit statement of his attitude towards time: 'O, let the hours be short/ Till fields, and blows, and groans applaud our sport!' (I.iii.295–6), which pertinently concludes the encounter.

All three spaces have by now been presented, and all three have been associated with the different projects which are going to fill out the play's plot. In the space of rule, the initial project is thwarted by the intrusion of external circumstances; in that of misrule, time appears short-winded, and the project of betrayal formulated by Hal (who is the spurious element in that space) also makes it short-lived; while in that of rebellion it appears characterised by impetuosity and presumptuousness. The idea that the conflict between the three main spaces is going to be a conflict between different conceptions of time is thus suggested right from the start. Quite surprisingly, however, the king's time is presented as the least stable and the most powerless. Henry's inability to formulate a project of his own, unaffected by external pressures, condemns the time of state politics and the locus of political power to the instability of unplanned action.

But it is in Act II (with a coda in III.i.) that we encounter the most interesting treatment of time and a clearer juxtaposition of, and confrontation between, the two destabilising axiologies of the play, those of misrule and rebellion.

In the sequence of scenes which I am going to discuss, time is on the one hand *used* as a dramaturgical tool to produce contrasts by suggesting simultaneity and on the other *evoked* as a topic for reflection. In the first scene, which is set in Rochester, time is repeatedly mentioned and specified as a relevant element of the plot. The first line, spoken by one of the two Carriers ('An it be not four by the day I'll be hanged'), signals the man's impatience to leave for London, to which he and his companion have to transport goods and passengers; Gadshill enters asking 'what's o'clock?' (31) and is answered by the First Carrier 'I think it be two o'clock' (32); when he further asks the Carrier 'what time do you mean to come to London?' (40–1), he is answered 'Time enough to go to bed with a candle, I warrant thee' (42–3). Obviously, 'two o'clock' has a different meaning for the Carriers and for Gadshill: the former are concerned to leave as soon as possible in order to deliver their goods, to get their passengers to their destinations in due time and not to spend too many hours of the day travelling; while for Gadshill, who is 'one of the squires of the night's body', two o'clock is the right time for purse-cutting. Scene ii, with the highway robbery and the trick played on Falstaff by Hal and Poins, who rob the robbers of their booty, presumably takes place a little later, the same night. By the end of the scene, Hal's night of revels seems to be concluded after Falstaff, Gadshill and Bardolph have fled. Leaving the prince and Poins on the highway, we are abruptly introduced to the presence of Hotspur, *solus*, Hamlet-like, reading a letter (the first of many epistolary intrusions from a different space and time in the space of rebellion). One of his possible allies in the dangerous enterprise of revolt has forsaken him. Nevertheless, in the dialogue which he starts with the absent and unknown (to us) sender of the letter, Hotspur shows a courageous heart: he will proceed relentlessly in his project.

In the first moments of this scene, the evident discrepancies – linguistic, stylistic and situational – with the preceding one prevent us from appreciating Hotspur's mood and from siding with the seriousness of his undertaking. However, by the end of the Hotspur scene, emotion and sympathy have been raised, mainly thanks to the dialogue which follows the appearance of Lady Percy (the encounter is an antecedent of that between Brutus and Portia in *Julius Caesar*, II.i.233–309); so that when, with equal abruptness, the Eastcheap scene is revealed, we feel that the pressure of estrangement is also working in the opposite direction: for a few moments, in fact, laughter is blocked and we are compelled to absorb the irreconcilable diversity of the two worlds.

The technical need to interpose a scene which takes place in a different space between two scenes showing the space of Hal's revels does not by itself fully account for the interpolation of the incongruous fragment. More compelling seems to be the need to contrast Hal's wild night with the serious and pathetic thoughts and activities which *in the meantime* are keeping his rival awake. In this case, it is not clear whose interests are served by the perception of the discrepancy. Certainly, however, the audience's tendency to side with the prince is blurred, and we are compelled to discern and discriminate; even to choose between the time and space of comedy and those of tragedy, between the laughter that accompanies Falstaff's cowardice and Hal's idleness and the pathos that attends on Hotspur's desperate courage; and finally, we are made to consider that events and motivations are neither neutral nor transparent and that our shifts in sympathy from the prince to his rival have been meticulously planned, directed and monitored.

Hotspur's monologue (a dramatic privilege which he shares with Hal and which gives him a chance to make the audience appreciate his point of view) closes with yet another mention of time ('I will set forward tonight', 35) which, again, presents rebellion's time as wilful and rash. In his dialogue with Lady Percy, then, Hotspur repeats his intention to leave 'within these two hours' (36–7), and we leave him making preparations for the journey.

At this point, the text makes a temporal leap of more or less 24 hours, and once again presents two scenes which seem to be taking place simultaneously, probably the following night.[14]

In II.iv, the first tavern scene of the sequence, time is again a conspicuous topic, while we have an explicit comparison between Hal's and Hotspur's time. The first 100 lines of the scene are occupied by Hal's ungenerous jest towards Francis. This, which is suggested by Francis's busy although unconsequential running here and there and answering calls with 'anon, anon', reveals yet another attitude towards time which is peculiar to this character. It has been argued that Francis lacks both memory – he cannot answer the simple question about his age – and forward vision and that 'he is the man who is never capable of questioning his immediate predicament, . . . lacking what Augustine called *distensio animi*, memory and project'.[15] In his 'dialogue' with Francis, Hal is precisely exposing the man's lack of future perspective: to his question 'when', which requests the specification of a time in the future, Francis in fact replies again with 'Anon, anon.' (61–3)[16] The prince's reply is jestingly didactic in its superfluous listing of possible future times, while the redundancy of the drawer's name is perhaps meant to prompt a further 'anon' from him ('Anon, Francis? No, Francis, but tomorrow, Francis; or, Francis, a-Thursday; or indeed, Francis, when thou wilt', 64–6); but the drawer further confirms his perception of the present time as merely 'anon' when, to Hal's direct question 'What's o'clock, Francis?', he again replies 'Anon, anon, sir.'[17]

Hal's final comment on Francis's 'fewer words than a parrot' and on his unconsequential running here and there triggers the thought of 'the Hotspur of the north':

> *Prince.* That ever this fellow should have fewer words than a parrot, and yet the son of a woman! His industry is up-stairs and down-stairs, his eloquence the parcel of a reckoning. I am not yet of Percy's mind, the Hotspur of the north, he that kills me some six or seven dozen of Scots at a breakfast, washes his hands and says to his wife, 'Fie upon this quiet life, I want work'. 'O my sweet Harry', says she, 'How many hast thou killed today?' 'Give my roan horse a drench', says he, and answers, 'Some fourteen', an hour after; 'a trifle, a trifle'.
>
> (96–106)

The shift from Francis to Percy has always been considered a sudden and almost inexplicable change of subject; this has led commentators to explain it as prompted by Hal's declaration, in line 90, about his being 'of all humours', and therefore as a contrast with Hotspur's gloomy bent on war. The interpolation of the comment on Francis between l. 90 and the mention of Hotspur starting on l. 99, however, remains unexplained unless Francis, too, is included as one of the elements in the comparison;[18] and it seems to me that the incongruity vanishes if we acknowledge time as the element which triggers the associative link which brings Percy into Hal's mind. The 'Hotspur of the north' (and the mention of Hotspur's space of action is not irrelevant) is evoked by Hal in a parodic mood in which his rival's headstrong way of living his time is equated to Francis's amnesic (namely, not historically-oriented), nonprojectual and inconsequential sheer present (see, 'at a breakfast', 101, and 'an hour after', 106).[19]

Twice more time is specified in the scene, and on both occasions in connection with an interference from a different space. When the hostess announces that 'a nobleman of the court ' (283), 'an old man' (289) is at the door and asks to speak to Hal, Falstaff's comment is 'What doth gravity out of his bed at midnight?' (290; the gentleman's appearance seems to him improper, for he comes from a space whose time is the day). Together with the call to duty from the king, who sends word to the prince that he 'must to the court in the morning' (330–1), the messenger brings the 'villainous news' (329) of the rebellion of those who, in Falstaff's words, are 'That same mad fellow of *the north*' and '*he of Wales*' (331–2; my emphasis). This first attack on the space of misrule, brought jointly by the king and the rebels, is followed a little later by the attack of justice: 'The sheriff and all the watch' (483), accompanied by the Carrier whose passengers have been robbed the night before, are at the door. In the brief exchange between Hal and the Sheriff at the end of the latter's visit, clock time is again specified:

> *Sher.* Good night, my noble lord.
> *Prince.* I think it is good morrow, is it not?
> *Sher.* Indeed, my lord, I think it be two o'clock.
>   (516–18)

The two invasions from an alien space have spoiled the night's fun. In an impatient projectual mood which he manifests for the first time, before Falstaff 'fast asleep behind the arras' (521–2), Hal seals the sequence and the night with words which dispel the lazy atmosphere of the tavern. The space which contains misrule has been invaded by the pressure of its rival axiologies and, besides, the coming of day disbands the night's revels:

> I'll to the court in the morning. We must all to the wars, and thy place shall be honourable. I'll procure this fat rogue a charge of foot, and I know his death will be a march of twelve score. The money shall be paid back again with advantage. Be with me betimes in the morning; and so, good morrow, Peto. (536–42)

Between Hal's night in Eastcheap and his interview with the king the following morning, we are introduced to the heart of rebellion. The scene in Bangor, like the one in Warkworth, takes place during the night, and its location – immediately after the Eastcheap night and before Hal's encounter with the king the following morning – means that we perceive it as taking place simultaneously with the tavern events in II.iv.[20]

Unlike Hal's, Hotspur's night is packed with events, of which the most important is the agreement between him, Mortimer and Glendower about the 'indentures tripartite' to be drawn and 'sealed interchangeably' (III.i.76–7). Space in this scene is mainly the map of the country, a model territory and a figure of dominion by which

the rebels are measuring their influence and building up their expectations of future sway. South-east, west and north, reduced to contractual items, are the terrains on which the rebels are constructing
their potential power. Time, intensely projectual, is again charged
with the haste to achieve the desired results which we by now
recognise as Hotspur's main characteristic, and which is repeatedly
signalled in the scene.[21] The night is spent drawing the deed of
partition and in the encounter with the ladies; Hotspur says to
Lady Percy that he will soon leave ('And the indentures be drawn
I'll away within these two hours', 254–5), and the scene is concluded
with yet another hint of his haste as compared to the attitude of
'slow' Mortimer:

> *Glend.* Come, come, Lord Mortimer, you are as slow
>   As hot Lord Percy is on fire to go:
>   (257–8)

The following two scenes have closings which present the re-
maining two spaces of the play, which are both equally projected
towards the meeting with the enemy. In III.ii., once the news that
the rebels' forces have gathered in Shrewsbury reaches Henry, the
king's time, too, becomes forward-bent. (Henry's time, however,
remains inhabited and determined by the moves of others):

> *King.* . . .
>   On Wednesday next, Harry, you shall set forward,
>   On Thursday we ourselves will march.
>   . . .
>   Our business valued, some twelve days hence
>   Our general forces at Bridgnorth shall meet.
>   Our hands are full of business, let's away,
>   Advantage feeds him fat while men delay.
>   (173–80)

The effects of the invasion of justice and war into the space of
misrule start to be felt in the following scene. Falstaff complains
that he has been robbed of a ring in the tavern and the Hostess
replies by accusing him of not paying his debts. Hal, who joins
them, does not appear to have changed attitude after his interview
with his father; rather, he seems to be profiting from his recovered

friendship with the king ('I am good friends with my father and may do anything', III.iii.180–1); and rather than reform his friends in view of the war, he seems to be willing to bring the tavern's space of misrule into the final conflict:[22]

> *Prince.* . . .
> Go, Peto, to horse, to horse, for thou and I
> Have thirty miles to ride yet ere dinner-time.
> Jack, meet me tomorrow in the Temple hall
> At two o'clock in the afternoon:
> There shalt thou know thy charge, and there receive
> Money and order for their furniture.
>
> (196–201)

In the last two lines of this speech, however, Hal's impatience to meet Hotspur and the impression that he is inflamed by patriotism are somewhat quelled by the formal tone suggested by the sudden use of verse for his speech and by the rhyme which appears in the closing lines ('The land is burning, Percy stands on high, / And either we or they must lower lie', 202–3).

In Acts IV and V, it is messages to and from the rebels and 'rebel letters' that are responsible for the border-crossings of time and space. Letters are delivered to Hotspur before the battle, but he 'cannot read them now' (V.ii.80).[23] Why does he not? What might their function be, given that we are never going to be allowed to know their contents? Again, border-crossing seems to be the point. By now, signals of discomfiture have gathered over the rebels' heads, and the spectators may imagine that the unread letters contain more defections on the part of prospective allies. For letters to the rebels, as we know by now, contain betrayal since a letter cannot but convey absence: 'it is only letters that arrive at the battlefield: death is their destination.'[24] Here, again, time and space play an important role. For, by definition, letters come from a different time and a different space. Those letters, then, apart from conveying absence, reveal that the betrayal of the rebellion has already been planned and executed and that the death sentence on the rebels was in fact pronounced in a time in which the rebellion still nourished expectations of solidarity and help: those that even now were still thought to be co-conspirators, have at a certain moment in the past forsaken the rebellion. It is here, maybe, that Hotspur realises for the first time that he – as one of his last sentences will reveal – is being

made 'time's fool'. The letters remain sealed: we, like Hotspur, know
that death has already been decreed and is now trying to force the
boundaries of rebellion, that death, coming from afar and from the
past, is the message of the unsealed letters. By refusing to read
them, Hotspur is making a last desperate attempt to keep away the
death sentence they carry.

When he meets Hotspur on the battlefield, Hal speaks in spatial
terms of the impossibility of them both living on the same historical
scene:

> Two stars keep not their motion in one sphere,
> Nor can one England brook a double reign
> Of Harry Percy and the Prince of Wales.
>
> (V.iv.64–6)

while Hotspur acknowledges the coming of his own death in terms
of time:

> But thoughts, the slaves of life, and life, time's fool,
> And time, that takes survey of all the world,
> Must have a stop.
>
> (80–2)

However, neither rebellion nor misrule are actually vanquished.
York and Wales are the spaces where the first is still 'busily in
arms' (V.v.38), and the king's prospective closing leads us to meet
the circumstance of 'such another day' (42); besides, we also perceive from Hal's complicit aside to Falstaff in V.iv ('if a lie may do
thee grace/ I'll gild it with the happiest terms I have', 156–7) that
misrule has by no means been dispersed.

The spaces – as well as styles and persons – that we encounter
in Part One are comparatively independent from each other and
remain in the end conflictual. Although there have been a number
of border-crossings (war and justice have violated the space of
misrule and rebellion has openly insinuated itself into both the
opposing spaces), the boundaries of each sphere have not been fatally
affected by those attacks and by the end of the play they seem to
have been reconstituted – except for the uncertainty of Hal's position.
The lasting violation of spaces will be a decisive feature of the next
play.

2 *HENRY IV*: BORDER-CROSSING, SICKNESS AND CORRUPTION

Rather than considering the second play as a revision and even an *undoing* of the meanings of the first (as Yachnin does), I prefer to describe it as enacting a process of corruption whose seeds are already present – albeit hardly stressed – in Part One.[25] Various forms of sickness now attack the core of the three spaces and, in the end, the axiologies which militate against the king are defeated by a process of pollution which changes their very nature; but even the natural body of the king is attacked by corruption, and illness decrees the end at least of that power which is associated with the illegitimate Henry IV.

In *2 Henry IV* there are repeated and open allusions to sickness, bodily decay, old age and the prospect of death; at the same time, the violations of what in Part One are comparatively independent and 'healthy' spaces become more and more frequent and aggressive. Border-crossing thus becomes the agent of malady: almost literally, a foreign body is insinuated into a healthy organism where it produces disease and corruption. Repeatedly, inversions and exchanges of attributes are given explicit verbal expression, and these represent an attack on the axiological integrity of the various spaces, whose nature is finally perverted.[26]

In his first appearance in I.ii., Falstaff questions his Page about the doctor's examination of his urine; 'He said', the Page answers, 'the water itself was a good healthy water; but, for the party that owed it, he might have moe diseases than he knew for' (2–4): Falstaff's, then, is a hidden disease, impossible to detect physically. In the same scene, we witness Sir John's first encounter with justice. After attempting to avoid the encounter by pretending to be deaf, he tries to exorcise the presence of the Lord Chief Justice and to undermine his sphere of action by alluding to an illness which supposedly affects him and to his age:

I am glad to see your lordship abroad, I heard say your lordship was sick. I hope your lordship goes abroad by advice; your lordship, though not clean past your youth, have yet some smack of age in you, some relish of the saltness of time; and I most humbly beseech your lordship to have a reverend care of your health.

(I.ii.93–9)

The Chief Justice does not seem to be affected by Falstaff's allusions to his health. It is Falstaff, instead, who appears troubled by the thought of illness. First, he mentions the king's sickness ('I hear, his majesty is returned with some discomfort from Wales', 102–3; 'And I hear, moreover, his Highness is fallen into this same whoreson apoplexy', 106–7), which he describes at length, simply annoying the officer: 'This apoplexy, as I take it, is a kind of lethargy, and't please your lordship, a kind of sleeping in the blood, a whoreson tingling' (110–12). The attempted attack on the king is rejected by the Chief Justice: 'What tell you me of it? Be it as it is' (113), but Falstaff repeats the assault with a more precise diagnosis of causes: 'It hath it original from much grief, from study, and perturbation of the brain; I have read the cause of its effects in Galen, it is a kind of deafness' (114–16). But 'deafness' is Falstaff's malady, as the Lord Chief Justice promptly retorts. The exchange that follows reveals that it is Sir John who has been infected by the disease he has mentioned and defined:

> *Ch. Just.* I think you are fallen into the disease, for you hear not
>   what I say to you.
> *Fal.* Very well, my lord, very well. Rather, and't please you, it is
>   the disease of not listening, the malady of not marking, that I
>   am troubled withal.
> *Ch. Just.* To punish you by the heels would amend the attention
>   of your ears, and I care not if I do become your physician.
>   (117–24)

The last attack on the integrity of the space of misrule is launched by the king: 'The king has severed you and Prince Harry' (202–3), says the Lord Chief Justice, and although Falstaff and Hal will meet again later on in the play, we know that the process of separation is already under way.

After the exit of the Lord Chief Justice, Falstaff enquires of the Page about his cash in hand; and, again, he comments on the emptiness of his pockets in terms of sickness:

> I can get no remedy against this consumption of the purse;
> borrowing only lingers and lingers it out, but the disease is in-
> curable. (237–9)

Then, passing from metaphor to the literal meaning, he curses his gout:

A pox of this gout! or a gout of this pox! for the one or the other plays the rogue with my great toe. 'Tis no matter if I do halt; I have the wars for my colour, and my pension shall seem the more reasonable. A good wit will make use of anything; I will turn diseases to commodity. (244–50)[27]

Act Two is, as in Part One, almost entirely devoted to the space of misrule and develops the idea of the corruption and dissolution of the Eastcheap world. When we next see Falstaff (in II.i.) he is being sued by the Hostess, who is trying to have him arrested on account of his debts and the breach of a marriage promise. Again the Lord Chief Justice crosses the border of Falstaff's space. Those wrongs, he says, must be redressed promptly: the one 'with sterling money, and the other with current repentance' (119–20). But, while the Justice is trying to patch up the quarrel, a further disturbance breaks in. This time it is war, news of which is brought by Gower from the king and the Prince of Wales, together with a letter giving details of the present situation. From line 135 to line 162, the scene presents the interesting configuration of a divided space. While the Chief Justice is absorbed in the reading of the letter, Falstaff tries to recover what is left of his space and succeeds in softening the Hostess's heart and in having her withdraw her action. By the end of the exchange, the Hostess promises to give him supper and to invite Doll Tearsheet to cheer him up. But after the Hostess and his other friends are gone, Sir John loses control of the situation. Once the space he dominates has dissolved, he is left alone with the Chief Justice and Gower and obliged to share the space of their present preoccupations and the subject of their conversation, which he tries to do to no effect. His repeated questions – 'What's the news, my lord?' (164), 'I hope, my lord, all's well. What is the news, my lord?' (167), 'Comes the King back from Wales, my noble lord?' (172) – are left unanswered by the Chief Justice, who thus, by breaking a basic conversational rule, manifests his utter contempt for Sir John. For the first time in the whole sequence, the audience, too, may tend to abandon Falstaff in his pathetic attempt to gain credibility in the sphere of state politics. His invitation of Gower to dinner and Gower's refusal do not raise laughter, for Falstaff's endeavour to captivate Gower's sympathy appears disturbingly grotesque and out of place; and there is more than a chance that we may share the Chief Justice's scorn and agree with his final verdict on the fat knight: 'thou art a great fool' (189–90).

In the following scene, the space we are in is even more equivocal and more distorted. The first part of the conversation between Hal and Poins was the starting point of Auerbach's essay on 'The weary prince'.[28] However far one may be from sharing Auerbach's interpretation of the scene as the epitome of Shakespeare's tendency to attribute dignity only to 'high' characters (the most surprising of Auerbach's examples of this is Shylock), one cannot but agree with the importance that he attributes to the Prince's sadness. The blending of styles – which Auerbach reads, through the intrusion of the 'humble' element represented by Poins and 'small beer', as a shame to Hal's greatness – is certainly relevant in this scene; for no other reason than simply because it is here that Hal remarks – and makes the audience realise – that there is a (stylistic) difference and discrepancy between him and his 'friends'. Indeed no such discrepancy is noticeable in the tavern scenes, where Hal seems to be perfectly at home in the 'low'-style discourse. In the scene with Poins, the discordance of styles is being openly enunciated and presented, as it were, as one of the problems that arise at this stage in the dissolution of the space of misrule and in Hal's gradual assumption to the space of power. The mixture of styles and persons is now for the first time seen as a disease in the body both of the story's development and of the text's decorum.

The reason the Prince gives for his sadness is his father's illness. But Hal's weariness may well derive from a more complicated mixture of feelings. He knows that in the world's eyes his father's sickness is not an adequate reason for his sadness ('it is not meet that I should be sad now my father is sick', 38–9), but perceives that the real reason behind his sadness is unspeakable: the mortal disease affecting the very heart of the space of rule is also infecting the space of misrule, and will in the end decree its dissolution. Besides, Hal's weariness, and the very fact that he speaks of his sadness, are also a hint to the audience: a melancholy separation is near, and in a short time the spectators will have to cope with the prince's betrayal of his former friends and the dissolution of the comic plot. While, on the one hand, by revealing his sadness, Hal is trying to increase the audience's sympathy through its appreciation of his divided mind, on the other, by showing contempt for his 'low' friend Poins, he is preparing the audience for his final desertion of Falstaff.

The next time we see Hal at the Boar's Head (II.iv.) is also the last.[29] The prince is wearing a drawer's costume – at this stage the disguise is necessary for him to meet his former friends on the same (stylistic) level. By the end of the scene, time in the tavern undergoes an acceleration which is wholly extraneous to the rhythm of laziness that we tend to associate with the space of misrule; the prince's last verbal jest is left incomplete ('You, gentlewoman, –', 346), for war knocks at the door in the person of Peto. Hal's farewell to Falstaff's world is couched in a formal style which once more signals the (stylistic) gap:

> By heaven, Poins, I feel me much to blame,
> So idly to prophane the precious time,
> When tempest of commotion, like the south
> Borne with black vapour, doth begin to melt
> And drop upon our bare unarmed heads.
>
> (358–62)[30]

and his farewell to Falstaff is cold and distant ('Falstaff, good night', 363).

A further (Bardolph's) knocking at the door summons Sir John to court, away from Doll and the prospect of yet another night of revels. After a last boast of self-praise ('You see, my good wenches, how men of merit are sought after', 371–2), Falstaff pronounces a warm farewell to the women ('Farewell, good wenches: if I be not sent away post, I will see you again ere I go', 374–5). And while not a single word has accompanied Hal's exit, Falstaff's departure is followed by tears of deep nostalgia.

The comic plot is soon to find other participants, in a space which is even more affected by war and almost obsessively corrupted by the thought of old age and death.

In his home in Gloucestershire, old Justice Shallow has gathered a company of ragged men for conscription. While waiting for Falstaff's arrival together with Justice Silence, he strikes the keynote which is going to colour the whole encounter: nostalgia for the mad days of his youth at Clement's Inn and the thought of his old acquaintance:

> *Shal.* . . . Jesu, Jesu, the mad days I have spent! And to see how
>   many of my old acquaintance are dead!
> *Sil.* We shall all follow, cousin.
> *Shal.* Certain, 'tis certain, very sure, very sure. Death, as the
>   psalmist says, is certain to all, all shall die.
>
> (III.ii.32–7)

Shallow's inane comments on death go on for a while. He asks
Silence about an old common friend:

> *Shal.* Death is certain. Is old Double of your town living yet?
> *Sil.* Dead, sir.
> *Shal.* Jesu, Jesu, dead! A drew a good bow, and dead! A shot a
>   fine shoot. John a Gaunt loved him well, and betted much
>   money on his head. Dead!
>
> (40–5)

After Falstaff has examined and 'pricked' the men, Shallow resumes the topic, and asks Sir John about Jane Nightwork (obviously,
a prostitute). Falstaff himself seems to be affected by the thought of
old age: the woman is living, he says, but she is 'Old, old, Master
Shallow' (201). His answer gives the JP an opportunity to produce
more silly and entirely tautological comments, this time on old age:
'Nay, she must be old, she cannot choose but be old, certain she's
old' (202–3).

But corruption also makes its appearance in other forms in this
scene: Bardolph and Falstaff accept money from Mouldy and Bullcalf
to free them from conscription; besides, according to Falstaff, Shallow's account of his 'mad days' at Clement's Inn is sheer corruption
of the truth (again, an instance of distortion of past events), 'every
third word a lie' (301). Here, again, the thought of old age affects
Falstaff, who produces a melancholy comment in a reflective mood,
an entirely new note in his humour : 'Lord, how subject we old men
are to this vice of lying!' (297–8).

But the sphere of rule, too, is affected by an incurable disease
which endangers the life of its very heart, the King. We see Henry
for the first time in III.i., but his illness has already been hinted at
on several occasions. From his first speech, moreover, we know that
sleep has abandoned him.[31] But sickness is not simply attacking the
King's natural body: in the shape of rebellion, it is attacking the
body politic and the country itself. To Warwick and Surrey, Henry
speaks of the danger coming from the north as of a malady which
has attacked the body of his kingdom:

> *King.* Then you perceive the body of our kingdom
>   How foul it is, what rank diseases grow,
>   And with what danger, near the heart of it.
>
> (38–40)

Warwick takes over the metaphoric suggestion and further elaborates it:

> *War.* It is but as a body yet distemper'd,
>   Which to his former strength may be restor'd
>   With good advice and little medicine.
>
> (41–3)

Other hints at sickness appear in the same scene. To Henry's preoccupations about the large number of soldiers in the rebels' army, Warwick answers by recalling that rumour may corrupt the truth ('Rumour doth double, like the voice and echo, / The numbers of the feared', 97–8); then he explains Henry's present state of mind with his illness:

> Your Majesty hath been this fortnight ill,
> And these unseason'd hours perforce must add
> Unto your sickness.
>
> (104–6)

The next and last time we see the King (IV.iv.), he is again projecting a crusade, this time in a sort of delirium.[32] If the present ordeal meets with success, Henry says, 'We will our youth lead on to higher fields, / And draw no swords but what are sanctified' (3–4). But the news that the rebels have suffered a defeat hardly cheers him, and the thought of illness returns implacably: 'And wherefore should these good news make me sick?' (102). The end, we know, is near:

> I should rejoyce now at these happy news,
> And now my sight fails, and my brain is giddy.
> O me! come near me, now I am much ill.
>
> (109–111)

But, before he dies, Henry is still to experience a final violation of his space in what is perhaps the most serious of the trespasses perpetrated by the heir apparent. The theft of the crown, by which Hal performs his premature appropriation of the space of rule, accelerates the King's death: 'This part of his conjoins with my disease, / And helps to end me' (IV.v.63–4).

But sickness has attacked the rebels' camp as well: when acting as messenger from John of Lancaster, Westmoreland remarks on the paradox of seeing the Archbishop in arms. He comments on the absurdity of York's transformation in terms of linguistic translation, and remarks that his presence produces a corruption of the nature of rebellion (IV.i.32–52). Quite pertinently, the Archbishop answers by claiming that his transformation into a warrior was dictated by the sickness of the whole realm and the necessity to cure it. His speech, a long medical metaphor (53–87), employs in thirteen lines no less than eleven expressions related to sickness ('diseas'd', 'burning fever', 'bleed', 'disease', 'infected', 'physician', 'diet', 'rank minds', 'sick', 'purge the obstruction', 'veins of life'). The encounter between the rebels and the emissaries of the King ends with John of Lancaster's arrival (the most fatal of all the border-crossings happening in the rebel's space) and with the rebels being sent to death. Quite pertinently, while they are drinking with Lancaster to what they still believe is their reestablished friendship, Mowbray feels 'on the sudden something ill' (IV.ii.80). The fatal disease, this time, has come from the King's sphere; rebellion is defeated in much the same way as misrule is going to be defeated. But misrule lingers on longer, and we are still to encounter what is left of Falstaff's world in Act Five.

Again, the last scenes of the play give us the impression that the various fragments take place simultaneously. While Falstaff and Bardolph visit Shallow in Gloucestershire (V.i.), the news of the king's death is given to the Lord Chief Justice (V.ii), and we first see the prince as Henry V who reconciles himself with the judge and promises to 'frustrate prophecies' (127); and while Pistol brings Falstaff news of the king's death (V.iii), Quickly and Tearsheet (we are driven to think, as an effect of Henry's reconciliation with justice) are brought to jail (V.iv). The last scene of the play seals the triumph of power and the unification of rule with justice by means of another betrayal. If it is true that Hal has mocked 'the expectation of the world' (V.ii.126), he has certainly not frustrated the spectator's forecasts. Time is finally redeemed, although by means of a cruel dramatic sin: the annihilation of the universe of comedy.[33]

There remains to discuss the moment where we encounter what is perhaps the most lengthy and elaborate, but also the most ambiguous meditation on (historical) time and change in the whole canon.

The passage, it seems to me, enunciates two distinct views of historical time and change, which reveal two opposed historiographical conceptions: on the one hand we have Henry's conception, the weak choiceless view of a world dominated by chance – or maybe by an inscrutable providence; on the other hand, we have Warwick's empirical view, which shows greater confidence in the possibility of formulating historical predictions. Warwick's somewhat facile forecast ('My Lord Northumberland will soon be cool'd', 44), obviously intended to soothe the king's anxiety, triggers Henry's meditation on our impotence in predicting what is in store for us:

> *King.* O God, that one might read the book of fate,
>   And see the *revolution* of the times
>   Make mountains level, and the continent,
>   Weary of solid firmness, melt itself
>   Into the sea, and other times to see
>   The beachy girdle of the ocean
>   Too wide for Neptune's hips; how *chance's mocks*
>   And *changes* fill the cup of *alteration*
>   With divers liquors!
>   (III.i.45–53; my emphasis)

Henry's speech is remarkably confused – as is his state of mind – for it oscillates between the idea of inspired prophecy (the conjunction of the expressions 'read the book of fate' and 'see the revolution of the times' evokes the prophecies produced by astrologers) and that of mere chance. The shape of events is written in the 'book of fate', and to read in that book the changes that time will bring is not given to us. To signify change, Henry chooses the alterations which take place in nature: mountains being made level and the ground being invaded by the waters; but he insists on a weak explanation of change – one which does not apply to the kind of mutational phenomena he has described – indicating 'chance's mocks', the unforeseeable tricks produced by mere chance, as the various causes ('divers liquors') which actually bring about changes ('fill the cup of alteration').[34] What is interesting in Henry's speech is his insistence on the idea of *change* and the hidden thought which it reveals. Although the images of his speech are taken from the natural world, and although the starting point of his meditation seems to be the change in attitude on the part of the Percies, it is evident that the kind of change he is envisaging if he should be defeated by the rebels is one which will take the form of the transference of power to a different person. Not improperly, in fact, the

word he uses is *revolution*. The word's meaning is ambiguous: Henry
might here simply be suggesting a 'process of change' in a linear
causative chain of events,[35] but he might also be using *revolution* in
its astronomical (and etymological) sense, where it connotes a revolving, a cyclic movement in a course which ends where it started
(in this way he might be connecting the idea of prophecy to astrology and at the same time alluding to the possible repetition of his
act of usurpation). To a modern reader, however, the word conveys
the political connotations which are connected with the kind of
change which is produced by the overthrow of an established government, a connotation by no means improbable in the passage
quoted, since it has been shown that by the end of the sixteenth
century the word was already on the way to acquiring its modern
meaning.[36] That this last meaning is at least coexistent with the old
ones is further shown by the fact that immediately following these
lines Henry evokes the revolution he himself produced by overthrowing Richard,[37] although he evokes the event by recalling the
change in attitude of the Percies:

> . . . It is but eight years since,
> This Percy was the man nearest my soul;
> Who like a brother toil'd in my affairs,
> And laid his love and life under my foot;
> Yea, for my sake, even to the eyes of Richard
> Gave him defiance.
>
>   (60–65)

But the course of Henry's meditation on time and (historical)
change is at this point complicated by yet another different theme:
that of political prophecy and of Richard's ability – which contrasts
with his own impotence – to produce a foretelling of future events:

>   But which of you was by –
> [*To Warwick*] You, cousin Nevil, as I may remember –
> When Richard, with his eye brimful of tears,
> Then check'd and rated by Northumberland,
> Did speak these words, now prov'd a prophecy?
> 'Northumberland, thou ladder by the which
> My cousin Bolingbroke ascends the throne'
> . . .
> 'The time will come, that foul sin, gathering head,

Shall break into corruption' – so went on,
Foretelling this same time's condition,
And the division of our amity.

(65–79)

Warwick's speech in answer to Henry's tends to steer the king's
weak and confused acknowledgement of his impotence towards
the idea of political prediction, by suggesting that careful observation of human behaviour is all that is needed to make the foretelling
of future events possible. Warwick at the same time explains how
Richard was able to foresee what was to happen eight years later
and suggests that the present situation, too, if examined in the light
of past events, will allow predictions to be made:

War. There is a history in all men's lives
    Figuring the nature of the times deceas'd;
    The which observ'd, a man may prophesy,
    With a near aim, of the main chance of things
    As yet not come to life, who in their seeds
    And weak beginnings lie intreasured.
    Such things become the hatch and brood of time;
    And by the necessary form of this
    King Richard might create a perfect guess
    That great Northumberland, then false to him,
    Would of that seed grow to a greater falseness,
    Which should not find a ground to root upon
    Unless on you.

(80–92)

In other words, if we observe the events in the life of a person,
we can detect a pattern, or, as it were, a sort of personal behav-
ioural norm in accordance with which each of us tends to act; and,
by observing this pattern, we can predict 'with a near aim' what
this person's future actions will be ('the main chance of things as
yet to come').[38] Thus, predictions may be made by observing the
'seeds' and 'weak beginnings', the basic tendencies of human behaviour. In other words, Warwick is suggesting that a reading of
the future presupposes the capacity to read the past.[39]

Warwick's speech, I believe, should be read as a more general
and complex statement than is suggested by Yachnin's reading of
it as 'a pragmatic analysis of personality types'.[40] Indeed, the passage

illustrates a historiographical procedure which places inference at the basis of historical research: although Warwick is exposing the procedure in the direction of prediction which goes from cause to effect, his speech may imply the contrary direction – the eminently historiographical one which proceeds from effects to their causes.

Indeed, it seems not improper to connect Warwick's idea of reading the 'seeds' and 'weak beginnings' to the circumstantial and conjectural model (particularising versus generalising) described by Carlo Ginzburg as the basic paradigm of historiography.[41] In his essay, Ginzburg envisages the possibility of formulating *retrospective prophecies* starting from the close, microscopic, analysis of details, a procedure which he sees as common to all the historical sciences. His claim is that scraps and marginal data, the fingerprints, as it were, of past events, allow the historian to grasp and discern a reality which would otherwise be unattainable, and that minimal details and circumstances have often been the key elements in the understanding of more general phenomena.

What Warwick is talking about is essentially the same procedure, although he is concerned with applying it in the direction of historical prediction. Indeed, the two perspectives share a method of close reading and of sign interpretation that allows both diagnosis and prognosis, and both are founded on intuition and on inferential procedures.[42]

It is easy to see how closely the conjectural paradigm applies to the (historical) dramatist. Unable to produce generalisations owing to the constraints of the genre, the dramatist cannot but produce a particular experience, whose decoding cannot but be indirect and conjectural.

But Warwick's idea of change taking place in time and his stress on the observer's activity also epitomises the spectator's experience, which is obviously the mirror image of the dramatist's. The 'weak beginnings' of the conflict, which we saw 'intreasured' in the first play and which Henry was not able to read – let alone dominate – have grown to produce the second play's 'necessary form'. Through the ten acts of the sequence, the audience has been driven to forecast 'with a near aim' the present state of affairs. This, however, is not the end of the story. To remind us at the same time that historical 'closings' are always open-ended and that the closing of a history play is never a conclusion, the play enacts two different endings: John of Lancaster's forecast of a campaign to conquer France as historical prediction and the Epilogue's promise that 'our humble author will continue the story, with Sir John in it' (*Epil.*, 27.8) as dramaturgical projection.

Notes

1. P. Yachnin, 'History, Theatricality and the "Structural Problem" in the *Henry IV* Plays', *Philological Quarterly* LXX (1991), 163–79, p. 164. Recently, the 'structural problem' has been discussed also by S. Hawkins, 'Structural pattern in Shakespeare's histories', *Studies in Philology* LXXXVIII (1991), 16–45.
2. 'History', p. 164.
3. Ibid., pp. 164, 163, 173.
4. I wish to point out that in the second play legality occupies a sphere of its own, that of the Lord Chief Justice, who never shares the same scenic space with Bolingbroke.
5. In the wake of Dover Wilson (ed.), *1 Henry IV* (Cambridge: Cambridge University Press, 1946) and Tillyard (op. cit.), Sherman Hawkins has restated this claim, speaking of 'a premeditated second part' (*'Henry IV*: the Structural Problem Revisited', *SQ* XXXIII [1982], 278–301, p. 281). In his later essay ('Structural Pattern') Hawkins is less explicit on this point.
6. H. Jenkins, *The Structural Problem in Shakespeare's 'Henry IV'* (London: Methuen, 1956), p. 26.
7. 'History', p. 168.
8. Ibid., pp. 168–9.
9. G. Melchiori discusses the importance of the exceptional prescription of costume ('painted full of tongues') in the 1600 Q stage direction (the prescription is absent in F) and suggests that the actor playing Rumor might reappear immediately after as Lord Bardolph, 'the bringer of false news, the personification of Rumor in the world of history'. 'The Primacy of Philology', in K. Elam (ed.), *Shakespeare Today*, pp. 39–50, 44.
10. This claim, like many others in this book, is certainly of the kind that would be challenged by Richard Levin as an 'ironic' reading. Levin's article on 'Performance-critics vs Close Readers in the Study of English Renaissance Drama', *MLR* LXXXI (1986), 545–59, has raised in radical (although ironic) terms the serious question of the spectator's perception as different from the reader's. His conclusion against the extremities of both performance-critics and ironic readers, however, leaves the issue unsolved. Granted, as Anthony Dawson argues, that performances cannot deliver, and audiences cannot 'absorb, the same kind of meaning that reading can produce' ('The Impasse Over the Stage', *ELR* XXI [1991], 309–27, p. 317), one fails to see why criticism should not construct readers' (ironic) meanings and why a performance should not use those – and other – hidden, implied, indirect or even possible meanings and convey them with its own communicative

tools. On this topic, see H. Berger, *Imaginary Audition* (Berkeley: University of California Press, 1989).

11. The way in which time and space are represented in literary texts has produced a number of differently focused theories. From a dramaturgical perspective, Elam is interested in the construction and reception of time as it is transmitted through the organisation of the play's syntagmatics in connection with action development. A dramatic text, he holds, is discontinuous and incomplete; the audience, therefore, needs to actualise the logical connectives suggested by the text's organisation in order to fill in the gaps and complete its furnishing. *The Semiotics of Theatre and Drama* (London: Methuen, 1980), Chapter 4. Such implicit connections are, I believe, particularly relevant to historical drama for they constitute the most efficacious substitute for the category of causation. Bakhtin considers the representation of time and space in literary texts (what he calls the *chronotope*) as the way in which literature takes hold of historical reality and masters it. Space and time are, in texts, fused into an inseparable whole: time, Bakhtin says, is in literary texts a fourth dimension of space ('Discourse in the novel'). Lotman attributes an exceptional importance to the way in which space is represented in texts, holding that through a particular space configuration we tend to simulate notions which are not of a spatial nature, but are ways of representing cultural, social, religious and moral models. Lotman shows how such antitheses as high/low, open/closed, right/left, inside/outside, and so on, are used to represent hierarchies, moral evaluations or value judgments and so on. *The Structure*, pp. 217–31; see also 'The Notion of Boundary' in *Universe of the Mind. A Semiotic Theory of Culture* (London: Tauris, 1990), pp. 131–42.

12. See M. Hunt, 'Time and Timelessness in *1 Henry IV*', *Explorations in Renaissance Culture* X (1984), 56–66.

13. The editor of the Arden edition, A. R. Humphreys explains 'squires . . . beauty' as 'Since we serve the night's excitements, do not complain that we are inactive by day'; he also signals a possible pun 'night–knight': ' "Squires of the body" were a nobleman's attendants.' But perhaps the most interesting passage of Falstaff's speech is the possible topical allusion to Elizabeth–Diana, 'our noble and chaste mistress, the moon'; Falstaff alludes to some form of royal protection in the play's situation ('under whose countenance we steal') and to its legitimation in the future when Hal will be king. Kastan comments on these lines, saying that 'for Falstaff this is not a submission to authority but an authorization of transgression'. ' "The King has Many Marching in His Coat": or, What Did You Do During the War, Daddy?', in I. Kamps, (ed.), *Shakespeare Left and Right* (London: Routledge, 1991), pp. 241–58, 248.

14. In II.iii. Hotspur is leaving Warkworth for Bangor and tells his wife: 'Whither I go, thither shall you go too:/ Today will I set forth, tomorrow you.' (116–17) In III.i. Hotspur has joined Mortimer and Glendower in Bangor, and Lady Percy is with them. As regards Hal, we leave him on the highway in II.ii., presumably towards the break

of day, given the intense activity during the night which started at two o'clock in the inn-yard at Rochester; and find him again in II.iv. at the 'Boar's Head' in Eastcheap, again at night (see, 'this present twelve o'clock at midnight', 92–3); it seems reasonable to suppose that this is the night immediately following the robbery, given Hal's impatience to follow up the joke played on Falstaff.

15. G. Martella, '*Henry IV*: the Form of History', unpublished, p. 8. To a certain extent, Francis shares these characteristics with Henry's impotence of prediction and project. The same idea of the unconsciousness of the present is expressed in *Macbeth*: '*Thy letters have transported me beyond* / This *ignorant* present' (I.v.56–7; my emphasis).

16. E. P. Thompson argued that 'in general, the populace has little predictive notion of time'. 'Eighteenth-century English Society: Class Struggle without Class?', *Social History* III (1978), 133–65, p. 158.

17. That with his question Hal is simply testing Francis's awareness of time is shown by the fact that the question comes immediately after his own 'this present twelve o'clock at midnight' (92–3).

18. Certain editors also suggest that the connection may lie in 'Francis's busy-ness, or his limitation of ideas' (Humphreys); or that 'Perhaps, too, this thought of Hotspur is prompted by Francis's feverish activity'. D. Bevington, *Henry IV Part 1* (Oxford: Oxford University Press, 1987).

19. Bevington suggests that 'Like Francis, Hal is being pulled simultaneously in two directions, and has not devised as yet a better response than Francis's own "Anon, anon, sir!"' (ibid., p. 60); interpretations of the passage are in M. Rose, *Shakespearean Design* (Cambridge, Mass.: The Belknap Press of Harvard University Press, 1972), pp. 50 ff.; Sheldon P. Zitner, 'Anon, Anon: or, a Mirror for a Magistrate', *SQ* XIX (1968), 63–70; Tillyard, op. cit., p. 275.

20. In III.ii, the dialogue between Henry and Hal is interrupted by Sir Walter Blunt, who communicates to the king 'That Douglas and the English rebels met / The eleventh of this month at Shrewsbury' (165–6). This piece of news locates the Bangor scene earlier than the preceding night (a few days are needed for the journey, and Henry answers Blunt that 'this advertisement is five days old', 172). The possible anachronism, however, does not cancel the impression of simultaneity between the two preceding scenes.

21. No other reason than a need to stress Hotspur's impetuousness can be given for his imprecation 'A plague upon it! I have forgot the map' (III.i.4–5) while the map is before him; and the same can be said of his quarrel with Glendower and his complaint that 'He held me last night at least nine hours / In reckoning up the several devils' names' (150–1). These two lines, however, run counter to the hypothesis that Hotspur's previous night was the night in Warkworth, although, again, the spectator's perception of its simultaneity with the highway robbery is not likely to be affected by this punctualisation. That Hotspur's time is precipitous is stressed even in Lady Percy's description of his way of speaking in Part Two (II.iii.24–5).

22. Falstaff seems to pick up the feeling when he seals the scene by

asking the Hostess for breakfast and adding: 'O, I could wish this tavern were my drum.' (204–5).

23. Goldberg develops the idea that rebellion is strictly allied with writing while there is an 'ideological and logocentric suppression of any connection between power and writing'. 'Rebel Letters: Postal Effects from *Richard II* to *Henry IV*', *Renaissance Drama* New Series, XIX [1988], 3–28, p. 13. It should be remarked, however, that in the second play of the sequence letter-writing and the reception of written messages are mainly connected with the king and his entourage.

24. J. Goldberg, ibid., p. 12.

25. The idea of revision largely depends on the importance that we attribute to Hal's 'reformation' in the battle. If we don't expect absolute coherence from Hal's behaviour and see his final conversion as a sequence of comparatively irregular false starts, we tend to attribute much less importance to Shrewsbury as the expected moment of his reformation. There is even a danger that we may mistake for patriotic involvement his aggressiveness and 'unruly disposition' if we conclude that Shrewsbury constitutes his reformation. Is Hal not simply harnessing to his father's service the riotous habits which he normally puts to quite different use in the tavern and on the highway? Jenkins remarks that 'The only man at court who believes in the Prince's reformation, the Earl of Warwick, believes that it will happen, not that it has happened already' (op. cit., p. 25).

26. Among these inversions, see Mortimer's statement that success will follow thanks to the fact that 'the Bishop / Turns insurrection to religion' (I.i.200–1); we encounter another verbal and conceptual inversion in I.ii.:

> Ch. Just. . . . God send the prince a better companion!
> Fal. God send the companion a better prince!
> (I.ii. 199–200)

When planning with Poins to dress as servants, Hal describes the disguise as an exchange of attributes:

> From a god to a bull? A heavy descension! It was Jove's case. From a prince to a prentice? A low transformation, that shall be mine. . . .
> (II.ii. 166–8)

Later on, Westmoreland remarks on the transformation of the Archbishop of York into a man of war and a rebel. Using a linguistic metaphor, he asks York: 'Wherefore do you so ill translate yourself' (IV.i.47) from a discourse of peace into the 'tongue of war' (49), 'Turning your books to graves, your ink to blood, / Your pens to lances, and your tongue divine / To a loud trumpet and a point of war?' (50–2).

27. In this speech, Falstaff makes use of two inversions: the one between pox and gout and the turning of disease into a commodity. This last reminds us of Pistol's speech in *Henry V* (V.i.84–93).

28. 'Der Müde Prinz' in *Mimesis* (Bern: Francke, 1946); English transl., *Mimesis* (Princeton: Princeton University Press, 1953), pp. 312–33.

29. In the dialogue which opens Falstaff's encounter with the Hostess and Doll, venereal diseases are one of the topics of conversation.

30. Peto, in his role of war messenger, is allowed a verse speech (352–7). Earlier I remarked on a similar formal closing with the switch to verse in Part One, at the end of III.iii.

31. Henry develops the conventional kingly theme of sleep which abandons the great on account of their cares and responsibilities while it visits the untroubled subject. In the preceding scene, Falstaff put forward a similar claim to greatness: 'the undeserver may sleep, when the man of action is called on' (II.iv.372–3).

32. In IV.iii.75, John of Lancaster informed us that the king is 'sore sick'; to Lancaster, in turn, has been attributed by Falstaff 'a kind of male green-sickness' (91) on account of his sober habits ('thin drink', 89); 'green sickness', Humphreys explains, is 'anaemia incident to unmarried girls'.

33. L. Falzon Santucci says that 'the task that faces Shakespeare at this point . . . is that of guiding *2H4*, and the audience, as swiftly and credibly as possible out of the world of comedy into that of serious historical drama; the closure must authenticate seriousness and not the irreponsible Falstaff world'. ('Theatrical Transactions', *Strumenti Critici* XV [1991], 317–33, p. 327)

34. Commentators remark that the imagery in ll. 46–51 is analogous to that of Son. 64. 5–8, and also recall a passage of Ovid's *Metamorphoses* (xv. 262 ff.) in Golding's translation (1567).

35. Melchiori's reading in the footnote to this passage in G. Melchiori, *The Second Part of King Henry IV* (Cambridge: Cambridge University Press, 1989).

36. The modern meaning is reported in the *OED* as first occurring after the 1688 revolution. As I have shown elsewhere (P. Pugliatti, 'Shakespeare's names for rebellion', in C. Nocera Avila, N. Pantaleo and D. Pezzini [eds], *Early Modern English: Trends, Forms and Texts* [Fasano: Schena, 1992], 81–93), it seems that the transition from a conservative meaning, deriving from astrology and indicating a revolving movement leading back to the starting point, to the modern one indicating a sudden breach with the past, was achieved through an intermediary phase where the word started to mean a 'change in condition'. In its five occurrences in Shakespeare's canon (*Hamlet*, V.i.88, *Antony and Cleopatra*, I.ii.125, *Love's Labour's Lost* IV.ii.68, Son. 59.12 and the one I am discussing here), the word seems to me to be well on its way to the modern meaning. It is quite possible, therefore, that the semantic change in English is to be attributed to Shakespeare. Christopher Hill has shown that the word acquired its modern political implications long before the 1688 revolution. 'The Word Revolution', in *A Nation of Change and Novelty* (London: Routledge, 1990), pp. 82–101.

37. Three and a half lines which appear in Qb (in Qa the entire scene is omitted) and do not appear in F are interposed between the end of the passage quoted and the beginning of the evocation of Richard:

> O, if this were seen,
> The happiest youth, viewing his progress through,
> What perils past, what crosses to ensue,
> Would shut the book and sit him down and die.
>
> (53–6)

Whatever the reasons for the omission of these lines in F, it should be noticed that the first half of l. 53 ('With divers liquors!') is completed by the otherwise inexplicably short l. 57 ('Tis not ten years gone'); and that the meaning of the added (or subtracted) lines contradicts Henry's wish to foresee future events. The lines, in fact, express the idea that even if it were possible to read the future we would become passive and sit still, waiting for death.

38.   The word *chance* here does not have the same meaning as in Henry's speech; Warwick simply means 'the way in which things will fall out' rather than a capricious and therefore unforeseeable turn of events.

39.   This idea appears, once again in connection with prediction or prophecy, in *Macbeth*. The expression is used by Banquo when he questions the witches about his future: 'If you can look into the seeds of time, / And say which grain will grow, and which will not . . . ' (*Macbeth*, I.iii.58–9).

40.   'History', p. 173.

41.   C. Ginzburg, 'Spie'.

42.   Ginzburg mentions the word *intuition* only in the last page of his essay. His claim is that the human sciences, confronted by the dilemma of choosing a weak scientific status and reach remarkable results or choosing a strong one and reach less remarkable results, should choose the first, opting for the 'elastic rigour' of conjectural paradigms.

8

The Strange Tongues of *Henry V*

Cath. A strange tongue makes my cause more strange, suspicious.

Henry VIII, III.i.43

BOTH RABBIT AND DUCK

The critical reception of *Henry V* indicates that the play may be considered one of the definitely ambiguous or ambivalent works of world literature: perhaps, Shakespeare's most conspicuous achievement in the reasoning *in utramque partem*. There have, in fact, been critics who argue resolutely for a celebrative reading and critics who argue as resolutely for its contrary; and there have been – more and more frequently in the last decades – critics who claim, and often brilliantly show, that the play 'points in two opposite directions.'[1]

It is, indeed, impossible to write or speak about *Henry V* without taking sides in the king's trial and without accordingly pronouncing a verdict, although all such trials end by rehearsing the usual catalogue of arguments: those in favour of Henry (many and self-evident) and those against (fewer and more indirect: his banishing and 'killing' Falstaff, his implicit acceptance of Canterbury's 'bribing', the violence of his speech before Harfleur, the killing of the French prisoners after Agincourt, his sending his old friend Bardolph to death, the charges of Court, Bates and Williams, and a few more optional accusations which vary from essay to essay). Obviously, however, it is not only on Henry that a verdict is pronounced: part of the critical energy is, in fact, spent in connecting the judgement that the play seems to pass on the most celebrated of English kings to what we may guess about Shakespeare's political attitude.

Generally speaking, partisans of the apologetic reading are explicit in arguing for Shakespeare's (conformist) intention to produce an epic celebration of Henry; on the contrary, those who point out the evidence which the play produces against Henry, suggest that these are not part of a conscious project.[2]

Goddard, for instance, produced one of the sharpest and most univocal responses to the play, piling up evidence to show that Henry, far from being depicted as the 'ideal king', appears to be the perfect ruthless Machiavellian. However, although Goddard believes that Shakespeare's Henry and the battle of Agincourt are strongly deglorified in the play, he contends, or at least implies, that deglorification was not a deliberate act: 'If Shakespeare had deliberately set out to deglorify the Battle of Agincourt in general and King Henry in particular it would seem as if he could hardly have done more.'[3]

The implication of this view may be either that Shakespeare's intention was to glorify Henry and Agincourt but that 'the text' eluded his intention and suggested a different picture (we have already heard it held that texts are stronger than authors) or that the conscious project (for obvious reasons of survival) was that of glorifying the king and the battle, but a deeper deglorifying intent (unconsciously) emerged in spite of the poet's efforts to keep it in check.

From a different perspective, Dollimore and Sinfield discuss the working of ideology in Shakespeare's representation of history, and they choose *Henry V* as a test-case. They, however, attribute the cracks in the ideological (conformist) consistency of the play to a mechanism of contradiction which is indicated as necessary and physiological: the idea is that ideology tends to incorporate the alternatives that it is engaged in neutralising.[4] In other words, here again we get the picture of somebody (consciously?) supporting the dominant ideology (epic celebration of Henry) who nevertheless unconsciously incorporates here and there unfavourable elements which are introduced as the physiological antibodies of ideology. Again, in this case, no deliberate intention is ascribed to the dramatist.

There is another position that I should like to mention, which assigns to the author a higher decisional capacity.

Norman Rabkin starts from Gombrich's well-known description of the picture of an ambiguous zoomorph being (rabbit or duck?) and concludes that, like that drawing, *Henry V* is constructed in such a way as to seem *either* one thing *or* the other.[5] Rabkin's idea is, therefore, that, having skilfully and deceptively included two opposite views in the same piece of writing, Shakespeare is daring us to choose one of the two figures he has woven into his carpet. In other words, Rabkin believes that – as happens with the mutually excluding plots which torment the reader of *The Turn of the Screw* – only one of the pictures may be chosen as the true one. Although Rabkin argues that 'Shakespeare's habitual recognition of the irreducible complexity of things has led him, as it should lead his audience, to a point of crisis',[6] he is too tempted by what he has brilliantly described as the play's 'rival gestalts' ever to consider that the two visions may not be contradictory and that the point of crisis may well consist in the fact that Shakespeare is trying to present a polymorphous or polyphonic political picture, namely, *both* a rabbit *and* a duck.[7] In other words, that the play is neither a riddle nor a trick; that, in spite of its contradictions, it is not an ambiguous political statement; on the contrary, it is a clear political assertion about how ambivalent political and historical issues can be. The complexity of the picture lies precisely in the fact that no choice is to be made between the conflicting portraits of Henry and among the diverse possible readings of the events.

Incidentally, the 'both-and' paradox was a recognised reasoning pattern in Renaissance thought. As a potentially dangerous procedure, it is discussed in that treatise of political reasoning *sub specie rhetorica* which is Puttenham's *Arte*. Puttenham disapproves of *Amphibologia*, defining it as a 'vicious speach' which occurs 'when we speake or write doubtfully and that the sence may be taken two ways'. Puttenham passes a clear judgement on the political dangerousness of this mode of reasoning, that he characterises as a linguistic malady able to breed social and political diseases. Amphibology, he argues, ends by producing ambiguities which are uncontrollable and which may induce political subversion. (Jack Straw's and Jack Cade's rebellions and Captain Ket's sedition were stirred, Puttenham holds, by 'certain propheticall rymes, which might be constred two or three wayes as well as to that one whereunto the rebelles applied it'.)[8]

Henry V stages amphibology by means of a series of peculiar procedures which are, broadly speaking, linguistic. They include first of all the two main languages which are used (English and French), the way and the circumstances in which they are used and the discrepancies which derive from their use; the regional linguistic variations (or better, the comic, mock-regional distortions of English), the use of various, socially connotated discourse types; the mixture of different genres and styles, the distribution of verse and prose, etc. Finally, one particular instance of dia-logue – or of reaction of one statement on other statements – concerns the Choruses. The way in which in *Henry V* these different, recalcitrant elements are woven together is the play's peculiar contribution to a representation of disharmony: by deploying so explicit and endemic a plurilinguism, by crediting a number of social discourses and of political perspectives, the play depicts a universe of discourse – and a historical context – which appears as a war-zone where the users of language engage in struggles for primacy and conflicts of interest. Languages, dialects, styles and social discursive varieties mark the boundaries (and differentiate the spheres) of the various ethnic, national and social components. And that the many disturbing and disuniting effects of many-voicedness are deployed in the play in which national unity is celebrated is, to say the least, noteworthy.[9]

HENRY'S 'STRANGE TONGUES' AND THE LANGUAGES OF THE CONQUERED

In *2 Henry IV*, trying to soothe the anguish of the dying king at Hal's 'headstrong riot', the Earl of Warwick interprets the Prince's disposition to turn things to his own advantage in linguistic terms:

> The Prince but studies his companions
> Like a strange tongue, wherein, to gain the language,
> 'Tis needful that the most immodest word
> Be look'd upon and learnt; which once attained,
> Your Highness knows, comes to no further use
> But to be known and hated.
>
> (IV.iv.68–73)

It appears that between this moment and the beginning of *Henry V*, having 'gained' – and hated – the strange tongue of his former riotous companions, Henry has turned to learning, again to his own advantage, the many languages of power: as Canterbury, in praise of the King, says in I.i.38-59, those of divinity, commonwealth, affairs, war and policy.

Henry's linguistic ordeal, however, is not yet concluded. The stage of his conquest is, in fact, a tangle of different languages and the conquest is largely a matter of linguistic integration. The King is going to meet more strange tongues and discourses on the way to national unity and to foreign conquest, although from now on it is not going to be a matter of learning – but rather of submitting, disfiguring or turning those strange tongues into some form of 'English'.

Many of the conflicts that are enacted in *Henry V*, starting from the literal conflict of the war which follows the invasion of France, are in fact represented as linguistic conflicts. In the course of the play, Henry will have to come to grips with his enemies' native tongue, with the dialects of the components of his regionally variegated army (in a sense, Henry himself, whose Welsh origin is underlined, is a 'stranger'). He will be touched, albeit peripherally, by what remains of the 'strange tongue' of his former companions and by the shreds of the comic convention which becomes more and more extraneous to his person (until what remains of the comic plot is liquidated in the person of Bardolph); in a strange tongue, or better in a bastard tongue that is meant to be French but looks more and more like English, he will conquer a woman for a wife whom he has already conquered as the daughter of his vanquished enemy; he will have to face the challenge of the conflicting discourses which raise doubts as to the holiness of his war and his right and honourable cause, and which pose questions about the leader's responsibility for the death of his subjects in battle. He is going to encounter the non-neutrality of alien discourses, the views and evaluations which belong to a perspective that challenges his own: words and forms, as Bakhtin says, 'populated by intentions'. In short, while conquest and unity imply the necessity of removing linguistic and cultural differences, these seem to resist the tendency to eliminate diversity and are, till the last scene of the play, presented as problematic.

NATIONAL AND REGIONAL HETEROGLOSSIA

Henry V is a play written by an English playwright for an English audience. It is not properly, however, a play written *in English*. There are scenes written in French (III.iv), which presumably were not understood by a large part of the contemporary audience and which may still create problems for both audience and actors, scenes in which both languages are spoken and which, therefore, require an onstage interpreter for both the English character on the stage and the English spectators (IV.iv and part of V.ii), and scenes where the French King, Dauphin and nobility signal their being French by introducing here and there expressions or exclamations in that language, although for the audience's benefit they mainly speak in English.

That the play's 'traffic' is to present 'two mighty monarchies' inside whose national confines different languages are spoken is not enough to explain the linguistic situation described above. In *1 Henry VI*, in fact – an even more Frenchified play – only a very small number of French words are spoken, and the convention that prescribes that characters, whatever their nationality, understand each other in the author's and audience's language obtains. In *Henry V*, not only is French spoken in a number of circumstances, but also, linguistic difference is signalled as problematic: lack of knowledge of English is, in different degrees, pointed out as a source of trouble: from simple incomprehension to the possibility of losing a husband to that of losing one's head.

Why is heteroglossia presented as a problem in *Henry V* while it is not in *1 Henry VI*? Why is the encounter of Lord Talbot with the Countess of Auvergne (*1 Henry VI*, II.iii) so entirely monolinguistic and therefore perfectly communicative? Why does the Pucelle speak to the English lords and the English lords to her with never a shadow of linguistic impediment while Katherine is shown as *having to* learn the English tongue ('il faut que j'apprenne à parler', III.iv.4–5) before she meets Henry? And why is the French soldier Monsieur Le Fer in danger of losing his life (IV.iv.) simply for not being able to grant Pistol a ransom *in English*? Is the scene simply yet another comic interlude or does it remind us, in a curious way indeed, that even that image of cowardice named Pistol is now, linguistically too, the master of his better?

Obviously, losing one's language or at least having to learn the victor's is one of the prices that a conqueror imposes on the conquered. What makes the difference between the two plays, then, seems to be simply the fact that in *Henry V* a *conquest* is staged while its sequel stages a *loss*. But precisely if we grant this truism, the persistent thematisation of the impediments created by linguistic difference and language learning in *Henry V* appears paradoxical.

The learning of the conqueror's language, in fact, is by no means taken for granted and seems to encounter resistance right up to the last scene of the play. Why does Henry describe the English tongue as 'rough' and his own capacity to teach it as weak? ('Our tongue is rough, coz, and my condition is not smooth', V.ii.304–5): the adjective *rough* may illustrate a positive value of plainness and simplicity, in contrast with the elaborate elegance of French, but it may also indicate that English is not easy to teach and learn; and why should it be suggested that Kate is 'not apt' (303) to learn it? Finally, it is significant that the only article of the treaty which is presented as problematic is the one that concerns the *naming* of Henry, in formal documents, as heir to the throne of France *in French and in Latin* ('in French, Notre très cher filz Henry, Roy d'Angleterre, Héritier de France; and thus in Latin, Praeclarissimus filius noster Henricus, rex Angliae, et Haeres Franciae': V.ii.357–60). The document does not include the conqueror's language: the French tongue, it would seem, will not stoop to England's will (indeed, Henry's 'condition' as foreign pretender and heir to the throne of France is as awkward as was the 'condition' of James Stuart as foreign pretender to the throne of England).

If Henry's linguistic conquest of France is not as successfully performed as his military and political conquest, the linguistic integration of Wales, Ireland and Scotland seems at first sight to be less problematic. Although Fluellen 'cannot speak English in the native garb' (V.i.79–80), there is no incomprehension between him, the Welsh, the Scottish and the English captain. Indeed, unlike what happens with the French, all these characters speak English, albeit in a remarkably corrupt form.[10]

It may be agreed that, as Dollimore and Sinfield have remarked, 'the jokes about the way Fluellen pronounces the English language are, apparently, for the Elizabethan audience and many since, an adequate way to handle the repression of the Welsh language and culture';[11] but it may also be that the situation is not as simple as that: in Fluellen's, Jamy's and Macmorris's 'disfigured' English, a way of speaking where difference is made explicit, a form of resistance to cultural integration is in fact objectively represented. If the process of unification tends to kill the native tongues, nevertheless the marginal cultures still express some form of centrifugal force, if nothing else, by corrupting the 'garb' of the prescribed unitary language.

The process, which becomes comedy in Shakespeare, is explained as a recurrent cultural phenomenon by Bakhtin:

> The victory of one reigning language (dialect) over the others, the supplanting of languages, their enslavement, the process of illuminating them with the True Word, the incorporation of barbarians and lower social strata into a unitary language of culture

and truth, the canonization of ideological systems, philology with its methods of studying and teaching dead languages . . . , all this determined the content and power of the category of 'unitary language' in linguistic and stylistic thought. . . .

But the centripetal forces of the life of language, embodied in a 'unitary language', operate in the midst of heteroglossia. At any given moment of its evolution, language is stratified not only into linguistic dialects in the strict sense of the word . . . but also . . . into languages that are socio-ideological: languages of social groups, 'professional' and 'generic' languages, languages of generations and so forth.[12]

In *Henry V* neither the English tongue nor the True Word of ideologically saturated discourses succeed in eliminating differences by imposing a 'unitary language of culture and truth'. Indeed, we have ample evidence in the play of the persistence of heteroglossia also in the form of differently oriented kinds of discourse. Henry's toughest encounter with the resistance of a non-neutral language 'populated by intentions' and with a challenge to the unitary discourse of the holiness of his war is, of course, his dialogue with the soldiers Court, Bates and Williams on the eve of Agincourt (IV.i), an obvious instance of the use of marginal voices to undermine a celebrative reading of the events. It should be pointed out that the three soldiers' view of the imminent battle, their indifference to and incomprehension of the 'right cause' for which they are sent to die is strengthened by the fact that it represents the view of a group: the three soldiers, in fact, stand for the whole army involved in the enterprise. Indeed, Alexander Court, John Bates and Michael Williams, whose position is made even more dramatically relevant and 'true' by their being given names and surnames,[13] express the only serious opinion of the 'vulgar', that is to say, of those who followed Henry only because 'to disobey were against all proportion of subjection' (IV.i. 148–9). What we see of Henry's army apart from them is much less creditable, since it comes either from the company of thieves and cut-purses or from what is explicitly presented as an instance of military fanaticism (Fluellen's in particular). Nothing in the play endangers our sympathy with Henry's enterprise so much as this scene, which comes close to destroying everything the play has been presenting up till now as justification for the invasion of France. However we read the play, there remain the questions of why a celebration should be so perilously endangered, why the balance of arguments should be so delicate and uncertain and, most of all, why so profound an ideological conflict should be shown if a celebrative mood were the sole perspective of the play.

CONFLICT AND THE COMIC PLOTS

Other forms of incomprehension arise between the two spheres of the comic plot which, from a certain point on, seem to be utterly incompatible. Indeed, the Welsh (Fluellen's) is the rising one, while the English (Pistol's) is clearly doomed to disappear. Captain Gower's rebuke to Pistol in defence of Fluellen (V.i.) literally determines the death of Pistol's bravadoes and his final disappearance from Henry's universe, which clearly can no longer contain this last, disowned residue of his past revels:

> *Gow.* Go, go; you are a counterfeit cowardly knave. Will you mock at an ancient tradition, begun upon an honourable respect, and worn as a memorable trophy of predeceased valour, and dare not avouch in your deeds any of your words? I have seen you gleeking and galling at this gentleman twice or thrice. You thought, because he could not speak English in the native garb, he could not therefore handle an English cudgel: you find it otherwise; *and henceforth let a Welsh correction teach you a good English condition.* Fare ye well.
>
> (V.i.72–83; my emphasis)

Let a Welsh correction teach you a good English condition.[14] Indeed, right from the start, the division has been incurable. In the two comic spheres of the play not only are different languages spoken, but these, in turn, betray different *conditions*. They do so because they are differently positioned with reference to the King, and their position largely depends on the way the comic conventions are treated. The 'old' comedy, that derives from the *Henry IV* plays, maintains its non-conformist, subversive character, while the 'new' comedy of Fluellen and his fellow captains is presented as submissive and traditionalist ('Will you mock at an ancient tradition . . .').

Moreover, the collapse of the 'old' comic plot is carried out by means of a series of interferences which make it more and more alien to comedy (or which strengthen its non-conformist character *as comedy*). Indeed, from the start, the comic conventions themselves seem to be polluted by the discrepant language of pathos. The first and most contradictory of these discrepancies is, of course, Falstaff's sickness and death (the news of his illness literally *interferes* with the comic quarrel between Pistol and Nym over the Hostess). The series of subsequent pathetic collapses that follow (the dramatic cruelty of the deaths of Bardolph and Nym and the even more incongruous and inexplicable, although indirect, news of the Boy's death),[15] culminates in Pistol's farewell speech, which immediately follows Gower's rebuke and exit:

> *Pist.* Doth Fortune play the huswife with me now?
> News have I that my Doll is dead i' th' spital
> Of malady of France;
> And there my rendezvous is quite cut off.
> Old I do wax, and from my weary limbs
> Honour is cudgell'd. Well, bawd I'll turn,
> And something lean to cut-purse of quick hand.
> To England will I steal, and there I'll steal:
> And patches will I get unto these cudgell'd scars,
> And swear I got them in the Gallia wars.
> 							(V.i.84–93)

Here we are made to think on the one hand that with these lines the long scene of Pistol's – and of his companions' – theatrical life has come to an end; on the other hand, the projection forward assures us that Pistol is going to survive (we may even hypothesise that by sparing Pistol Shakespeare is leaving the possibility of his return in a future play open).

Almost up to the end of *2 Henry IV*, the comic plot agreed with, and was supported by, the Prince. In *Henry V*, again, we have agreement between comedy (the 'new' comedy, this time) and Henry. Here, however, the King's support has, so to speak, defaced comedy, drawing it into a conformist sphere of action. What remains of the old, subversive comedy does not even touch the King. We will never know whether Henry recognises Pistol in their only encounter (IV.i.), although we more than suspect that he is conscious of sending his old friend Bardolph to death (in III.vi. 104–9 Fluellen names Bardolph as the man to be executed and describes him with accuracy); and we may be reminded of Falstaff's words to Hal in an entirely different situation: 'Do not when thou art king hang a thief' (*1 Henry IV*, I.ii.59–60). Indeed, if languages and dialects are distorted, the nature of comedy and laughter is no less perverted: while non-conformist comedy has been polluted by pathos and melancholy and eventually marginalised, what remains is a loyalist form of comedy, incongruous because fully 'authorised'. Nothing, in any case, seems to guarantee the advent of a unitary form of national comedy.[16]

What has been withdrawn from Henry's former friends, however, is the King's sympathy, not ours. The audience has mixed feelings: while our sympathy for the pedantic Fluellen is by no means undisputed, we do resist, up to a certain point, the many attacks that are launched against the 'old' comedy. Thus, we are likely to side with Pistol – a more and more marginalised character who lacks the language of conformism which would integrate him into the bright future of national unity – when he is allowed to pronounce his farewell speech. Pistol's monologue quoted above is a mock-counterpart of so many tragic farewell speeches; a mock-counterpart which, however, lends dramatic relevance to the character's disappearance. Whatever moral judgement the audience may pass on Pistol's plans for stealing and purse-cutting, the speech shows one last spark of the 'old' comedy's fire. Pistol may be going to disappear forever, but he may also survive and even come back. What his speech shows, in the last analysis, is in fact his capacity to oppose resistance to the attacks of both Fortune and the 'new' form of legalitarian comedy.

But the most serious and insidious conformist attack that the 'old' comedy faces in the play comes from its own ranks, even if it seems directly inspired by the King. This attack comes in the Boy's long monologue in III.ii.; a speech which, incidentally, makes an independent character out of what was until then only a functional element, so that we may the better regret his death. What is noteworthy is in the first place the fact that the attack comes from one who is both younger and socially lower even than Bardolph, Nym and Pistol; one, however, who speaks the language of wisdom and honesty that the king's former friends have never been able to speak; but, above all, the fact that the Boy's critical attitude in this speech curiously recalls Hal's in his famous monologue in 1 *Henry IV* (I.ii.190–212):

> *Boy.* As young as I am, I have observed these three swashers. I
> am boy to them all three, but all they three, though they would
> serve me, could not be man to me; for indeed three such antics
> do not amount to a man. . . . They would have me as familiar

with men's pockets as their gloves or their handkerchers: which
makes much against my manhood if I should take from another's
pocket to put into mine; for it is plain pocketing up of wrongs.
I must leave them and seek some better service: their villany
goes against my weak stomach, and therefore I must cast it up.
(III.ii. 28–32 and 49–57)

With whom does an audience side after so sensible a speech?
Things, by this time, have become utterly confusing. A battle is
ahead of us, and the audience's feelings cannot but side with the
hero; and the Boy's speech (an uncompromised speech, since it
comes from 'one of us') contributes to the drifting and drowning of
those who do not side explicitly with heroism and do not labour for
a glorious victory. After all, a certain amount of conformism is
maybe one of the few common denominators of all audiences.

THE DISCREPANT VOICE OF THE CHORUSES

Prologues, Epilogues and Choruses, apart from introducing, commenting and concluding the action, are, not metaphorically, cues in
a dialogue. Being direct addresses to the audience, they aim at getting
a specific, although silent, response and, as seems the case with
Henry V, the acceptance of a certain reading of the text that they
introduce. In other words, they may represent an external way of
determining a certain viewpoint. External, because in the first place
they are not part of the action, and in the second place they contem-
plate the action from a temporally removed perspective, that of the
contemporary audience.[17]

Henry V has six such appeals to the audience, which introduce
the five acts and close the play. Apart from expressing both the
material and moral inadequacy of the stage and of the company to
represent the exceptional events of Henry's reign, Prologue and
Choruses illustrate the virtues of the ideal king, anticipate the content of the following act and fill in the gaps by relating the events
that are not going to be represented. Their function, however, is not
only metadramatic, since they also suggest, more or less directly, a
number of evaluations.

The voice responsible for these fragments obviously belongs to a
member of the company: an actor, a stage-manager or the author

himself; one, in any case, who is professionally engaged in the staging of the play and who therefore knows of the material inadequacies
of the stage to evoke so huge an argument. What evaluations are
transmitted to the audience by the Chorus, then, are felt as coming
from a perspective that is nearer – temporally, but also socially – to
them than most of the perspectives that are to be found in the play.
Nearer, and therefore, more trustworthy (psychologically, if not
historically). And what this voice tells us is all in favour of the
glorious king. Indeed, if a reader were to read only these introduc-
tory and concluding speeches and disregard the body of the play,
none of the doubts so far raised about the celebrative intention of
the play would arise.

However, the voice of the Chorus runs the risk of losing reliability
and likewise its privileged contact with the audience, for on many
occasions it affirms things that are belied by the action. These apparent discrepancies have generally been treated as so many textual
cruxes. And they probably are. Nevertheless, until their textual status
is coherently and satisfactorily established, we may suggest an interpretation in the light of what has been argued so far regarding the
play's conflicting views.

Discrepancies of this kind include first of all the contrasts between
the way in which heroism is depicted by the Choruses and the kind
of 'heroes' we are shown in the action. These contrasts are particularly sharp in the case of Acts II and V, where the comic scenes with
their anti-heroes immediately follow the exit of the Chorus.

The hypothesis that the Choruses are a later interpolation may,
indeed, explain some of the minor inconsistencies, but it leaves the
interpretation of the play even more open to further speculation
about its incongruity as epic celebration. Why, in fact, should the
need to add these unequivocally celebratory passages have been
felt if not to buttress the uncertain celebrative mood of the play?[18]
But the most blatant discrepancy comes from the last Chorus, which
overturns the optimistic mood with which the play closes and finally
flouts the rules of the celebration game. The last speech of the play,
delivered by Henry, has just sealed the king's conquest of France
and of Katherine in a euphoric tone:

> *K. Hen.* Prepare we for our marriage: on which day,
> My Lord of Burgundy, we'll take your oath,
> And all the peers', for surety of our leagues.
> Then shall I swear to Kate, and you to me;

And may our oaths well kept and prosp'rous be!
                    (V.ii.388–92)

That neither conquest is shown on the stage as an accomplished fact is not, by the time Henry's and the play's last words are pronounced, noteworthy. A prospective ending, in fact, indicates, in terms of theatrical conventions, that what is announced verbally is going to happen.[19] And even supposing that some of the contradictions that have been enacted have left a mark in the consciousness of a few spectators, we may surmise that by now they have all been wiped out.

Moreover, the story of King Henry V closes with a promise of immortality which is unique in the stories of kings that Shakespeare had written until then: Henry does not die (years later, Henry VIII will be granted a similar immortality). In the audience's eyes the fact that Henry's death falls outside the temporal limits of the play suggests that *he is going to live*. The effect is that of a life eternal and, given the euphoric final tone, eternally happy.[20] The non-death of Henry is certainly what the spectators expect, whatever sector of the playhouse they are occupying.

After the final speech, the royal train disappears, leaving behind a promise of life: peace and prosperity for the country and a happy marriage for the royal couple. Then, the final Chorus enters the empty stage. It speaks of what will follow: events that the audience knows ('which oft our stage hath shown'), but whose memory the play has succeeded in dispersing: Henry's death, the loss of what has been conquered and a bloody civil war. And while the Chorus speaks, we discover, or are reminded, that, in spite of what the play's final words had promised, Henry is going to die, and that happiness and prosperity will last only a 'small time'. What we have been made to see and to believe was, we now perceive, as ephemeral as the play's two-hour traffic. The audience cannot but be disappointed.

Indeed, Henry dies in untimely fashion, even before we leave the playhouse, and in as short a time all his conquests are lost. What the final Chorus tells us, in plain words, is that *all* (the play's *all* as well as history's *all*) was for nothing.

Notes

1. N. Rabkin, 'Either/Or', p. 34. For a summary of the divergent opinions on *Henry V*, see G. Holderness, 'Prologue', pp. 62–3.

2. One of the exceptions is Cox (op. cit., Chapter 6), who elaborates a notion of 'opacity' as the main characteristic of Henry (versus the 'transparency' of, for example, Richard III), which he qualifies as a theatrical dissimulating capacity. This capacity, which Puttenham indicated as an essential expression of power ('Qui nescit dissimulare nescit regnare', *The Arte*, p. 186), constitutes, Cox argues, the supreme ambiguity of Hal (and of King Henry), while it in turn reflects the theatrical opacity of public Elizabethan figures of power (the Queen, of course, but also Essex and Raleigh).

3. H. C. Goddard, *The Meaning of Shakespeare* (Chicago: University of Chicago Press, 1951), p. 256. Richard Levin said that Goddard is 'probably the most relentless ironizer of our time' and that 'when he comes to *Henry V* . . . everything in the play he disapproves (that is, everything favourable to Henry) is dismissed as part of the apparent meaning, a sop to the groundlings, whom Shakespeare wanted to deceive' ('Performance critics', p. 547).

4. 'History and Ideology: the Instance of *Henry V*', in J. Drakakis (ed.), *Alternative Shakespeares* (London: Methuen, 1985), pp. 206–27. S. Greenblatt expresses a similar view: 'we may suggest that the subversive doubts the play continually awakens serve paradoxically to intensify the power of the king and his war even while they cast shadows upon this power'. 'Invisible Bullets. Renaissance Authority and Its Subversion', in J. Dollimore and A. Sinfield (eds), 18–47, p. 43.

5. 'Either/Or . . .', pp. 34–5. The passage quoted by Rabkin is in E. H. Gombrich, 'Psychology and the Riddle of Style', *Art and Illusion* (London: Phaidon Press, 1960), pp. 3–25.

6. Op. cit., p. 61.

7. There exists, however, in Rabkin's work, an indecision between complementarity (and inclusiveness) and mutual contradiction. Although he speaks of coexistence and of the presence, in Shakespeare, of equally valid opposed elements, the paradigm which he evokes is Niels Bohr's principle of complementarity, where two different explanations of a given phenomenon which are considered equally valid are, nonetheless, found to be mutually exclusive.

8. *The Arte*, pp. 260–1. The passage is commented on by Stephen Cohen, who distinguishes in this section of the *Arte* the illustration of two kinds of ambiguity: a first type in which we have a true meaning masked by a false one; and a second type (*amphibology*) in which 'truth and falsehood are unknowable' and 'either option is equally likely'. *The Language of Power, the Power of Language* (Cambridge, Mass.: Harvard University Press, 1987), p. 16. S. Mullaney discusses amphibology as a figure of rebellion and treason which possesses 'unruly but generative force' ('Lying Like Truth', p. 43). On *Amphibologia*, see also C. Belsey, 'Love in Venice'. Assuming Cohen's distinction, it would seem that we should recognise a difference between what is

ambiguous (of dubious meaning, equivocal, lacking clarity) and what is ambivalent or amphibologic (admitting two non-exclusive meanings). The second is the kind of double meaning that concerns us here.

9. Discussing the issue of 'brotherhood' and the differences in language which create communicative problems in the play, A. Gurr remarks that 'the play is full of brothers (and sisters) who cannot communicate with each other'. 'A Performance Text for *Henry V*', in P. Kennan and M. Tempera (eds), *Shakespeare from Text to Stage* (Bologna: CLUEB, 1992), pp. 71–81, 80. W. F. Bolton finds all the premises of linguistic division in the first part of the play but claims that, by the end, Henry has achieved unity. *Shakespeare's English. Language in the History Plays* (Oxford, Blackwell, 1992).

10. A different linguistic situation is presented in *1 Henry IV* (III.i). Owen Glendower speaks English and gives a reason for it (he has been 'train'd up in the English court', 117), while his daughter, Mortimer's wife, only speaks Welsh. However, although there is no linguistic communication between husband and wife, there seems to be a deeper form of communion (a 'feeling disputation', 199). Moreover, Welsh is here granted the full status of an independent language because it has not been subjugated and is described, when spoken by the lady, as communicative in the way music is (201–4).

11. 'History and Ideology', p. 224.

12. M. Bakhtin, 'Discourse in the Novel', pp. 271–2.

13. Gurr remarks that the fact that these three ordinary soldiers are given forename and surname is 'a feature of this play which is unique in all Shakespeare' ('A Performance Text', p. 76).

14. *Teaching* and *correction* are other pervasive topics of the play. Languages, manners, the respect for ancient traditions, the 'discipline of the wars', in a word, the unitary language of a 'good English condition' have to be taught to the heteroglot, the ignorant and the recalcitrant.

15. We infer the Boy's death from Gower's words: 'Tis certain there's not a boy left alive' (IV.vii.5). As regards Nym, we know of his death from a passing mention by the Boy (IV.v.71–5).

16. The discussion of the way in which dramatic conventions are contaminated in *Henry V* would imply in the first place a reckoning of the verse–prose distribution (see, for instance, the surprising decision to prose the courtship scene in V.ii).

17. The external and contemporary position of the Chorus is stressed in the overt allusion to Essex's expedition to Ireland (V.0.29–35), which started in March 1599 and which, judging from the false forecast of a victory, had not yet come to an end when the Chorus was composed.

18. Gurr expresses the opinion that 'it is more likely that the Chorus was fitted to the play fairly early on, to strengthen a celebratory and patriotic reading'. *King Henry V* (Cambridge: Cambridge University Press, 1992), p. 7.

19. There are other occasions in which this convention is flouted. But when this happens, as with Bolingbroke's never-accomplished purpose of a voyage to the Holy Land at the end of *Richard II*, an additional meaning is to be attributed to the broken rule.

20. Lotman discusses the different framings of literary works as representing different world models. In particular, a text which closes with the victory of the hero establishes a model where the hero can neither die nor be discomfited (*The Structure,* pp. 209–17).

9
Jack Cade: An Unpopular Popular Hero

Until recently, the way in which Shakespeare represented Jack Cade's rebellion in Act IV of 2 *Henry VI* has been taken as one more piece of evidence of his loathing for the 'populace', even of his sharing of the Elizabethan ruling class's obsession with all kinds of disorder and dissension. Indeed, it is precisely the Cade episode that seems to have fuelled the tradition of Shakespeare as 'an enemy of the people'. However, a few recent critical readings have resumed the issue, reaching diverse conclusions, thereby suggesting that Shakespeare's representation of the uprising of 1450 is not as univocal as it might seem to be.

Greenblatt is interested in the ways in which different genres, responding to different historical pressures, represent the victory of the high over the low. The main problem, Greenblatt argues, is how to shield the victor's dignity from the danger of being tainted by the enemy's base condition; he therefore focuses on the killing of Cade by a small property-owner, Alexander Iden, and concludes that in Shakespeare's solution (which he terms 'simple, effective and, in its way, elegant'), 'the aristocrat has given way to the man of property, and heroic commemoration has been absorbed into a new genre, the history play'.[1] In other words, given the low status of the rebel, the new genre implies a lowering of the victor's social status.

Cohen argues that, although in 2 *Henry VI* 'rage and murderous hatred are pervasive within the ruling class, the poor and the working people are seen as so many fools and dolts, easily misled by a villain who promises them anarchy, wealth, and revenge against their enemies, the rich'.[2]

Rackin examines a series of characters in the first tetralogy that she sees as 'subverters of history'. Mainly women or lower-class persons, Joan of Arc, Queen Margaret, Jack Cade, Eleanor Cobham and her associates, Simpcox and his wife and the Duke of York, 'all share the Machiavellian attributes of treachery and selfish, amoral ambition that define them as demonic Others'.[3] Rackin argues that, although potentially dangerous, the theatrical energy of these characters is in the end contained and neutralised. Rackin's conclusion on the Cade scenes, therefore, is that, however 'Potentially subversive, they seem finally designed to justify oppression.'[4]

Hattaway argues that 'in this play, unlike Part 1, the commons do come to stand for values that are worth taking seriously'; in particular, 'the Cade rebellion . . . stands not as "comic relief" but as a vision both of the limits of government and of the consequences of aristocratic factionalism'.[5]

Patterson deals explicitly with the issue of the author's political stance and deploys arguments to redeem the dramatist from the old charge of antipopulism. Examining the Cade episode – one of the most convincing arguments for that charge – she argues for the existence, in Shakespeare's time, of a cultural tradition of popular protest and for Shakespeare's consciousness of that tradition and concludes that Cade is far from being part of it: he is, she affirms, 'an impostor aristocrat, a traitor to his class'; therefore, she adds, 'little is proved by demonstrating how inconsistent is Cade in his recapitulation of the ancient tropes of levelling'.[6]

Certainly, the importance that we attribute to the Cade episode derives from the fact that there, perhaps more than anywhere else, Shakespeare seems to take sides on a political issue of enormous importance, that real nightmare of the Tudor political establishment, namely, rebellion: the episode, in other words, seems to offer elements for our reconstruction of some kind of authorial intention and opinion.[7] However, the fact that the episode has been used to show both a populist and an antipopulist attitude on the part of its author indicates its suitability to support antithetic perspectives. That the episode is ambivalent is the point that I should like to make.

Departure from the historical sources is the main argument of my reading of the Cade scenes. However, if we look at the episode in isolation from the rest of the play, source manipulation seems to speak loudly against the rebels, their attitude and the motivations of their revolt and in favour of its repression and of the restoration of the King's control. On the contrary, if we consider the way in which the source material is altered in the whole play, the monstrosity of the rebels will appear as a consequence of the monstrosity of the power that rules over them and that – as the play suggests much more strongly than the sources – has seduced them into rebelling. In fact, although nearer to the sources than Part One, Part Two presents alterations which, however slight, are remarkably coherent and significant since they all seem to point to the same general effect: a levelling to the lowest plane both of those who intrigue at court for their own advancement and profit and of those who rebel out of material need and hunger.[8]

In the play, the Duke of York is depicted as being far more Machiavellian than Halle suggests. He is presented as plotting the ruin of 'good Duke Humphrey' of Gloucester and as finally agreeing to his murder; Margaret's ambition to rule her husband and to govern the country is seasoned with the unhistorical charge of her being an adulteress; equally unhistorical is Cardinal Beaufort's complicity in Gloucester's murder; his 'Blaspheming God, and cursing men on earth' (III.ii.371) even on his deathbed is the playwright's invention; Suffolk is accused of more and harsher acts of 'devilish policy' in the words of the Lieutenant who arrests him (IV.i.70–102) than he is in the chronicle. Moreover, in Act V the play gives prominence to the role of crookback Richard, thus hinting that the sequel to the story is going to be even grimmer and darker. But, above all, Cade's rebellion in the play is much more York's responsibility than it is in the sources, where it is said to have been inspired by York's friends and supporters. In Shakespeare, therefore, much more than in Halle or Holinshed, Cade is an instrument of the Duke's ambition (York in fact calls Cade 'a minister of my intent', III.i.355). This obviously makes the Kentish rebellion much less a popular revolt and much more an instrument of the power that it is apparently directed against. Finally, the initial episode of the play reveals a world where the experience of political rout (illustrated in the loss of Maine and Anjou) is dominant; accordingly, the final episode confirms a model of discomfiture and political disorder by presenting the victory of the rebel York and therefore the triumph of disloyalty and treason.

As regards the people in power, then, the play presents an image of mock-kingship ruled by an ambitious, ruthless and adulterous woman; it presents a villain who wants to be king and who, to further his ambitions to the throne, seduces the commoners into staging a 'popular' rising and finally inflicts on the nation the wounds of civil war; it brings to the foreground an ignorant noblewoman who wants to be queen and pursues her aim with the help of black magic; it presents a contentious and ruthless clergyman who plots for power, does not hesitate to instigate murder and is finally unable to repent even on his deathbed.

These alterations to the historical sources construct the image of an utterly inept kingship that has yielded up its rule to a totally corrupt, treacherous and seditious nobility, entirely oblivious to the interests of the nation. As a consequence of this 'abasement' and 'disfiguring' of the high sphere we find a parallel process of degradation in the low sphere, a process which involved significant changes.

Moreover, while Halle's account usually traced the events back to uncontrollable forces such as destiny or chance, or even divine providence, Shakespeare's version unequivocally relies on the 'second causes' driven by human ambition and the thirst for power.[9] However, lack of wisdom and of foresight together with a thirst for power and the machination of one's enemies also play a part in Halle's account of the tragic destiny of such persons as Suffolk and Gloucester.

Suffolk is described as 'beyng in high favor with the kyng, and in no lesse grace with quene Margaret'[10] and as expecting some concrete advancement because 'somewhat infected with the sede of vainglory' (Cxlix) for arranging the marriage between Henry and Margaret. He is also reported as having lawfully contrived to obtain what he considered the reward for his efforts in France by making a speech in the House of Commons and as having received, as a result of this speech and with the support of the Commons, what is presented as his rightful recompense, namely, the title of Duke. After this dispassionate account of the facts, we read one of the sentences that may have suggested to the dramatist Suffolk's adulterous relationship with the queen and his many treacherous plots. In the same sentence, Halle deplores Suffolk's thirst for power, but solely because it procured his ruin: 'This Marques thus gotten up, into fortunes trone, not content with his degree, by the meanes of the Quene, was shortely erected to the estate and degree of a Duke, and ruled the kyng at his pleasure.' (Cxlix^v–Cl)

Therefore, what Suffolk's *exemplum* teaches one is merely 'what securitie is in worldly glory and what constance is in fortunes smyling' (Cl), for the Duke, 'within foure yeres after, was in the same place [in Parliament], by the commons of the Realme, accused of many treasons, mispricions and offenses . . . and in conclusion, beyng exiled the realme, he was taken upon the sea, and made shorter by the hedde . . .' (Cl).

After this, Halle dispenses to the readers his somewhat amoral moral of the story. Suffolk would have had a better chance if he had remembered the advice of the *popyngay*, namely: 'when thou thynkest thy self in courte moste surest, then is it high tyme to get thee home to rest' (Cl). Later on, Suffolk is said to have been held by the Commons to be the chief procurer of Duke Humphrey's death, 'the moste swallower up and consumer of the kynges treasure' (Clvii) – although his responsibility for Gloucester's death is related as a simple suspicion.[11] However, quite unlike Shakespeare, the author of the chronicle does not commit himself with a guilty verdict nor show a judging attitude towards Suffolk.

What Shakespeare sees in Margaret as destructive ambition is described by Halle as courage and as virtue of a political nature. Here is how the chronicler describes Henry's newly-wedded queen on her first appearance: 'This woman excelled all other, as well in beautie and favor, as in wit and pollicie, and was of stomack and corage, more like to a man, then a woman.' (Cxlviii[v])

Margaret's 'manly' character (obviously high praise, coming from a man's pen) is emphasised in more than one passage. Her qualities, as described by Halle, are tainted only by fickleness, while the fact that she disowned her husband is presented as more or less necessitated by Henry's incapacity:

the Quene his wife, was a woman of greate witte, and yet of no greater witte, then of haute stomacke, desirous of glory, and covetous of honor, and of reason, pollicye, counsaill, and other giftes and talentes of nature, belongyng to a man, full and flowyng: of witte and wilinesse she lacked nothyng, nor of diligence, studie, and businesse, she was not unexperte: but yet she had one poynt of a very woman: for often tyme, when she was vehement and fully bente in a matter, she was sodainly like a wethercocke mutable, and turnyng. (Cl[v])

This manly woman, this coragious quene, ceased not to prosecute furthwith, her invented imaginacion and prepensed purpose . . . (Cli).

And although she joyned her husbande with her in name, for a countenance, yet she did all, she saied all, and she bare the whole swynge, as the strong oxe doth when he is yoked in the plough with a pore silly asse. (Cli)

Shakespeare unhistorically lowers the queen's motives to a mean desire to humiliate Eleanor Cobham (I.iii.138–40), whereas Margaret and Eleanor Cobham probably never met. Even worse, he makes her the instigator of Gloucester's murder. Margaret is in fact the first to suggest that the Duke should be suppressed:

> Believe me, lords, were none more wise than I,
> And yet herein I judge mine own wit good,
> This Gloucester should be quickly rid the world,
> To rid us from the fear we have of him.
> (III.i.231–4)

On this point, Halle simply suggests that the queen contrived to deprive the Duke of his protectorship and that she did not stop his enemies when they devised false accusations to ruin him:

> she excluded the duke of Gloucester, from all rule and governaunce, not prohibityng suche as she knewe to be his mortal enemies, to invent and imagyne, causes and griefes against hym, . . . of the whiche, diverse writers affirme, the Marques of Suffolke, and the duke of Buckyngham to be the chiefe, not unprocured by the Cardinall of Winchester . . . (Cli)

As for Margaret's adulterous relationship with Suffolk, it is only thanks to Shakespeare's version that we can read possible hints of it in Halle. All we know from the chronicle, in fact, is that Suffolk was 'in high favor with the kyng, and in no lesse grace with quene Margaret' (Cxlix), that he 'not content with his degree, by the meanes of the Quene, was shortely erected to the estate and degree of a Duke' (Cxlix^v–Cl) and that he was 'the Quenes dearlynge' (Clviii) and her 'chefe frende & counsailer' (Clviii^v).

Cardinal Beaufort is described by Halle as being neither a holy man nor exempt from ambition; unlike Holinshed's portrait of Wolsey, Halle's portrait of Winchester suggests a man unlearned and of a mean nature,

> more noble of blodd, then notable in learning, haut in stomacke, and hygh in countenaunce, ryche above measure of all men, & to fewe liberal, disdaynfull to hys kynne and dreadfull to his louers, preferrynge money before frendshippe, many thinges beginning, and nothing perfourmyng. His couetous insaciable, and hope of long lyfe, made hym bothe to forget God, hys Prynce and hym selfe, in his latter daies. (Clii–Clii^v)

Nevertheless, however negatively Winchester is judged by Halle, he is never connected with the plotting of Gloucester's death that Shakespeare unequivocally attributes to him. In the play, he dies in despair because of his sin and shows no sign of redemption. Warwick's comment after his death seals his many guilts: 'So bad a death argues a monstrous life.' (III.iii.30)

York's character and actions are considerably altered by Shakespeare. In the first place, the Duke's aspirations to the throne are somewhat ennobled in the source by what are presented as not purely personal motivations:

> Rychard duke of Yorke . . . , perceivyng the Kyng to be a ruler not Ruling, & the whole burden of the Realme, to depend in the ordinaunces of the Quene and the duke of Suffolke, began secretly to allure to hys frendes of the nobilitie, and priuatly declared to them, hys title and right to the Crowne. (Clii)

Halle speaks of York's 'gentle behavior' and mentions the popularity that the Duke gained by subduing the 'rude and savage' Irish nation (Clvii^v). Moreover – and what is more interesting for our present purposes – he ascribes to his friends and followers rather than to himself the actions designed to further York's claims to the throne and to stir up Cade's rebellion.

That Shakespeare's York is the perfect Machiavellian villain and the worthy father of crookback Richard is made obvious throughout the whole play. Not unlike his son in *Richard III*, York is allowed a privileged channel of communication with the audience. In two lengthy monologues (I.i.215–60 and III.i.331–83) and two asides (III.i.87–92 and V.i.23–31), he is allowed to speak his mind freely and to disclose his machinations. Consequently, no noble motive can be attributed to him. Moreover, Shakespeare grants him the final victory, cutting the action abruptly after the battle of St Albans and thus constructing a political model where the forces of evil eventually triumph.

Dame Eleanor Cobham, too, is given a chance to speak her ambitious mind 'privately', after having openly, and unsuccessfully, tempted her honest, unwavering husband with the lure of the crown. Shakespeare gives prominence to her character, thus strengthening the paradigm of ambition that pervades the play. In Eleanor we encounter a minor Lady Macbeth, although less resolute and 'manly' than her more famous sibling. Unlike Lady Macbeth, Eleanor is prompted by her jealousy for another woman as well as by personal ambition; she is ignorant and superstitious, given to sorcery, dreams and prophecies; like Lady Macbeth, although with less determination, she contrives to put on a 'manly' attitude in order to make up for what she considers her husband's 'womanly' nature:

Follow I must: I cannot go before,
While Gloucester bears this base and humble mind.
Were I a man, a duke, and next of blood,
I would remove these tedious stumbling-blocks
And smooth my way upon their headless necks;
And, being a woman, I will not be slack
To play my part in Fortune's pageant.

(I.ii.61–7)

Shakespeare also uses Eleanor's treason to signal the corruption of the clergy as well as of the nobility. One of Eleanor's associates, the priest Hume, is given a monologue (I.ii.87–97) to reveal that he is being paid both by the Duchess and by Suffolk and the Cardinal who, by bringing her to ruin, hope to destroy Gloucester.[12]

That personal ambition is the motor behind all political action and that treason is its only weapon, is made clear from the start in the masterly organisation of the play's first scene. In the opening segment of the scene, all the relevant characters of the play except Dame Eleanor are present: the King, Duke Humphrey, Salisbury, Warwick, Beaufort, York, Somerset and Buckingham have gathered to welcome Queen Margaret, whom Suffolk has wedded by proxy and escorted to England from France.

The first party to exit comprises the King, the Queen and Suffolk (at line 73). Gloucester, then, speaks his mind to the nobles and reveals his grief for the loss of Maine and Anjou decreed in the articles that have been signed to make the marriage possible. When Gloucester exits, leaving behind his prophecy that 'France will be lost ere long' (145), the Cardinal of Winchester reveals his fears concerning the popularity that Gloucester has gained with the common people. Buckingham then suggests that the Duke be divested of the protectorship, a suggestion that the Cardinal promptly makes his own:

This weighty business will not brook delay;
I'll to the Duke of Suffolk presently.

(169–70)

Immediately after Winchester's exit, it is left to Buckingham and Somerset to briefly express their hatred for the 'haughty' prelate and their fear that he might become protector after the displacement of Gloucester. When these two leave the stage (178), Salisbury displays his fears at 'the pride of Suffolk and the Cardinal / With Somerset and Buckingham's ambition' (202–3) and suggests that he, his son and York join Duke Humphrey while his actions 'do tend the profit of the land' (205). York openly agrees, but half-reveals his secret intentions in a brief aside (208). Finally, after Salisbury and Warwick leave the stage, he is left alone, the last link in the disquieting chain of treasons, to utter his first monologue. He then reveals that his agreement with Salisbury and Warwick and his appreciation of Gloucester are feigned and that he will exploit the situation only to further his ambition to take the throne:

A day will come when York shall claim his own;
And therefore I will take the Nevils' parts
And make a show of love to proud Duke Humphrey,
And when I spy advantage, claim the crown,
For that's the golden mark I seek to hit.

                                        (240–4)

What is left to be revealed, as far as the courtly plots are concerned, is soon shown in the two scenes that follow. Scene Two presents Eleanor Cobham's plans against Henry and Margaret, while Scene Three reveals the treacherous confederacy between Margaret and Suffolk. Shakespeare makes their plot known to the audience by deftly displacing and manipulating an episode that he found in Halle but which in the chronicle is not connected with any political issue. When Peter, the armourer's servant, presents the queen and Suffolk with a petition against his master 'for saying that the Duke of York is rightful heir to the crown' (I.iii.25–6), Margaret is encouraged to speak her mind to Suffolk:

Beside the haught Protector, have we Beaufort
The imperious churchman; Somerset, Buckingham,
And grumbling York; and not the least of these
But can do more in England than the King.

                                        (I.iii.68–71)

and adds her hatred for 'that proud dame, the Lord Protector's wife' (76).[13] The kind of league that Suffolk suggests to her excludes all the others, even the king:

> Although we fancy not the Cardinal,
> Yet must we join with him and with the lords
> Till we have brought Duke Humphrey in disgrace.
> As for the Duke of York, this last complaint
> Will make but little for his benefit:
> So, one by one, we'll weed them all at last,
> And you yourself shall steer the happy helm.
>
> (94–100)

Here we may sense that Suffolk is making even Margaret his tool, especially if we remember his lines at the end of *1 Henry VI*:

> Margaret shall now be queen, and rule the king;
> But I will rule both her, the king and realm.
>
> (V.vii.107–8)

By this time, the audience is conscious of the fact that no one is safe at court; that loyalty has been banished, that ambition holds sway, that the last thing that crosses the mind of those in power is the common weal, that the king is excluded from all important actions and decisions, and that a civil war grounded on the meanest type of personal ambition is bound to follow.

However, there is still a healthy part of the nation, quite evidently presented as such and towards whom the sympathies of the audience are clearly oriented. This is unequivocally embodied in Duke Humphrey and in the common people who love him (the Nevils are presented as acting in good faith, although they support York's claim). Henry is more on the side of this party than on that of the ambitious nobility, but he is too weak and too easily deceived ever to allow the sane and wise to prevail.

The common people's love for Gloucester and the epithet of 'good Duke Humphrey' are reported by Halle.[14] Indeed, the chronicle is explicit, although not detailed, in describing the Duke as noble and disinterested, as well as presenting him as an experienced politician and in attributing his ruin to the envy of his enemies. In the play, Gloucester's righteousness is made clear in his opposition to his wife's ambitious plans, and is recognised even by his enemies (see

York's tribute in II.ii.72–3). But most of all we are made to recognise from his own speeches the honest man whose only concern is the good of his country. Shakespeare gathers the hints present in the chronicles and uses them to build up a major political confrontation, based on a sharp contrast between a healthy party and a diseased one among those wielding power. As in a mirror, the play also shows on the one hand the honest and virtuous among the common people (those that follow Gloucester) and, on the other, the 'idle rascals' (those that follow Cade).[15]

Moreover, in political terms, the play seems to affirm that there are popular claims which are considered acceptable and well-grounded, while there are, of course, others that are not. In particular, while the use of popular revolt to further the people's claims is condemned, the practice of petition is considered legitimate.[16] But the play seems to go further than that, suggesting that even certain acts of rebellion are justified. The possibility of an uprising by Gloucester's followers after his death, in fact, produces fear only in those who plot his murder, while their rebellion is seen as an acceptable form of protest by Salisbury and Warwick and by the king, since it is prompted by anger at the perpetration of a hideous crime.

The commoners are mentioned very early in the play, and it is clear from the start that they are treated in two different and opposite ways: with fear and scorn in the words of the ambitious nobles, and with sympathy in the words of Gloucester.

The first to mention the common people in connection with the affection they have for Gloucester, and therefore as a menace to the privileges and power of the nobles, is the Cardinal:

> What though the common people favour him,
> Calling him 'Humphrey, the good Duke of Gloucester',
> Clapping their hands, and crying with loud voice
> 'Jesu maintain your royal excellence!'
> With 'God preserve the good Duke Humphrey!'
> I fear me, lords, for all this flattering gloss,
> He will be found a dangerous Protector.
>
> (I.i.157–63)

The Cardinal cynically suggests that popular favour is to be manipulated for one's own ends: he knows, in fact, that it is one of the ingredients of power and a potent tool for its maintenance and furtherance, and therefore potentially dangerous when it is held by the enemy.[17]

The commoners are mentioned with scorn and hatred by the Duchess of Gloucester when, after she is found guilty of high treason, she is subjected to the humiliation of being led through the streets of London, and of being made an object of ridicule and contempt by the crowd. The epithets that she uses here show her haughty mind: to be followed by 'the giddy multitude' (II.iv.21), looked at with 'their hateful looks' (23), scorned by 'a rabble' (32), laughed at by 'the envious people' (35) and by 'every idle rascal' (47), constitutes the most cruel punishment that could be devised for her.

Margaret's perspective is by no means less cynical than the Cardinal's. Her cue is, again, the favour that Gloucester has won with the commoners. The power conferred by popular favour and the nightmare of popular rebellion are here clearly evoked by the queen:

> By flattery hath he won the commons' hearts,
> And when he please to make commotion
> 'Tis to be fear'd they all will follow him.
> (III.i.28–30)

Suffolk's view is no different; his fear of popular rebellion equals that of the others. This is how he speaks of the commoners in connection with Gloucester, suggesting that he be murdered rather than venture a regular trial that might provoke popular protest:

> The King will labour still to save his life;
> The commons haply rise to save his life;
> And yet we have but trivial argument,
> More than mistrust, that shows him worthy death.
> (III.i.239–42)

York not only shares the view that the commoners should be manipulated, he also puts this manipulation into practice, provoking popular commotion in the hope that this will help him get the crown. In the long monologue that he pronounces in III.i.331–83, he reveals that he has 'seduced' Jack Cade 'To make commotion as full well he can' (358) and shows his political deftness in his plan to observe the humour of the common people and study their possible reactions before proclaiming his intentions:

> By this I shall perceive the commons' mind,
> How they affect the house and claim of York.
>
> (374–5)

Gloucester's attitude is obviously different, and it is towards his honest perspective that the audience's appreciation is directed. The word *commonweal*, unknown to the others, is pronounced by the Duke in connection with the discredit cast on him by Eleanor's treason. To Margaret, who hurls his wife's shame at him, Gloucester replies with the assurance of a clean conscience:

> Madam, for myself, to heaven I do appeal,
> How I have lov'd the king and commonweal.
>
> (II.i.182–3)

Gloucester again reveals sympathy for the poor ('the needy commons') when he pleads his honesty and good faith in answer to York's accusation of having 'stay'd the soldiers' pay' (III.i.105):

> No; many a pound of mine own proper store,
> Because I would not tax the needy commons,
> Have I dispursed to the garrisons,
> And never ask'd for restitution.
>
> (III.i.115–18)

However, the 'needy commons' are not only evoked in the nightmares and pleadings of people in power, although the fact that they are frequently mentioned by itself makes them a relevant social background for political misdemeanour. They also appear on the stage, in a number of capacities and roles.

In I.iii, they first appear in the role of petitioners (one of them is the Armourer's man, Peter, whose petition is against his master 'for saying that the Duke of York was rightful heir to the crown': 25–6). Their petitions are meant to be delivered to Gloucester, and it is understood that they expect that the Lord Protector will answer their supplications in the affirmative. But the men mistake Suffolk for Gloucester and are compelled to deliver their petitions to the wrong person. Here is the first petition, in which the righting of an evident wrong is requested:

Mine is, and 't please your Grace, against John Goodman, my
Lord Cardinal's man, for keeping my house, and lands, and wife,
and all, from me.

(I.iii.16–18)

Suffolk reacts scornfully, and becomes furious when he reads the
second petition, one that accuses him:

Thy wife too! that's some wrong indeed. What's yours? What's
here? [*Reads*] 'Against the Duke of Suffolk, for enclosing the commons of Long Melford.' How now, sir knave! (19–22)

The only petition to receive Suffolk's and Margaret's attention is
Peter's, because it furthers their aim to get rid of York by proving
him guilty of high treason. The others are dismissed by the queen,
who tears them up in the face of the petitioners:

And as for you, that love to be protected
Under the wings of our Protector's grace,
Begin your suits anew, and sue to him.
(37–9)

Following the verdict pronounced by Gloucester, Peter and
Horner, his master, attempt to prove the truth of their assertions in
single combat. This episode, too (II.iii.59–91), which ends with the
victory of the servant, shows a reversal of power relationships.
Although both socially and physically the stronger, Horner is morally
the weaker: in his presumptuousness, he boasts of an easy victory
but has drunk too many cups of sack and is therefore easily overcome
by his servant.[18]

Indeed, there are also liars and impostors among the commoners.
Saunder Simpcox, 'the lying'st knave in Christendom' in the words
of Gloucester (II.i.125), takes advantage of the king's good faith by
telling him that St Alban has restored his sight after a life-long
blindness. He and his wife are whipped for their fraud. However,
to the account in his source Shakespeare adds a line that informs us
of the motive for the fraud and therefore mitigates their guilt: as
Simpcox's wife says plainly, 'Alas! sir, we did it for pure need.'
(150)[19]

It is, again, two commoners who perpetrate the crime of Gloucester's
murder. They are shown after they have done the deed, and one of

them, unlike those who had commissioned the murder, shows pity and remorse:

O, *that it were to do!* What have we done?
Didst ever hear a man so penitent?
(III.ii.3–4; my emphasis)

Not unlike the sorcerers, these men have been bribed and corrupted by those in power; not unlike Simpcox and his wife, they have acted 'for pure need'.

The episode that shows that popular risings are acceptable when they are prompted by a right cause is the commoners' revolt following Gloucester's murder (III.ii). What the text makes clear is that no one is thinking of taking up arms against the rebellious citizens; instead, the King's opinion is that satisfactory explanations of Gloucester's death must be provided, so that the crowd may be appeased.

Undoubtedly, the revolt is presented as acceptable owing only to its lack of a properly popular character: what has pushed the commons to revolt, in fact, is their rage at the traitorous murder of a nobleman and their wish to shelter a 'pious' king who is unable to protect himself and the country against the plots of a corrupt nobility. All the same, however, the rebellious citizens are presented as infinitely healthier than, and morally superior to, the nobles that they accuse. Moreover, their action is lent dignity by the attitude of Warwick and Salisbury – who try to appease them by enquiring about the murder – and by what is presented as their sensible request that the traitor Suffolk be either executed or exiled. Finally, their rebellion is given weight and formal sanction by the King's decision to banish Suffolk.

Thus when it comes to the elimination of Suffolk (IV.i.), the shipmen that carry it out are presented as executioners and avengers rather than as murderers. The fact that before sentencing Suffolk to death the ship's captain throws at him the long catalogue of his acts of 'devilish policy' (70–102) makes us perceive Suffolk's elimination as an execution rather than as a murder, and therefore as an act of popular justice.

It is only at this stage, when good and evil have been clearly distributed, that Jack Cade makes his appearance.

The elaborate compositional process which the Cade episode went through shows the exceptional importance that Shakespeare attributed to its representation. Its various stages may be reconstructed with some confidence. It is clear that Shakespeare was not satisfied with Halle's account of the episode. He may have consulted other accounts and found that they offered a similar treatment. He must then have abandoned his main source and the historical event proper and turned to more than one alternative book and to other events, searching for elements that might fit his representational purpose. Thus, he met with a different – although similar – story set in a different time: that of the peasants' revolt under Jack Straw, the time being 1381. The most abject acts that Cade and his followers perform in Shakespeare's play come from the accounts that Grafton, Holinshed and maybe the anonymous play *The Life and Death of Jack Straw* give of that event. In those reports, Shakespeare learned of the rebels' loathing of learning and books and of their sending clerks and lawyers to death; he came across accounts of the destruction of the Savoy and of the Inner Temple and of the burning of all written records; and finally he read about the motivations for the uprising and took in the verbal vesture of the rebels' communist dream.

We may imagine the dramatist taking notes of these elements or marking the margins of his books to underline those references which seemed to suit his purpose, and establishing, while reading, parallels not only between the 1381 revolt and the uprising of 1450 but maybe also between those two and other, more recent, disorders: the 1517 xenophobic prentices' rising which he had just represented or was soon to represent in the three folios of *The Book of Sir Thomas More* that are attributed to his hand; and maybe other disorders, nearer in time, like the Hackett rebellion in July 1591 or the June 1592 feltmakers' revolt before the Marshalsea prison in Southwark.[20]

While reading these accounts, a rich network of intertextual associations and a dialogue of diverse voices started to take shape in his mind. One text reacted to the other so that one event explained, and was explained by, the other: the 1381 revolt was therefore assumed as a critical comment on other similar events. Finally, the conflation of two distinct but similar episodes made it possible to transcend the contingent so that Cade's rebellion assumed the status of a *prototype*. What a modern theorist of historiography would call a 'limited generalisation' was instinctively adopted so that rebellion was awarded the status of a general political issue;[21] an issue which, in turn, was perfectly understandable and familiar to the theatrical audience.

Once these associations were mentally established, the next problem was how to render the episode. Shakespeare decided on the comic convention. However, the kind of laughter that came to his mind was not the liberating and festive laughter of the carnival tradition; it was the grim, bitter, moralistic laughter that comes from the grotesque, a laughter that proclaims some kind of disease. He, then, decided to embitter and ridicule the tradition of both revolts, representing the rebels as a bunch of laughable, although violent, individuals. The motives for the 1381 rising, which seem to be taken seriously both by Grafton and by Holinshed and which are narrated not without sympathy in the chronicles, are devalued in the play and rendered irrational and inconsequential. Thus Cade's communist dream and the kinds of reform that he promises are abased to little more than wild revelling:

> *Cade.* . . . . There shall be in England seven halfpenny loaves sold
>   for a penny; the three-hoop'd pot shall have ten hoops; and I
>   will make it felony to drink small beer. All the realm shall be
>   in common, and in Cheapside shall my palfrey go to grass.
>   And when I am king, as king I will be, –
> *All.* God save your Majesty!
> *Cade.* I thank you, good people – there shall be no money; all
>   shall eat and drink on my score, and I will apparel them all in
>   one livery, that they may agree like brothers, and worship me
>   their lord.
>
> 　　　　　　　　　　　　　　　　　　　　　　　(IV.ii.62–72)[22]

That the enterprise and its leader are not taken seriously even by the rebels, is made clear on Cade's first appearance in Dick the Butcher and Smith the Weaver's side-play, which cuts Cade's boasts of nobility and his claims to the throne down to size (IV.ii.31–60).

The burning of the men of law's houses, the destruction of the Savoy and of the Inner Temple and of all the official records, which the sources relate as having been perpetrated by the Kentish rebels in 1381, are attributed in the play to Cade and his followers. Cade's incongruous utopia involves the project of making a *tabula rasa* of all cultural records, to which Shakespeare adds the purpose to 'kill all the lawyers' (IV.ii.73), showing the arraignment and killing of the Clerk of Chartham. Historical (1381) and non-historical materials are here mingled, with the addition of ludicrous motivations and with a stress on the rebels' loathing of writing and of books and the consequent indiscriminate killing of those who 'can write and read and cast accompt' (IV.ii.81–82), let alone those who can speak foreign tongues (something which may have pleased the illiterate in the audience). The Clerk of Chartham confesses that he can write his name and is therefore found guilty. Cade's verdict is,

> Away with him, I say: hang him with his pen and ink-horn about his neck.
>
> (IV.ii.103–4)

However, there is no pathos in the poor man's death, for the scene verges on sheer farce. Similarly, the killing of Sir Humphrey Stafford and of his brother are denied the dignity of tragedy (Sir Humphrey 'can speak French; and therefore he is a traitor', 159–60); no ideals are behind the burning down of the Savoy and of the Inner Temple and the destruction of all written records; indeed, this last action is made an object of derision even by John Holland and Smith the Weaver, who produce a few aside comments to Cade's suggestion that, after the destruction, all the laws of England come out of his own mouth:

> *Hol.* [*Aside*] Mass, 'twill be sore law then; for he was thrust in the mouth with a spear, and 'tis not whole yet.
> *Wea.* [*Aside*] Nay, John, it will be stinking law; for his breath stinks with eating toasted cheese.
> *Cade.* I have thought upon it; it shall be so. Away! burn all the records of the realm; my mouth shall be the parliament of England.
> *Hol.* [*Aside*] Then we are like to have biting statutes, unless his teeth be pull'd out.
>
> (IV.vii.7–16)

The general effect of these distorting and debasing strategies is a complete devaluation of the seriousness of the rebels' enterprise, and therefore a drastic reduction of their dangerousness. However, it is for fear of these rebels and of their mock-rebellion that the King has run away and that the whole commonwealth is on the verge of collapse.

Even allowing for the uncertainties which come from the text's corrupted transmission, we may still remark a few more subterranean stylistic devices which contribute to the construction of a levelling strategy: there are moments when Cade is allowed to speak verse, thereby acting on the same level as the nobility (IV.ii); and moments when, in the mouth of the emissaries of the runaway King, to speak verse is by no means more dignified or more sensible than to speak prose (and is certainly more incongruous). One of these is when Lord Say is brought in to the presence of Cade, who accuses him of a series of 'cultural' crimes: 'Thou hast most traitorously corrupted the youth of the realm in erecting a grammar-school' (IV.vii.30–2); 'thou hast caus'd printing to be us'd' (33–4); 'thou hast men about thee that usually talk of a noun, and a verb, and such abominable words as no Christian ear can endure to hear' (36–9).[23] Say's answer to these absurd accusations is no less absurd, and is obviously such as to condemn him: unaware of the kind of crimes of which he is being accused, he starts his defence with a Latin sentence referring to Kent as 'bona terra, mala gens' (54) which causes Cade's obvious reaction: 'Away with him! away with him! he speaks Latin' (55); to which, in a last desperate effort to save his life, Say answers by quoting Caesar's *Commentaries* and is thereupon beheaded.

It remains to be seen how a divided perspective could be generated by the satirical mode; and whether the author could expect that a play which presents such a ludicrous face of rebellion would be read as supporting the interests of all the components of the variegated audience he was addressing. Generally speaking, in fact, the satirical and the grotesque modes require full agreement between sender and receiver as to the object in which the deformity is held to reside. But can we say that only Cade and his followers are the object of derision? Have we not witnessed, throughout the first three acts of the play, the grotesque aberrations of power? The idea that monstrous rulers cannot but generate monstrous subjects, in fact, has been carefully engineered in the course of the first three acts. Before Cade appears, we have been assailed by the absurdly gratuitous violence of the nobles, which the ineptitude of the 'saintly' king is unable to repress: the rulers we have seen, then, are no less ludicrous and wild than the ruled. After the disappearance of 'good Duke Humphrey', the idea that the high are no better than the low – indeed, that in the end they are responsible for the monstrosity of a demented uprising – is by no means a simple suggestion between the lines.

If Cade and his followers are grotesque and almost subhuman, the power which produced them and whose instrument they are is by no means the comparatively dignified power of the chronicles; it is the abased, degraded and sickly power that the play systematically constructs; if the rebels are a fickle and ignorant mass, those who are responsible for the public weal are treasonous and even criminal; if the rebellion is a mock-rebellion, the power that takes it seriously and deploys an army to halt it is no less a mock-power; if the rebels' expectations are depicted as 'basely' materialistic and incongruous, the acts of the nobility are certainly not inspired by noble ideals. The deformity of the rebels, then, holds a mirror up to the deformity of the party in power. The political lesson is there for those who want to see it.

My point about the possibility of a divided reception would be more sustainable if records of a theatrical success of *2 Henry VI* had survived as they have of Part One. In the absence of witnesses, to make assumptions about the kind of reception that the play may have had by its first audience is mere conjecture. However, the very textual history of the play – one of the thorniest in the canon – the three quarto editions which it went through, the probable memorial reconstruction, the names of the actors Bevis and Holland which are still attached to two of its characters, its careless and hasty transmission, the many Folio variants probably due to the intervention of the censor, may in the final analysis testify to the frequent use of the text in the theatre.

If mine were not mere speculation, then we would have one more element to argue that the play may have reached with diverse but equally pertinent messages the various sectors of the playhouse. One part of the audience must indeed have felt that the representation of the Cade rebellion supported the interests of those who repressed the frequent broils that broke out outside theatres and prisons; another part, the one that was more intensely aware of social contradictions, may have registered with satisfaction the exhibition of the many perversions of authority and perceived the Cade episode and the events that led up to it as a dramatic presentation of those contradictions. *2 Henry VI* might then be one more case in point to support what Dollimore has shown, namely, that 'Despite all the propaganda to the contrary, it was quite possible for people to see that disorder was often generated from the top down rather than from the bottom up'.[24]

Notes

1. 'Murdering Peasants', pp. 24, 25.
2. D. Cohen, *The Politics of Shakespeare* (London: Macmillan, 1993), p. 60.
3. *Stages of History*, p. 75.
4. Ibid., p. 219.
5. *The Second Part of King Henry VI*, p. 20.
6. *Shakespeare and the Popular Voice*, p. 49.
7. The other Shakespearean locus which has invariably been read as evidence of its author's political conservatism is Ulysses' speech on 'degree' in *Troilus and Cressida* (I.iii.75–137). However, the situation is different in the two passages, especially from the point of view of the source from which the 'opinion' comes. While, in fact, the *Troilus* speech, however authoritative in tone and persuasive in its rhetorical organisation, can be viewed as just one of the possible axiological positions in a virtual debate, a position which is attributed to one character, the Cade scenes impose themselves by the truth-value of direct representation. As such, they more strongly imply the 'arranger's' (if not the author's) standpoint, and therefore a less mediated attempt at shaping the audience's reactions. Paradoxically, in a dramatic text the evaluations imposed by representation, although less directly expressed, may work more strongly than those suggested by explicit declarations.
8. The main source of *2 Henry VI* is Halle's chronicle. Probable sources are Holinshed, Grafton, Foxe and the anonymous play *The Life and Death of Jack Straw.*
9. See, for instance, the following passage, where the seed of all discord is seen in God's displeasure with Henry's marriage:

> But moste of all it should seme, that God with this matrimony was not content. For after this spousage, the kynges frendes fell from hym, bothe in Englande and in Fraunce, the Lordes of his realme, fell in diuision emongest themselfes, the commons rebelled against their sovereigne Lorde, and naturall Prince, feldes were foughten, many thousandes slain, and finally, the kyng deposed, and his sonne slain, and this Quene sent home again, with as muche misery and sorowe, as she was receiued with pompe and triumphe. (Cxlviii^v)

Halle expresses the opinion that, if Duke Humphrey had not been murdered, the house of Lancaster would not have been destroyed; his comment on this point is: 'This is the worldly judgment, but God knoweth, what he had predestinate, & what he had ordeined before, againste whose ordinaunce prevaileth no counsail, and against whose will avayleth no stryuinge.' (Clii)

As regards the issue of first and second causes, M. Hattaway remarks that 'If there is a grand design it is only dimly glimpsed, for the emphasis of Shakespeare, if not always of his characters, rests firmly upon efficient and not final causes.' (*The Second Part of King Henry VI*, p. 1).

10. *The Union*, p. Cxlix. Page reference is henceforth given in parenthesis.

11. That Gloucester's death was procured by his enemies is recorded by Halle as a popular conviction. Halle says that 'all indifferent persons well knewe, that he died of no natural death, but of some violent force: some iudged hym to be strangled: some affirme, that a hote spitte was put in at his foundement: other write, that he was stiffeled or smoldered betwene twoo fetherbeddes' (Cli^v). Moreover, Gloucester is said by Halle to have been granted a trial where he could defend himself and plead his innocence, while in Shakespeare he is liquidated before the day appointed for his trial.

12. Halle only says that Suffolk was suspected of having some responsibility for the Duke's murder.

13. Margaret's hatred for Eleanor Cobham is unhistorical. The discovery of Eleanor's treason and her condemnation, in fact, are reported by Halle as having taken place long before Margaret's arrival in England in 1445.

14. See also Foxe: 'Of manners he seemed meeke and gentle, louing the common wealth, a supporter of the poore commons, of wit and wisdome discreet and studious, well affected to religion, and a friend to veritie, and no les enemy to pride and ambition, especially in hauty Prelates, which was his undoing in this present evill world: And which is seldome and rare in such princes of the calling, he was both learned himselfe, and no lesse giuen to study, as also a singular fauourer and patrone to them which were studious and learned . . .'. The passage does not appear in the first edition of Foxe's *Actes and Monuments of Martyrs* (1563) but in the second (1583, 'newly recognised and inlarged by the Author'). My repeated attempts to obtain vol. I of the 1583 edition (*The first Volume of the Ecclesiasticall Historie, Containing the Acts and Monuments of Martyrs*), where the story is told, have been in vain: to the staff's surprise, it had disappeared from its place on the shelves of the British Library. My reference edition is, therefore, the 5th imprint (*Actes and Monuments of Matters Most Speciall*, 1596; the passage is in vol. I, p. 647).

15. However, Cade's followers are in the end 'redeemed', even though their rehabilitation is conditional to their giving up the claims for which they had revolted. Once the 'corrupting' influence of Cade is uprooted, they cease to be dangerous and become 'sensible' persons whom the political power may in turn manipulate. It is clear, besides, that even between Cade and his followers there is a hierarchy of power relations, that – exactly like those in power – Cade knows how to use the commoners to further his own ambition; significantly, those who occupy the lowest position even in this sphere are viewed with greater sympathy.

16. See I.iii.1–36, where the blame falls clearly on the use that Suffolk and Margaret make of the petitions.

17. Cade seems to be no less cynical in exploiting his followers when, assuming an attitude of aristocratic scorn, he calls them 'base peasants' (IV.viii.21).

18. The legal aspects of trial by battle in Shakespeare are discussed by Keeton (op. cit., pp. 211–22), who examines this episode (pp. 214–16).

19. See my discussion of the episode, *infra*, pp. 213–17.

20. See Patterson's discussion of the possible connection of the Cade episode with contemporary popular risings and the evidence that she produces for it in *Shakespeare and the Popular Voice*, Chapter 2.

21. Limited generalisations in historiographical narratives are assertions similar to general laws, in that they are more general than simple descriptions; however, they are 'limited' or 'restricted' in that they 'are rooted in *transitory regularities*' and therefore, as explanations, they are not valid for all times and places, but rather depend on certain conditions which may be temporal, social, geographical, cultural, etc. These generalisations, therefore, constitute corrections to the concept of 'uniqueness' in history, in that they serve to connect certain classes of events to certain contexts and circumstances. See C. B. Joynt and N. Rescher, 'The Problem of Uniqueness in History', *HT* I, (1961), 150–62.

22. In the account of both of Shakespeare's probable sources, the rebels' claims to equality are justified in Christian terms:

> At this time, there were a certaine of suche kinde of people as is aforesayde, that beganne to stirre in England and namely in Kent, and sayde they were in great seruitude and bondage: But sayd they, in the beginning of the worlde, there were no bond men: neyther ought there to be any nowe, except it were such a one as had committed treason agaynst his Lorde, as Lucifer did to God. But sayde they we can haue no suche battayle, for we are neyther Angelles nor spirites, but men framed and formed to the similitude of our Lordes, and therefore sayde they, why should we then be so kept under lyke beastes and slaues? (R. Grafton, *A Chronicle at Large*, London, 1569, p. 330)

The same attitude we encounter in Holinshed, when he relates the arguments with which John Ball enflamed the spirits of the poor people:

> When Adam delu'd and Eue span,
> Who was then a gentleman?

and so continuing his sermon, went about to prooue by the words of that proverbe, that from the beginning, all men by nature were created alike, and that bondage or seruitude came in by injust oppression of naughtie men. For if God would haue had anie bondmen from the beginning, he would haue appointed who should be bond & who free (*Chronicles*, 437.I.63–71).

Much less favourable to the rebels is the account that, by the middle of the eighteenth century, David Hume will give of the same rising, thereby showing that the obsession with sedition is by no means exclusively Elizabethan and Jacobean:

> One John Ball, also, a seditious preacher, who affected low popularity, went about the country and inculcated on his audience the principles of the first origin of mankind from one common stock, their equal right to liberty and to all the goods of nature, the tyranny of artificial distinctions, and the abuses which had arisen from the degradation of the more considerable part of the species, and the aggrandizement of a few insolent rulers. These doctrines, so agreeable to the populace, and so conformable to the ideas of primitive equality which are engraven in the hearts of all men, were greedily received by the multitude, and scattered the sparks of the sedition which the present tax raised into a conflagration. (*The History of England from the Invasion of Julius Caesar to the Abdication of James the Second, 1688, 1754–1761*, Boston: Phillips, Sampson and Co., 1858, vol. II, p. 283).

23. Shortly after reporting the outcome of the battle of St Albans, Halle launches into praise of the newly discovered technique of printing: 'In which season, the craft of Printyng was first inuented in the citie of Mens in Germanie, to the great furtheraunce of all persons, desiryng knowledge or thyrstyng for litterature.' (Clxx^v)

24. J. Dollimore, *Radical Tragedy* (New York and London: Harvester, 1989 [1984]), p. XXIV.

Part III
Thresholds and Margins

10

'Bastards and else': Less than History

The unfacts, did we possess them, are too imprecisely few to warrant our certitude.

J. Joyce, *Finnegans Wake*

In the past, historians could be accused of wanting to know only about 'the great deeds of kings', but today this is certainly no longer true. More and more they are turning toward what their predecessors passed over in silence, discarded or simply ignored. 'Who built Thebes of the seven gates?' Bertolt Brecht's 'literate worker' was already asking. The sources tell us nothing about these anonymous masons, but the question retains all its significance.[1]

The latter extract opens one of the most remarkable enterprises in the retrieval of historical marginality. Carlo Ginzburg's exemplary story of Domenico Scandella, *alias* Menocchio, a sixteenth-century miller from Friuli in Northern Italy, is not only concerned with his trials for heresy and final burning by the Holy Office; more importantly, it engages in the reconstruction of a fragment of what we call 'the popular culture'.

That Tudor chroniclers ignored social history and that their works were exclusively 'the bokes of great prynces and lordes' is a fact. Understandably enough, for the Tudor historian history was the story of political power, the 'visible' facts, in which the life of unknown, invisible individuals was not included even as a background.

Let me report two influential opinions on the non-role of common people in public affairs and, therefore, in history and in history books. The first to speak is Sir Thomas Smith, Secretary of State during the reign of Elizabeth. After illustrating the first three 'parties of the Commonwealth of England' (gentlemen, citizens or burgesses, and yeomen artificers), he passes to the fourth and last:

181

The fourth sort or classe amongest us, is of those which the olde Romans called *capite censij proletarij* or *operae*, day labourers, poore husbandmen, yea merchantes or retailers which have no free lande, copiholders, all artificers, as Taylers, Shoomakers, Carpenters, Brickemakers, Bricklayers, Masons, &c: These have no voice or authoritie in our common wealth, and no account is made of them but onelie to be ruled, not to rule other. . . .[2]

The second is George Puttenham:

who passeth to follow the steps, and maner of life of a craftes man, shepheard, or sailer, though he were his father or dearest frend? yea how almost is it possible that such maner of men should be of any vertue other then their profession requireth? Therefore was nothing committed to historie but matters of great and excellent persons. . . .[3]

Indeed, this view of political history, that has made 'such maner of men' (and all manner of women) a lost crew, has long been, and still is, dominant, although it was principally for 'such maner of men' and women that power projected the means by which it exercised its strength. It seems, moreover, that the story keeps repeating itself:

Even today the culture of the subordinate class is largely *oral*, and it was even more so in centuries past. Since historians are unable to converse with the peasants of the sixteenth century (and, in any case, there is no guarantee that they would understand them), they must depend almost entirely on written sources (and possibly archaeological evidence). These are doubly indirect for they are *written*, and written in general by individuals who were more or less openly attached to the dominant culture. This means that the thoughts, the beliefs, and the aspirations of the peasants and artisans of the past reach us (if and when they do) almost always through distorting viewpoints and intermediaries.[4]

A part of Shakespeare's historical imagination was devoted to admitting into the body of greater events the residues and scraps of history, what the chroniclers considered as background or 'noise' in the stories of kings and dynasties and to admit them as fully respectable parts of the picture. In the secluded space of the playhouse, those who had 'no voice or authority' in Smith's *respublica*, were allowed some freedom of speech: in Shakespeare's plays, they spoke and revealed their minds to other voiceless, although presumably noisy, people, filling the small time which was allowed them with their voice – in verse or more frequently in prose, in conventional or unconventional tones, on important or unimportant matters. Sometimes they are merely the instruments of the great, other times they reveal an independent mind; on a few occasions they are identified by a name and by a few traits of their personality, on others they stand for a group or a trade or a category of persons; their needs and aspirations may be treated seriously or made the object of laughter and scorn; they may be used to serve the interests of the people in power and may even show a mind prone to those interests; their connection with the events of greater history and their role in the play's plot may be one of structural necessity but it may also be wholly accessory from a structural point of view, and therefore perform a different kind of function; they may appear by themselves or in the company of their likes or may be introduced in the presence of kings and princes and made to converse with them; they are even, on a few occasions, called onto the historical proscenium to chide their betters, to remind them of their responsibilities and to awaken their political and moral conscience.

If we read Shakespeare's history plays reversing the focus of our attention, we discover a world of persons who compose, if not a project of invisible history, at least a significant subtext which is certainly worth bringing to the surface. If we look at them closely, these anonymous figures which seem at a first glance to be designed as a background to the deeds of the great become a whole crowd which throngs with its needs against the doors of the palaces of power; a crowd which, albeit fragmentarily, seems able to tell its own story.

But what can the function of this subtext be; what credentials can those elsewhere voiceless figures present for their inclusion in a historical play; whence does the shady area of invisible history derive its legitimation, whence its capacity to persuade and even to present an independent set of values, since it cannot rely on the basic justification of truth which legitimates the well-lit area of greater history; to what extent and in what way does the presence of its obscure side influence the interpretation of visible history; and, finally and most cogently, what can we glean from the representation of those background figures about Shakespeare's attitude towards the poor

and the marginalised? Answers to these questions seem again to
rest on the reader's focus of attention rather than on the texts' clear
allegations; again, there have been contrasting evaluations, particularly in attempts to reply to the last of my questions.

Margot Heinemann has commented on the dignity and weight
of Shakespeare's marginals, deploring the fact that in modern pro-
ductions 'these characters are routinely presented as gross, stupid
and barely human – rogues, sluts and varlets with straw in their
hair, whose antics the audience can laugh at but whose comments
it can't be expected to take seriously', and that 'directors of our
national companies make them all walk with their feet wide apart
and their bottoms stuck out, in contrast to the aristocracy who stand
up properly.'[5]

Larry Champion has remarked that 'secondary characters and
diversionary episodes can point to flaws either in the ruler or in the
society, often exposing the seam between the rhetoric of patriotism
and national harmony, on the one hand, and the reality of social
conditions and the Machiavellian schemes by which power is maintained, on the other'.[6]

Richard Helgerson holds a different view of Shakespeare's
marginals. Discussing Shakespeare's histories in connection with
the historical romances of the Henslowe playwrights, he affirms
that since Shakespeare's main interest in the history plays was the
consolidation of monarchic rule, he excluded the ruled, and dis-
tanced the king from the people, 'mingling king and clown only
when the latter can function as a type of the former, a lord of
misrule whose banishment will effect the cleansing of the monarchic
body and realm'. On the contrary, Helgerson argues, the Henslowe
plays, though not unconcerned with monarchic power, 'represent
such power from the point of view of those who suffer its harshest
consequences'.[7]

Derek Cohen argues that 'The poor in Shakespeare's history plays
. . . tend to be violent, stupid, aggressive, vacillating, sycophantic,
vicious, brutal and unkind';[8] and that, not unlike such marginal
social entities as Jews, blacks and women in other Shakespeare plays,
'the poor are endowed with qualities that make them unincorporable
into the mainstream of power politics'.[9] Cohen rightly problematises
the issue, posing interesting questions about our criteria for evaluating the treatment of poverty and marginality in those plays (are the
criteria we use 'those fostered by the plays, our own notions and
ideologies, Shakespeare's own, or those of the histories of poverty

and violence over the last four centuries?);[10] but he brands any attempt to argue for Shakespeare's sympathy – or even ambivalent attitude – towards the marginals as a nostalgic revival of the kind of old historicism which produced the works of Tillyard, Chambers, Dover Wilson and Bradley; a revival of that 'ideological and economic individualism' which prospered in periods 'when it was only with reluctance that ideological "deficiencies" in Shakespeare were acknowledged'.[11]

Obviously, the way in which we evaluate the issue of the author's stance depends on what we think we may expect from those texts; more particularly, it depends on our effort to place them in a historical perspective. If we complain that Cade 'is not given the chance to seem the revolutionary hero that many of his followers would have celebrated';[12] if we wonder why the nobles opposing the monarchy 'are represented as plausible (though not always desirable) alternative governments . . . while the poor who would assume power are represented as megalomaniac and absurd' or we even consider relevant that 'At no time do the pretenders to the throne offer a redistribution of wealth';[13] if we tend to read all statements and acts as either openly subversive or obviously functional to the maintenance of power;[14] if we fail to consider how deeply and unequivocally antipopulist most contemporary writings are (Shakespeare's alleged antisemitism in The Merchant of Venice should always be measured against Marlowe's in The Jew of Malta), then we are certainly evaluating through 'our own notions and ideologies': a temptation which I will try to elude.

Certainly, Shakespeare's commoners are not many, and they never rise, in number and in sort, above the figures of power. But they are frankly popular, and in many cases they are summoned at fateful junctions of the story, where they are allowed to have their say about the momentous events at hand. Often, in fact, non-historical characters figure as axiological markers, and other times they express their group's problems and viewpoint, somehow disturbing the prevailing perspective of 'visible' history.

The invention of non-historical events and the summoning of non-historical characters, therefore, allows the dramatist to lay down an arena where a multiplicity of voices are allowed to take part in the dialogue. These forms of polyphony are often employed to reveal symptoms of social pathology or, more simply, the dissenting perspective or the uneasiness of a category, a trade, or a group of people (the obvious instance of the use of marginal voices to undermine a

celebrative reading of the events is the Court, Bates and Williams
episode in *Henry V*, IV.i.85–235).[15] Sometimes one of those persons
is allowed to assume the consistency and relevance of a character
or a quasi-character: soldiers, gardeners, citizens, apprentices,
women, who may have a name or be nameless, are from time to
time summoned to the historical proscenium and allowed to speak
their mind with the wisdom of their class or trade (or of what is
conventionally understood as its rhetorical equivalent), as they were
never allowed to do in a history book.

To these voices coming from the obscure side of history are often
entrusted messages of peculiar political relevance. The horror of
civil war, for instance, is never expressed with like dramatic emphasis as when, in *3 Henry VI* (II.v.55–122) two anonymous characters (a father that has killed his son and a son that has killed his
father) are summoned to show the devastating effects of the conflict
through their private grief. Besides – and more importantly – the
presence of the king as a grieving witness, on the one hand connects
the anonymous characters and the imaginary incident to the core of
true and great history while, on the other, it shows the kind of
political and moral relevance that historical events assume when
seen from below.

Thus the mimesis of the greater, visible history crystallised in
history books is rendered more varied and complex by the light
which is shed on the obscure zone of invisible history, while, at
those moments during which the dramatist explores the unrecorded
possibilities of lost truths, a sense of the individuality, peculiarity
and uniqueness of the represented events emerges, so that the intuition of the particular and distinct is transmitted from the margins
to the core of historical events: what prevails at these times is, indeed,
not the *exemplum* but the *memorabile*, not history as model but history as singularity and exception.

In other words, the lighting of the obscure areas makes possible
the enactment of a number of individual, diverse and sometimes
disturbing perspectives and the introduction of different voices and
different social discourses, many of which are presented as highly
creditable and worthy of the audience's attention; these, in turn,
give a peculiar flavour of verisimilitude to the greater historical
events in which they take part. But, above all, to have rendered
visible and memorable the contradictions and the trivialities of the
experience of common people is an instance of historiographical
irreverence which can be made to coincide with a political option.

Remarking a common mistake, Peter Burke says that 'Villon and Rabelais were of course familiar with the little tradition of their day, the culture of the tavern and of the market-place; but they were also familiar with the great tradition, and they drew freely on it. They were not unsophisticated examples of popular culture but sophisticated mediators between the two traditions'.[16] We may, therefore, tend to interpret the imaginary portraits and speeches of the women, soldiers, sailors, apprentices, servants, vagrants, rebels and the like that appear in Shakespeare's plays as the ventriloquism of an intellectual, for we know that the literary reconstructions of popular culture are never a faithful reproduction of the real voice of the common people. It could be argued, in other words, that, not unlike what happens with the 'low' characters that people the world of Rabelais, with the parsons, the vagabonds, the prostitutes and the innkeepers that people the world of Cervantes or with the crowd of anonymous characters that are assigned the role of protagonists in Brecht's plays, Shakespeare's inhabitants of the obscure side of history speak to us with a voice and exhibit a frame of mind that can hardly be attributed to their real counterparts. There are, however, differences that should be considered: in the first place, unlike both Rabelais and Cervantes, Shakespeare wrote for the theatre, and unlike Brecht, he wrote for an audience which was also composed of illiterate common people; even allowing some bias in the following description by Gosson, the persons for whom Shakespeare wrote and by whose shillings he made his living were 'an assemblie of Tailers, Tinkers, Cordwayners, Saylers, olde Men, yong Men, Women, Boyes, Girles, and such like'.[17] Besides, he himself was a commoner and the actors of his company were commoners. He was, therefore, familiar and possibly in sympathy with the lower classes and their way of thinking, while he certainly had an ear for their way of speaking. In other words, the social 'residues' that appear in his plays must have come to him from observation and may, therefore, be considered as elements witnessing some sort of social reality. The representation of this reality, besides, served the purpose of filling in the gap which separated his audience from the historical worlds represented. Shakespeare may have felt that diversity is rendered more easily accessible when some sort of familiarity makes it intelligible and he may have entrusted to his historical imagination the task of translating, at least in part, difference into similarity. But above all, unlike what happens in the worlds of Cervantes or Rabelais, in the case of Shakespeare's histories the marginals are put in direct contact with the great events and persons that made the history of England. Shakespeare's marginals, in fact, do not live in a popular, secluded world of their own; they are not sheltered by the romantic niceties of a more or less sophisticated literary genre that has been created to *contain* them – in both senses of the word; on the contrary, they are introduced into an epic genre in which they do not belong and where they risk their identity and, occasionally, their life.

Puttenham, it seems, did not attend theatrical performances; if he had, the fact that 'such maner of men' and women might be committed to history and be thereafter kept as historical characters in the spectator's collective memory, that they should be allowed to converse with princes and contribute to shaping the opinions of a popular audience would certainly have appeared to him subversive (of literary decorum, if nothing else).[18] In the eyes of the audience, on the contrary, these elements were of vital importance: some of these inventions may have served as an interface between past and present; some of the non-historical voices and their statements may have been evoked precisely as familiar issues in the dialogue with otherness. But also, more radically, they constitute a scandal of historiography, for they are instruments to 'make greatness familiar' by exposing it, on the historical scaffold of a playhouse, to the censure of those who are fit 'onelie to be ruled'.

To the attempt to move closer to a few of these characters I will devote the last part of this book.

THE INSTRUMENTS OF POWER: LAW AND POLICE OFFICERS

2 Henry IV deploys nearly the whole hierarchy of law and police officers, from beadle, sergeant and constable to Justices of the peace to the Lord Chief Justice. However, the maintenance of order, the enforcement of laws and statutes and the defence of the country are entrusted to such people as Fang and Snare who tremble at the idea of what may happen to them if they try to arrest Sir John Falstaff (II.i.), to the beadles who have to suffer the whip of Doll's and Quickly's sharp tongues while they arrest them (V.iv.) and to the two senile JPs in Gloucestershire who are wholly unable to perform the military duties connected with their office and fail to perceive that the crime of corruption is being committed under their eyes

(III.ii, V.i, V.iii.,V.iv, V.v.). The whole picture speaks of inefficiency, total lack of professionalism and cowardice, although it seems to invite us to laughter rather than to blame. However, we may ask ourselves whether the police and law officers of Shakespeare's time deserved to be treated so contemptuously – albeit in the extenuating circumstances allowed by comedy – and, more generally, whether the administration of justice authorised such a negative picture.

Contemporary treatises and handbooks on the duties of the JPs are obviously engaged in stressing the prestige of the office and in affirming the efficiency of those who held it, their integrity and the attachment that these amateur administrators admittedly showed to the performance of their duties.[19] Certainly, the official and élite perception of the office of JP – whose status was that of a landed gentleman – depicted this pivotal figure, that was the principal link between the central government and local administration, as one of prestige and unfailing attachment to the ideal of order (although inefficiency in the inferior offices is seen as a possibility); William Lambarde, who was a JP in Kent from 1580 to 1601, is certainly our best witness to this view. A JP, he says, should have in the first place

> a knowledge to see and understand what things be good and to be followed, what other things be evil and to be eschewed; what persons are to be cherished, and what to be chastised. The second is an authority or power according to that knowledge to confirm the good in their well-doing and to reform the evil for their disobedience and excess. The last is a will or mind prompt and ready bent to do that which in knowledge we see, which by authority we may, and which of conscience and duty we ought to accomplish and perform.[20]

Lambarde further argues that the responsibility for administering justice should be felt both as a privilege and as a burden: 'It is a matter of no small weight, good neighbours and friends, for you and us to have the administration of country laws committed into our hands'.[21] The task is indeed heavy: 'How many Justices . . . may now suffise (without breaking their backes) to bear so manie, not Loades, but Stackes of Statutes, that haue . . . bene laide upon them?';[22] but, Lambarde acknowledges, it is rendered more arduous by the inefficiency of jurors and of the inferior offices, the Dogberries,

Dulls, Fangs and Snares whose behaviour must be closely watched;
he, in fact, mentions

> the slothfulness of jurors and inquests that will neither make
> presentment of constables or borsholders for not apprehending
> rogues as law hath enjoined them, nor yet discover the names of
> such foolish persons as under cloak of charity do give relief and
> alms to rogues when law forbiddeth them. . . .[23]

It would seem, therefore, that at least part of the picture we get
from *2 Henry IV* – that which concerns lower officers – is not unrealistic;[24] and although all descriptions stress the efficiency of the
system, certainly the need to set out the principles and rules of the
trade in so many handbooks may suggest that at least some officers
needed to be reminded of what was simply obvious, namely, their
duties of impartiality and rectitude. As Sharpe has remarked, in
spite of the unconditional praise which Lambarde bestows on the
English legal system, some of his statements 'have an apocalyptic
tinge, which, even if allowance is made for contemporary styles of
rhetoric, is suggestive of a genuine underlying anxiety on the part
of the speaker'.[25]
An even less monologic and monolithic picture of efficiency and
impartiality emerges when we read modern historians. Speaking
mainly of lower-rank officers, Emmison affirms that the number of
assaults they suffered and the number of successful 'self-rescues' of
prisoners performed, gives us 'a fairly reliable idea of the ineffec-
tiveness of the English police system';[26] Keith Wrightson says that
'even when local troops were raised and committed to the defence
of public order they could be far from reliable';[27] and Esther Moir
argues that the attraction of the office of JP, more than 'the wish to
rule' and 'the desire to serve the community', was to be seen in the
factions and quarrels, often violent, which divided the landed families and in the opportunity which the office of JP offered to either
settle or instigate disorder, to avenge supposed wrongs and ultimately to strengthen the position of the family and of its clients.[28] Moir
quotes an illustrious case: 'The guiding motive of Robert Devereux,
Earl of Essex', she says, 'was simply to build up his family territo-
rial interests'.[29] Nor is this only the view of a modern historian: in
1565, in fact, Nicholas Bacon complained that the office of JP was
often embraced because it afforded the possibility of 'overthrowing
an enemy or maintaining a friend, a servant, or tenant'.[30]

More recently, Keith Wrightson has advanced doubts about the very effectiveness of the whole system, in spite of appearances:

> The system of local administration and law enforcement built up over the centuries was an impressive monument to the institutional inventiveness of England's medieval kings, and through it the royal government was always potentially present in the localities. Yet, the effective presence of the government could be far less impressive, for it depended above all upon the diligence and cooperation of essentially amateur, unpaid local officers, ranging from the Justices of the Peace of the counties to the petty constables of townships and villages.[31]

If the official picture – as exemplified in Lambarde's view – was that of an efficient and equanimous system of surveillance and repression, the popular perception must have been different. People not only knew that there were chances to escape surveillance and avoid being caught (by corrupting an officer, by relying on the powerful system of relationships and connivances which obtained in small villages, on the protection of a powerful master and on the fact that constables disliked being the object of enmity and hatred on the part of the population); but also that, when they were caught, there was a good chance of being rescued following a successful assault on the officers;[32] and although many actually fell into the snares of justice and had to suffer its heavy hand, probably as many escaped punishment. Reluctance to enter legal procedures contributed to this: when the loss or injury was small, private prosecution was avoided because it was 'an expensive and troublesome matter' and 'might not seem worth the loss of time and money involved'.[33] Indeed, the actual rate of criminal prosecution under Elizabeth seems not to have been up to the standards of the laws and statutes issued by the political bodies and of the number of crimes actually committed; on the part of officers, the maintenance of good relationships among neighbours often prevailed over the necessity of enforcing the law: local police officers, Wrightson says, experienced 'the tension which could exist between the order demanded by the law and the problem of maintaining neighbourly relationships in the village'.[34] Recent research by social historians, in fact, has revealed a certain degree of 'potential disharmony within the village, and the high price at which such harmony as did exist was obtained'.[35]

However, it should not be overlooked that, apart from the efficiency of the system and the actual rate of criminal prosecution, the law had a symbolic value as ideology; that, as Sharpe put it, it was 'essential for curbing man's disorderly passions and thus preserving the body politic', that it represented 'an instrument of class oppression' and 'the one certain method of ensuring that the masses remained obedient'.[36] If, as is probable, this function was part of the people's way of perceiving the role of law and justice, it is arguable that the population might feel more menaced than protected by statutes which were 'an embodiment of the ideas and aspirations of the groups which ruled that population'.[37] Hostility towards law and police officers is more than mere conjecture and, as regards the county law authority – the most praised JP – there may have been on occasions a clear perception of his arrogance, nepotism and improbity; while constables, who had to surveil and punish petty offences, who closed unlicensed or 'superfluous' alehouses, who prosecuted those who did not go to church on Sundays and those who ate meat during Lent, collected taxes, and so on, were part of the community but little in harmony with it. As regards officers who tried actions against alehouses, Wrightson says that

> the most important aspect of their action was perhaps less instrumental than symbolic; for in attacking the major centres of popular sociability they were dissociating themselves from the customary behaviour of their neighbourhoods and aligning themselves with a definition of good order and social discipline derived from their social superiors, from the sermons of their ministers and the 'charges' and orders which they heard at quarter sessions.[38]

One of the ways to take revenge for the abuses which the common people suffered at the hands of those who were regarded as equal but were allowed some power to hurt, may indeed have been – apart from the physical resistance which led to self-rescue and from the passive reaction of noncooperation – that of ridiculing them or attacking their weaknesses: their incompetence, cowardice and corruptibility. *1* and *2 Henry IV* enact precisely this kind of popular 'revenge'.

Discussing the model of negotiation and compromise which he suggests as an alternative to the binarism of the subversion/containment description of power, Leinwand focuses on what he considers 'a mediatory, crossroads sort of figure in power relations', namely, the constable, who is engaged 'in negotiations which might confirm or contest the status quo'.[39] Leinwand examines the position of Dogberry, who has 'the unusual role of having to police, not one of his equals or neighbors, but the aristocracy'. The circumstances in which the constable acts in *Much Ado* are, Leinwand remarks, peculiar as concerns the containment effect which is expected from law-enforcing: 'Unable to control subversion within its own ranks, the aristocracy has to rely on a lowly constable to enforce its codes of conduct and its law.'[40] Within the play's social framework, 'both the aristocracy's dependence on the constable and the constable's investment in the codes of the aristocracy reveal the sometimes mutual, sometimes negotiable, and sometimes antagonistic relations between high and low'.[41] Leinwand's conclusion, on the basis of his discussion of the model of compromise as is shown in the 'constabulary effect' – both as regards Dogberry and as regards Elbow in *Measure for Measure* – is that 'Negotiation entails a process that acknowledges conflict and struggle; it can also engender authentic, if not revolutionary, change.'[42]

The *Henry IV* plays present a series of different situations which are not all ascribable to the model discussed by Leinwand; the circumstances in which in the two plays' officers are summoned to perform their duties deserve, therefore, to be discussed separately, for they highlight different circumstances and relationships which might be seen as different interpretations of the popular perception of law and police officers.

In *1 Henry IV* (II.iv), 'the sheriff and all the watch' (483) come to the Boar's Head. After the highway robbery, the sheriff says, 'A hue and cry / Hath follow'd certain men unto this house' (500–1); one of them is the 'gross fat man' (504) whom the prince is trying to protect, bidding him to 'hide . . . behind the arras' (493). Hal's reply is aimed not only to protect Falstaff ('The man I do assure you is not here', 505), but also – and more significantly – to point out that the person whom the sheriff is after is one of the prince's men ('For I myself at this time have employ'd him', 506). In other words, underlying the relationship of patronage that binds him to Falstaff, Hal is warning the sheriff of the powerful protection that the 'gross fat man' enjoys. The closing of Hal's reply, indeed, is more conclusive than a mere farewell ('And so let me entreat you leave the house', 511). Although the sheriff is aware of the warning (his reply opens with 'I will, my lord', 512) and maybe also of the fact that the prince is lying to him, he in turn takes the occasion to warn Hal of the seriousness of the crime committed by his protégé ('there are two gentlemen/ Have in this robbery lost three hundred marks', 512–13). In spite of the officer's good intentions, however, Falstaff is not going to be arrested: first thing next morning, in fact, Hal is going to pay back the money that Sir John has robbed ('O my sweet beef, I must still be good angel to thee – the money is paid back again', III.iii.176–7).

The second circumstance (Part Two, II.i) in which Falstaff risks being arrested is different from the point of view of the context of relationships which frame it. This time, the beadles who come to arrest Falstaff are acting on behalf of a popular suer (Quickly). The risk seems to be less real than the one Sir John ran in Part One, for Fang and Snare, the officers whom Quickly has summoned, are a prototype of inefficiency (even more inconclusive than Dogberry).

'Master' Fang, who makes show of great determination before Falstaff's arrival ('If I can close with him I care not for his thrust', 18; 'And I but fist him once, and a come but within my vice', 20–1),[43] is in reality no less scared than Snare, who is afraid that 'It may chance cost some of us our lives, for he will stab' (11–12). The two officers' reluctance to act when Falstaff, Bardolph and the Page appear is mirrored in Quickly's anxious suit: 'Do your offices, do your offices, Master Fang and Master Snare, do me, do me, do me your offices' (39–41); and when Falstaff shouts 'Keep them off, Bardolph!' (53), Fang and Snare, quite realistically, fear an assault resulting in the prisoner's escape. Consequently, Fang cries 'A rescue! A rescue!'[44] When the Chief Justice arrives (60), the two officers have been completely overcome by Quickly's hysterical cries and by the Page's insulting reply (55–9).

The arrival of the Chief Justice and his first authoritative words, 'What is the matter? Keep the peace here, ho!' (60), would seem to announce that the two officers' action and Quickly's suit are going to be backed by the higher authority; on the contrary, the text shows here an example of mediation which might seem to be in favour of the lower complainant but proves in the end to be in favour of Sir John. After chiding him for his bad behaviour and for abasing his rank ('Doth this become your place, your time, and business?', 64), and reminding him of his forsaken duty ('You should have been well on your way to York', 65) and after hearing the contents of Quickly's suit, the Chief Justice contrives a solution which appears to be in favour of the complainant but ends by favouring the maintenance of the *status quo* ('Pay her the debt you owe her, and unpay the villainy you have done with her; the one you may do with sterling money, and the other with current repentance', 117–20). The Chief Justice is performing a sort of *extempore* arbitration between the litigants,[45] following which Falstaff asks, and apparently obtains, deliverance from the two officers by claiming to be 'upon hasty employment in the king's affairs' (127). The arbitration, however, is not taken by the Chief Justice to its conclusion, and Sir John will succeed in not paying either of his debts.

The Hostess is here suffering from the same system of protections which she is going to invoke later on in her own favour when, to the beadles who have come to arrest Doll Tearsheet, she will say: 'O the Lord, that Sir John were come! He would make this a bloody day to somebody' (V.iv.12–13). In this last circumstance, Quickly and Doll are neither protected by a powerful person nor rescued by their friends. Prosecuted by two who are socially their equals but physically their betters, the two women may only use their tongues as a weapon. Quickly's comment ('O God, that right should thus overcome might!', 24) is maybe not a blunder, after all: in the play's world, right, indeed, only occasionally succeeds in overcoming might, and only when, as in the present case, officers are acting against their equals. (Quickly herself has experienced circumstances in which might has overcome right.)

It is not easy, however, to establish on whose behalf and for whose benefit both Hal and the Chief Justice are acting when contriving Falstaff's rescue. Sir John himself is a median element, both socially and dramatically. Inside the play's world he is socially a crossroads figure, and as a dramatic character presented to the community of theatregoers he 'belongs' to all the sectors of the playhouse and, therefore, enjoys the protection of high and low; mediatory and levelling as laughter is, he may be seen as an aberrant version of the elasticity of justice, of its capacity to punish but also to protect, to deal 'in terror but also in mercy'.[46] Thus, while his rescue might disturb those who enjoyed no protection, it might also console them by presenting the flexibility of justice.

Different in kind but equally critical of the system is the 'country comedy' connected with the two Gloucestershire JPs in Part Two.[47] Justice Shallow and his cousin Silence are certainly not the types who can embody the efficiency of the main executive instrument of Tudor legal power or legitimate the imposition of central authority throughout the country. Far from representing a monolithic model of surveillance and containment, they are by no means models of resistance either; simply, their senile and feeble-minded amateurism ridicules the 'admirable institution' of Tudor justice.[48] If Shallow's personal integrity is not questioned, his performance of duty is so devious as to allow crimes to be committed in his presence; and although his lies are presented as a feebleness of old age, they certainly do not warrant reliability.

It is thus a fact that, while treatises and handbooks strove in those years to present the Tudor organisation of justice as a perfect machinery for producing order and contriving obedience, the theatre could present its aberrations and deviations and, therefore, its (occasional) lack of stabilising potential.[49] Indeed, the vision of justice, the law, and crime presented in the *Henry IV* plays is neither moralistic nor stereotyped: it is a picture which, in degrading the office of law administration, also degrades the capacity of control of the central power. *Quis custodiet ipsos custodes*, given that the Chief Justice seems to be content with his symbolic role? Crime, we perceive, is committed, covered and even encouraged right in the palaces of power: indeed, justice has been lenient to Falstaff while he enjoyed the Prince's protection; but, as soon as protection is withdrawn, people – as happens to Quickly and Doll – may be arrested for no justifiable reason and can only hope to escape by being illegally rescued.

As regards the administration of justice, the *Henry IV* plays are critical in more than one sense: on the one hand, the sequence exposes a system of privilege through protection; on the other, it shows that the restraining force of justice is not unfailing, that its attitude of surveillance and repression is remarkably flexible and that its organisation is inefficient. Justice, in other words, is both partial and/or unreliable, and so, in any case, it is unjust.

It is not negligible that, before the occasionally gathered assembly of theatregoers, a company of actors contrived to dismantle the élite and role-conscious vision of a Lambarde in favour of a popular view. But, above all, the fact of imposing, albeit through laughter, a 'low' perception of justice in a public playhouse means showing the vitality of the popular voice and its consciousness of class distinctions.

WITCHCRAFT, PROPHECY AND SUBVERSION

Witchcraft is . . . a secret sense of power and superiority which can never really be tested or disproved.

                                                              Barbara Rosen

In the long title of *The Discouerie of Witchcraft*, Reginald Scot opens the list of idolatries and false beliefs with 'the lewde dealing of witches and witchmongers', 'the knaverie of conjurors, the impietie of inchanters' and 'the follie of soothsayers'.[50] Although witch-belief in England was little influenced by the violent fanaticism of the *Màlleus maleficarum*,[51] and although England produced, with Scot's book, what is maybe the only sceptical treatise on witchcraft of the age, those whose activities suggested the trespassing, in one way or other, of natural boundaries, were regarded with deep suspicion and legally prosecuted with determination. However, due to the limited influence of the Roman Catholic perspective, which on the continent tended to prosecute witchcraft mainly as heresy, England developed an independent view which regarded such phenomena as witchcraft and prophecy as obnoxious in a more practical way, in their effects as *maleficium* and as subversive activities more than as the outcome of a diabolical compact, as an activity which might cause maternal injury and breed disorder more than as religious heresy and as superstition.[52]

Indexed among dangerous, disorderly and destabilising behaviours – along with vagrancy, prostitution and to a certain extent mental disorder – witchcraft and soothsaying both evoked figures of sedition.[53] Prophets and witches alike were persons who practised a trade which exercised a great influence on the imagination of the common people and on whom, therefore, it was difficult to exercise control. Apart from their social deviousness and their moral uncleanness, which made them a social threat, able to spread moral and physical infection (even witchcraft, it was thought, could be transmitted), these unruly figures were associated with certain forms of political disorder, with the threat of rebellion and even with political radicalism;[54] witchcraft itself assumed the form of a political threat, for on certain occasions it was directed against the person of the sovereign;[55] and prophecy was intimately connected with political propaganda and with rebellion.

Since the reign of Henry IV statutes restricting the practice of prophecy were passed and severe punishments were devised for trespassers. Similar laws were enacted under Henry VIII (1541–42) and Edward VI (1549–50 and 1552–53). In 1562–63 and 1580–81, Elizabeth re-enacted a statute issued by Edward. Harry Rusche remarks that the opening words of Edward's statute acknowledge that 'the inherent political and propaganda value of prophecies was recognized and that the law was aimed at ending their usefulness as a potential means of arousing people to rebellion by instilling in them false hopes and confidence'. Rusche reports the first lines of the law, entitled *An Acte against fonde and fantasticall Prophesies*:

> Where now of late ... divers evill disposed parsons, mynding to stirr and move sedicion disobedience and rebellion, have of their perverse minds feyned ymagined invented published and practysed dyvers fantasticall and fonde Prophesyes, concerning the King's Majestie dyvers honorable parsons gentlemen and commons of this Realme, to the great disturbance and perill of the King's Majestie and this his Realme....[56]

Many characters in Shakespeare's histories are more or less explicitly connected with this complex set of beliefs and therefore embody the threat which came from it. Their social marginality may be 'natural' – as with women; ethnic – as with the Welsh; religious – as with priests; or it may be connected with the professional use of magical arts and the exploitation of magical powers as with sorcerers, prophets and necromancers.

Keith Thomas mentions a distinction which has been drawn between witchcraft and sorcery in a study of Azanda witchcraft, and says that it can to a certain point be applied to the English context:

> Witchcraft is an innate quality, an involuntary personal trait, deriving from a physiological peculiarity which can be discovered by autopsy.... Sorcery, on the other hand, is the deliberate employment of maleficent magic; it involves the use of a spell or technical aid and it can be performed by anyone who knows the correct formula.[57]

This distinction explains in part the fact that witches were almost invariably women, while sorcerers and necromancers (as well as prophets) were men, by introducing knowledge in the practice of sorcery and, conversely, by marking witchcraft with the 'natural' discrimination which derives from its innate quality.

It is not surprising, therefore, that many of the 'naturally' disorderly characters explicitly characterised as witches who appear in Shakespeare's plays are women: Margery Jourdain, Margaret of Anjou and Joan of Arc are creatures combining sensitivity and sexual disorder, namely the very qualities which associated witchcraft with prostitution.[58] Discussing mainly the first tetralogy and *King John*, Rackin examines those women to whom Shakespeare gives a chance to interfere with men's historical projects. Margaret of Anjou and Joan of Arc, Rackin argues, 'are typically defined as opponents and subverters of the historical and historiographic enterprise, in short, as antihistorians'. In the earlier histories, Rackin holds, the function of women is that of endangering the historical project which the male protagonists are trying to defend, and in *King John* they threaten 'to invalidate the patriarchal myths that Shakespeare found in his historiographic sources', implying that 'before the masculine voice of history can be accepted as valid it must come to terms with women and the subversive forces they represent'.[59] Interestingly, Rackin assimilates the treatment and function of women (the historical noblewomen who are nearest to the source of power) to that of other irregular or disorderly characters, whether or not they are historical: not unlike Jack Cade, Falstaff and 'low-life' characters in general (but Rackin also mentions the Duke of York in *2 Henry VI*), women represent the 'demonic other', for they directly attempt to oppose men's historical design. But, one may add, unlike their male counterparts, women – particularly in the first tetralogy – are witches, and some of them prophets; alternatively, they consort with witches, conjurors and corrupted priests and are guided by evil spirits; and one of them at least – Eleanor Cobham – is the cause of the ruin of the only honest political project of the sequence, that of good Duke Humphrey in *2 Henry VI*.

Telling the story of her own fall in *The Mirror for Magistrates*, Eleanor Cobham says that, 'not content to be a Duchesse great/ I longed sore to bear the name of Queene';[60] she therefore resorts to the 'art Magicke and wicked Sorcery' (90) of a group of professionals, among whom is a historical witch. Margery Jourdain or Jourdemain, named the witch of Eye, was a notorious witch, whose power in the practice of black magic the people highly esteemed: 'Both feendes and fayries her charmyng would obay,/ And dead corpsis from graue she could vprere –/ Suche an Inchauntresse, as that tyme had no peere' (96–8). She was burned in 1441, following an offence which seems to have been treason. Halle reports the story of Eleanor Cobham's accusation and conviction, connecting it with the 'divers secret attemptes' which were 'advaunced forward' against good Duke Humphrey of Gloucester:

At the same season, wer arrested as ayders and counsailers to the
sayde Duchesse, Thomas Southwel, prieste and chanon of saincte
Stephens in Westmynster, John Hum priest, Roger Bolyngbroke,
a conyng nycromancier, and Margerie Jourdayne, surnamed the
witche of Eye, to whose charge it was laied, that thei, at the
request of the duchesse, had deuised an image of waxe, repre-
sentyng the kynge, whiche by their sorcery, a litle and litle con-
sumed, entendyng therby in conclusion to waist, and destroy the
kynges person, and so to bryng hym to death.

He also reports that Eleanor was condemned to do penance in
three open places in the city of London and then 'adiudged to
perpetuall prisone in the Isle of Man'; that Southwell died in the
Tower before execution, Hume was pardoned, Roger Bolyngbroke
was 'drawen and quartered at Tyborne' and Margery Jourdain 'was
bernt in Smithfelde'.[61]

Significantly, Shakespeare takes up one of the episodes which
show the connections of witchcraft and sorcery with politics and
sedition, altering the sources slightly but in an interesting way which
strengthens the subversive potential of the plot. In the first place,
the function which is attributed to the woman is not that of an
ordinary witch: Margery Jourdain is allowed only a few lines in the
play (I.iv.23–6), but these are pivotal in the action. She takes part in
the conjuring of the spirit and then questions it, apparently with the
right formula, showing the technical competence which was attributed to sorcerers: Jourdain's is, in other words, not simply the
'natural' gift which was attributed to witches. But the most interesting variation is the addition of political prophecy to the activity of
the group. While Halle only mentions the casting of a wax image
of the king (a characteristic action by which witches contrived their
maleficium against a person), Shakespeare concentrates on prophecy,
thereby colouring the action with a clearer subversive tinge and, in
a way, enhancing the power of the witch by involving the use of
will and the exploitation of a conjuring competence.[62]

Shakespeare's policy in the depiction of Margery and of at least
two other of the women of the first tetralogy is therefore ambivalent: while, on the one hand, he enhances their power, on the other,
and by the same token, he renders them more disquieting and more
menacing. This attitude reveals the uneasiness which the representation of the domineering female must have produced at that time
and the contradictions it involved. The same contradictions in the

treatment of certain female characters are discussed by Leah Marcus. Marcus's localisation of certain traits of the character of Joan of Arc in relationship with the contradictory way in which Elizabeth was perceived by the people and by which she studied to present herself (mainly introducing elements of gender ambiguity in the spectacle of the 'woman on top' which procured so many anxieties to the contemporaries), highlights a number of details which, Marcus shows, Shakespeare did not find in his historiographical sources. The chapter which Marcus dedicates to Elizabeth is extremely suggestive and deeply disquieting, and its conclusion – very much in the line of duplicity – utterly convincing: while, Marcus says, a local reading of 1 Henry VI forces us to recognise that ' "Shakespeare" in this play is inextricable from something that looks suspiciously like political sacrilege', on the other hand, 'Even as the dramatist plants the specific details which could generate subversive thoughts about the queen, he makes them part of a structure so unstable that it refuses to settle into a single set of political implications.' Thus, the play's 'very unsettledness is its protection', for it creates 'such an open field for speculation that audience response is scattered as a prism scatters colors'.[63]

While Marcus discusses Joan at length, she only dedicates a few remarks to Margaret of Anjou, although sowing seeds which are worth developing. Marcus remarks that Parts 2 and 3 of Henry VI show that Margaret 'has succeeded Joan as the reigning "disorderly woman" upon Joan's death' and that the burning of Joan 'facilitates the emergence of another figure at least potentially "monstrous", whose bent is as yet unknown'.[64]

But why does Margaret appear so monstrous and so dangerous, especially in a context in which even greater cruelty is attributed to the male agonists? Certainly, the fact that she is a woman adds monstrosity to monstrosity; not so much, however, because it is not expected that a woman be as merciless and violent as a man; but mainly because she has gifts which her male partners lack; in particular, she has the rational capacity to produce historical predictions.[65]

The tetralogy reveals her power slowly and by subsequent steps. In 1 Henry VI she is simply a potentiality; in Part Two she is the sexually unclean domineering female steeped in the mud of dirty politics; in Part Three she is a warrior and an utterly cruel creature, and has completely freed herself even from the formal subjection to her husband: 'The Queen hath best success when you are absent' (II.ii.74) says Clifford to Henry to persuade him to leave the battlefield; besides, *she is now king*: 'You that are king, though he do wear the crown' (II.ii.90) says the future Edward IV. Witch and sexually unclean, prophetess and king is indeed an explosive mixture. But Margaret is also 'lunatic' (I.iii.254), and the discourse of madness cannot circulate like other kinds of discourse, for strange powers are attributed to it: that, in particular, of pronouncing a hidden truth and of announcing future events.[66]

But it is when she has lost her material power that Margaret becomes symbolically even more dangerous. In *Richard III* she finally succeeds in toppling men – noblemen, politicians, future kings and kings – for in the last act of the tetralogy she has finally crossed the boundaries of the natural. Richard calls her 'witch' (I.iii.164) and 'hag' (215), and speaks of her 'charms' (ibid.); Dorset calls her 'lunatic' (254), but she explicitly calls herself 'prophetess' (301). And it is indeed her prophetic gift which is seen as menacing, for prophecy is on the one hand intimately connected with sedition, and on the other it is seen as a gift of political far-sightedness, a gift which, in these circumstances, men seem not to possess.[67]

Margaret inspires the fear which is produced by the empirical prediction of political disasters. Unlike the 'drunken prophecies' which Richard claims to have spread in order to set Clarence against the king (I.i.33) – those 'prophecies and dreams' which Edward IV is said to hearken after (I.i.54) – Margaret's curse in I.ii. is an exact prediction of things to come. Linguistically, too, her curse has nothing of the inspired prophecy, whose characteristic is an ambiguity and obscurity which admits more than one interpretation;[68] Margaret names persons and circumstances, the way and the means of each one's end, mostly in the optative mood but also in the future tense ('The day will come . . .', 245). She is the oldest; she has seen the 'seeds and weak beginnings' (*2 Henry IV*, III.i.84–5) by which political far-sightedness may infer future developments. 'Margaret's curse', Garber says, 'becomes in effect the true plot of *Richard III*, placed in opposition to, and ultimately defeating, the "plots" and "prophecies" . . . Richard himself invents to gain the throne.' Moreover, Margaret's curse 'foresees what history has already told, and what the playwright – in his play – is about to tell'.[69] This is of course a general condition of prediction in a history play. 'Shakespeare', Garber remarks, 'uses the audience's own knowledge to validate his characters' predictions of the future', and thus 'the audience is invited, not to imagine, but to remember'.[70]

Margaret's knowledge comes from the fact that she has been

witness to the deeds of the previous generation; she knows the ways of politics and the effects of certain behaviour, and therefore she may anticipate events. Her deep contrariness, and the substance of her radical subversiveness, is in her being at the same time an antihistorian in the sense suggested by Rackin and a historiosopher, for she possesses a gift of political prognosis which she has acquired through her deep knowledge of the system of political events. But the optative form of her prognosis also shows her supernatural powers: prophetess as well as sorceress, she is not only able to predict through the observation of visible phenomena, but is also considered able to determine certain directions in the historical process. Moreover, as witches can do, she can transmit her gift to others.[71] She is, even in this sense, the disorderly woman, possessed at the same time with that 'secret sense of power and superiority'[72] which was the substance of witchcraft and with the self-assurance of her political sagacity. Subverter of history, she also practises a subversive form of historiography, that which substitutes a lay form of empirical prediction for the inspired prophecy of Biblical origin.

But any forecasting of events – and therefore also that form which came from the oracles of soothsayers – was considered eminently seditious by the regime. In prophecies, as well as in riddles, Mullaney argues, 'what we might dismiss as mere superstition constitutes in fact a rhetoric of rebellion'.[73] The prohibition on circulating prophecies was not suggested simply by the fact that the forecasting of events might either spread panic or determine false hopes and expectations; rather, it was thought that prophecies might influence political events and in particular that they might encourage sedition. Rupert Taylor says that 'In some cases prophecies helped make history' and that they were 'potent factors in English political affairs'. It seems that the Welsh were particularly fond of prophecies: 'They not only quoted them, but they believed them.'[74] On a few occasions, Shakespeare emphasises Welsh credulity, stressing the relationship of omens and forecasts with political events. In *Richard II*, a Welsh Captain alleges that 'lean look'd prophets whisper fearful change' (II.iv.11) and the appearance of certain signs which 'forerun the death or fall of kings' (15) to account for the withdrawal of his army.[75]

But it is Owen Glendower who best embodies this trait of Welsh popular culture. In *1 Henry IV*, Glendower insistently mentions the portents which he believes to have marked his birth, boasting of his capacity to summon spirits and devils, and is impatiently checked by the sceptical and pragmatic Hotspur. Mocking Glendower's credulity, Hotspur complains with Mortimer: 'He held me last night at least nine hours/ In reckoning up the several devils' names' (III.i.150–1). In the same circumstance, Hotspur mentions, as something which testifies to Glendower's superstition that he does not share, the Moldwarp prophecy:

> sometime he angers me
> With telling me of the moldwarp and the ant,
> Of the dreamer Merlin and his prophecies,
> And of a dragon and a finless fish,
> A clip-wing'd griffin and a moulten raven,
> A couching lion and a ramping cat,
> And such a deal of skimble-skamble stuff
> As puts me from my faith.
>
> (142–9)

That of the Moldwarp is one of Merlin's prophecies which were used to influence public opinion to the advantage of a political faction; in this case, in particular, to justify rebellion. Percy, Glendower and Mortimer, Rupert Taylor says, 'doubtless did not believe that Fate and Merlin had decreed the tripartite Convention among them, but they . . . were glad to make the best of what argument and justification the prophecy afforded them'.[76]

Holinshed says that the division of the country in the tripartite convention

> was doone (as some have said) through a foolish credit giuen to a vaine prophesie, as though king Henrie was the moldwarpe, curssed of Gods owne mouth, and they three were the dragon, the lion, and the woolfe, which should diuide this realme betweene them. Such is the deuiation (saith Hall) and not diuination of those blind and fantasticall dreames of the Welsh prophesiers.[77]

In Shakespeare's text, which is consonant with the comment produced by Holinshed (and Halle), the Moldwarp prophecy is divested of its political weight and of its capacity to justify and encourage rebellion, and is presented merely as an instance of (Welsh) credulity.[78] By introducing the difference in attitude which separates Hotspur and Glendower, Shakespeare is presenting a conflict between rationality and superstition and highlighting the distance between 'vain' prophecy and political prognosis; the latter, however, engages the spectators' skill rather than Hotspur's, for the present division, which simply disturbs him, allows the audience to prognosticate the rebels' incohesion at Shrewsbury and, ultimately, their defeat. Thus, that of prognosis becomes one of the main tasks of the spectators as well. The elements for a dramatic forecast that the play provides by revealing the incipient dissolution of the friendship between Hotspur and Glendower are of the type which comes from the close reading of the 'seeds and weak beginnings' of men's behaviour. This kind of forecast, made by the audience and based on observation, is going to prove true; while Glendower's 'vain' prophecy of the Moldwarp is shortly going to be falsified.

It has been remarked that, by prohibiting the practice of soothsaying, the Tudor regime was contriving a shift in the control of the forecast of future events from the hands of the church to those of the temporal power; and that this transference also marks a transformation of the historical and political efficacy of prophecy, for it signals the transition from providential to empirical historiography.[79] In spite of prohibition, however, popular forms of prophecy were still alive under Elizabeth, and were still held to deserve consideration either as a dangerous social practice or as propaganda which could be exploited to further some political project.[80]

Peter of Pomfret in *King John* is the kind of prophet who may exercise a remarkable influence on the people. The Bastard is conscious of his dangerousness, for he has been witness to the fact that Peter was followed by a multitude, arousing in them fantasies and 'idle dreams', and validating rumours:

> But as I travaill'd hither through the land
> I find the people strangely fantasied;
> Possess'd with rumors, full of idle dreams,
> Not knowing what they fear, but full of fear.
> And here's a prophet, that I brought with me
> From forth the streets of Pomfret, whom I found
> With many hundreds treading on his heels;
> To whom he sung, in rude harsh-sounding rhymes,
> That, ere the next Ascension-day at noon,
> Your highness should deliver up your crown.
>   (IV.ii.143–52)

Peter is only allowed one line to explain why he spread the ominous forecast of John's resignation: 'Foreknowing that the truth

will fall out so' (154) is his answer; John clearly shows his fear of
a prediction which may turn into political propaganda against him
and orders that Peter be imprisoned and executed on the very day
in which his prophecy is supposed to have effect. (It will fall out
that Peter's forecast proves true, but 'in a certain sense', as most
prophecies do.)

But the kind of popular prophecy which in the case of Peter may
turn against the king's power, is exploited in *King John* to the advantage of another political faction. This Machiavellic perspective is
in fact affirmed by the papal legate. Apart from the attempt to determine future events by exploiting his power of excommunication,
Pandulph utters to the Dauphin the prognosis of what is going to
happen in the lower strata of the population if, or rather when, the
king will have Arthur murdered. Pandulph anticipates that the event
is going to encourage popular interpretations of natural phenomena
as 'plainly denouncing vengeance upon John' (III.iii.159), to the
advantage of the Dauphin's interests.[81]

The new empirical political prognosis has learned to make the
best of popular credulity and ancient superstition; and it is not
without meaning that the humiliation of the inspired prophecy of
Biblical origin be entrusted to the voice of a Roman Catholic priest.

DISSENTING VOICES: MESSENGERS, MURDERERS, JAILERS AND A SCRIVENER

In that 'unflinching account of class pride and class resistance' that
is the *Henry VI* sequence,[82] even messengers – those characteristically
neutral emissaries of tidings – may pronounce memorable speeches.
Indeed, those of the first tetralogy are, among the histories, the
plays where class polarity is more explicitly marked. In the very
first scene of the tetralogy, the exposition of the main theme of the
sequence – the violent strifes which divide the nobles and will ruin
the country – is entrusted to a messenger. Interrupting the funeral
of Henry V, he dares announce, 'before dead Henry's corse' (I.i.62)
the news of 'loss, of slaughter and discomfiture' (59) in France, and
attributes the disaster not only to 'want of men and money' (69) but
also to the fact that the English nobles 'maintain several factions'
(71); instead of fighting, he tells them, 'You are disputing of your
generals' (73) and quarrelling about the way in which money can

be saved. His speech closes with an exhortation which verges on invective:

> Awake, awake, English nobility,
> Let not sloth dim your honours, new begot.
> Cropped are your flower-de-luces in your arms:
> Of England's coat one half is cut away.
>
> (78–81)

One might imagine that this Messenger and the other two who will follow announcing more mischances were among those who, seven years before, had fought with Henry at Agincourt and who, therefore, thought that they had contributed to a lasting conquest of France. But, whatever the source of their passion, they seem to have acquired a sharper consciousness of the common good than those who rule them, and to have taken upon themselves heavier responsibilities than their function entails, and even a certain power: not only the obvious power which derives from the possession of information but, for once at least, the power to add to the transmission of information the capacity to express an independent view, to judge and to chide openly their betters. Unlike Harrison's and Smith's commoners, these have got both voice and authority, and their voice is one of dissent.

They are not the only ones. Hired murderers prove almost invariably to be less cruel than the king or noble who employs them: 'I am best pleased to be from such a deed', says one of the Executioners when, in *King John*, Hubert makes preparations to kill Arthur (IV.i.85); the murderers who have been hired by Suffolk to kill 'good Duke Humphrey' of Gloucester in *2 Henry VI* regret the crime they have committed: 'O, that it were to do! What have we done? Didst ever hear a man so penitent?' (III.i.3–4).

But the most striking contrast between the brutality of power and the compassion of hired murderers is in *Richard III*. The planning and execution of Clarence's murder is rather elaborate. The two Murderers appear for the first time at the end of I.iii. They are addressed by Richard as 'my hardy, stout, resolved mates' (340),[83] and they seem to feel obliged to show that they deserve his praise: they are people, they answer, who talk little and act with determination. To Richard, who asks them to 'be sudden in the execution' (346), for Clarence may move them to pity, the 2nd Murderer answers:

Tut, tut, my lord: we will not stand to prate.
Talkers are no good doers; be assur'd
We go to use our hands, and not our tongues.
                                                    (350–2)

They will use their tongues, instead, and the 2nd Murderer is not
going to use his hands at all. The dialogue between the two men,
which takes place in the following scene, shows that the man is
taken by 'a kind of remorse' (I.iv.105); that he is striving to overcome the pangs of conscience ('I hope this passionate humour of
mine will change', 113–14); that he resumes courage only thinking
of the recompense ('Zounds, he dies! I had forgot the reward', 120);
that his overelaborate speech, where he pretends to disparage conscience, is in reality praise (''Tis a blushing, shamefaced spirit, that
mutinies in a man's bosom. It fills a man full of obstacles; it made
me once restore a purse of gold that by chance I found', 131–4);
nay, his speech is so convincing that it makes his fellow-murderer
hesitate too ('Zounds, 'tis even now at my elbow, persuading me
not to kill the Duke', 139–40). Clarence is aware that even the stouter
of the two (the 1st Murderer) is at odds with his conscience: 'Thy
voice is thunder, but thy looks are humble' (158), to which the man
answers declaring that his self is divided, that the worst part has
been sold to the king, but the best remains his: 'My voice is now the
King's, my looks mine own' (159). Further, they try to free their
conscience by throwing at Clarence the catalogue of his guilts (190–
9), and in the end the 2nd Murderer refrains from striking Clarence
and even warns him (too late) when the stroke of his companion is
falling on him ('Look behind you, my lord!', 258). The 1st Murderer
has resumed courage and committed the murder, but conscience
prompts his more compassionate companion to renounce his recompense ('Take thou the fee, and tell him what I say,/ For I repent me
that the Duke is slain', 267–8).[84]
     Later on in the play appears the name of Tyrrel, one whom gold
would 'tempt . . . to anything' (IV.ii.39). When Tyrrel appears in the
presence of Richard, the usual arguments are deployed on both
sides: by the murder, the sovereign would be freed from a mortal
enemy who is a menace to his rest, and the person who is going to
dispatch this enemy will gain his love and preference; on the part
of the prospective murderer, we hear the assurance that the murder
will be dispatched immediately. Only, this time, two children must
be killed ('those bastards in the Tower', 74). In the presence of

Richard, Tyrrel shows no scruple before the horror of the task; but he will delegate the murder to Dighton and Forrest ('two flesh'd villains, bloody dogs', IV.iii.6) who, in turn, 'Melted with tenderness and mild compassion,/ Wept like two children in their death's sad story' (7–8).

By buying the subjects' need, power has unexpectedly awakened their conscience. Most of the subjects' moral principles, indeed, cannot be bought, although their hands are ready to act at the sovereign's service in exchange for money. A fine example of this kind of deal is in the Scrivener's soliloquy in III.iv.

A scrivener's trade is characteristically one of silent words, his task the exact reproduction of graphic symbols, his pride the neatness and harmony of their lettering. His function, however, is not merely esthetic: by setting a text in a formal legal style, he gives it a dignity which is not simply exterior, validates its contents, makes them official and operative. Albeit in a peculiar way, therefore, he is responsible for the legitimation of the private original, for his handiwork is instrumental to the performance of the official acts of the regime.

In *Richard III* (III.vi) we have an opportunity to hear the considerations of the Scrivener who has just finished setting in a formal hand the accusation of Lord Hastings, an *a posteriori* justification, since Hastings has already been executed without trial:

> Here is the indictment of the good Lord Hastings,
> Which in a set hand fairly is engross'd,
> That it may be today read o'er in Paul's.
> And mark how well the sequel hangs together:
> Eleven hours I have spent to write it over,
> For yesternight by Catesby was it sent me;
> The precedent was full as long a-doing
> And yet within these five hours Hastings liv'd,
> Untainted, unexamin'd, free, at liberty.
> Here's a good world the while! Who is so gross
> That cannot see this palpable device?
> Yet who's so bold but says he sees it not?
> Bad is the world, and all will come to naught
> When such ill-dealing must be seen in thought.
> (III.vi.1–14)

Seemingly, all the Scrivener tells us is that the indictment was written and brought to him to be copied in a formal style before

Hastings was accused, and that, although he has detected the 'palpable device', he cannot openly denounce the ill-doing he has become aware of. But the speech also works at other levels, whose main points emerge from a consideration of the notion of *sequence* – the sequence of interrelated events which concern the composition and copying of the document (its translation into a formal *sequel* of words), that of the accusation and execution of Hastings and, finally, the sequence of scenes in which the speech is inserted. But let us see in greater detail how these topics emerge from the speech.

Lines 1–3 present the finished document and declare the immediate purpose for which it was set formally ('That it may be today read o'er in Paul's'); line 4 exhibits the neatness of the written chain of words ('and mark how well the sequel hangs together'), underlying its visual aspect. But the word *sequel*, apart from referring to the spatial arrangement of the text, also introduces the idea of time, which is specified in the following lines as 'the time which the copying of the document took' ('Eleven hours I have spent to write it over'); from now on, two time-sequences are confronted: in the first place, that of the writing of the original which, the Scrivener estimates, must have taken as many hours as the copy to be composed ('The precedent was full as long a-doing') plus the copying of the same in formal style (which took the last eleven hours); and in the second place that of the events which led to Hastings' apprehension and execution. These, he considers, must have developed independently from, and occupied a time much shorter than, the chain of actions which led to the completion of the official document which legitimised them; 'for', he ponders recollecting the time-sequence, 'yesternight by Catesby was it sent me' and 'within these five hours' (until five hours ago) Hastings lived, unaware of the indictment. This simply means that Hastings's death was decreed many hours before he had an opportunity to defend himself, even, that this opportunity was denied to him: a 'palpable device' indeed, to which the Scrivener can only answer with a mute reaction ('such ill-doing must be seen in thought'). But the Scrivener is also saying that, although he is responsible for the spatial *sequel* (the chain of words which compose the official text), he is not for the temporal *sequence*, the chain of events which led to Hastings' execution: the trick he has detected (the fact that the *sequel* was composed before the *sequence* of the accusation and condemnation began) is precisely what excludes his responsibility in the formal validation of the events. Moreover, this brief scene is part of a sequence (scenes v to

vii) where the *open expression of consensus* emerges as a necessary condition for the furthering of Richard's project of seizing power and where, on the contrary, we are shown how dissension may be manifested through silence.

In scene v, following the murder of Hastings, Richard manifests his need for an explicit approval of his actions on the part of the citizens. The Mayor is asked to speak to them, 't'avoid the censures of the carping world' (67), and Buckingham is sent after him to 'infer the bastardy of Edward's children' (74) and to add the suggestion that Edward himself was a bastard. When, meeting Buckingham again in scene vii (immediately after the Scrivener's soliloquy), Richard asks him impatiently: 'How now, how now? What say the citizens?' (1), Buckingham answers that 'The citizens are mum, say not a word' (3); he adds that they refused to cry ' "God save Richard, England's royal King!" ' (22), and further elaborates on the possible meaning of their silence:

> they spake not a word,
> But like dumb statues or breathing stones
> Star'd each on other, and look'd deadly pale.
> Which when I saw, I reprehended them,
> And ask'd the Mayor what meant this wilful silence.
> His answer was, the people were not us'd
> To be spoke to but by the Recorder.
>
> (24–30)

But Richard knows well what the citizens' response means: 'What, tongueless blocks were they? Would they not speak?' (42); that their mute response is not lack of reaction, but the only weapon they can use to manifest the denial of consensus. By their silent speech, the citizens have launched a challenge which perturbs the norms established by the ruling power and which might become the source of an alternative social norm; in short, by refusing to speak, they have communicated to Richard, who thought that he possessed their production of discourse, that this is still their prerogative.

In other words, the sequence enacts two kinds of mute reaction taking place simultaneously (technically, the Scrivener's soliloquy is a device to allow the episode with the citizens to 'take place' offstage); silence, however, has a contrary meaning in the two cases (by their mute reaction the citizens express their dissent, while the Scrivener hides his), although both episodes alike show that power attempts to own the subjects' language and that it strives to impose both the production of discourse and its suppression: while the citizens are being manipulated into speech to express consensus, the Scrivener's dissent is being controlled through the implicit injunction of silence – even a permanent abrogation of speech.[85]

Apart from controlling the subjects' use of language, power masters different kinds of discourse and may communicate through different channels – the oral address of public oratorial discourse as well as the written discourse of official documents – on which it imposes different kinds of response according to the different circumstances of enunciation and the different positions and statuses of the receivers. The citizens may be manipulated by one who can 'play the orator' (III.v.94) and asked to speak in favour of the tyrant because they can only surmise Richard's perfidy and double dealings; the Scrivener is obliged to silence because he has at his disposal the palpable witness of a *written document* which, as an element of the plot, is also a step in the sequence of actions; he may, therefore, reconstruct Richard's *treason* simply by reasoning on the circumstances of the document's *tradition* (one is tempted to evoke the common root, *tradere*, of both *tradition* and *treason*).

In other words, within a social framework in which the linguistic competence is distributed unequally, the Scrivener has an ambiguous position: he is both privileged (his trade makes him familiar with words) and hindered (although he can detect 'errors', he is not entitled to amend them: he cannot assume the function of editor of the written text); more able than the others to reconstruct meanings, he is not supposed to interfere with those meanings; although he has direct access to the discourse of power, he is bound to limit his action to recognising and reproducing only graphic symbols; by trade, his linguistic competence is voiceless, for he is used to disjoining sight from voice: his sight, indeed, has been developed over the other senses, hence, he is trained in *seeing in thought*; finally, although he is by contract excluded from the construction of meaning, his finished work ratifies that meaning: power has taken him into its service because he masters a valuable technique: writing is one with him, the writing instrument an extension of his body, and hence his body belongs to power. His competence allows him to detect errors (formal mistakes as well as 'ill-dealings' and 'palpable devices'), but his task does not imply emendation – on the contrary, his servile situation binds him to the reproduction of the errors of the regime: thus, although he may distinguish the spatial *sequel* of written symbols from the temporal *sequence* of actions, he cannot altogether disjoin his responsibility from that of Hastings's murderers. There is, however, a capital discrepancy which involves the whole situation and finally overturns it: the silence by which the Scrivener is hiding his dissent is patently broken in order that treason may be communicated in the dramatic form of the monologue. By negating silence and subtracting from power control over the subject's discourse-production, the dramatic form interferes with Richard's project of getting the crown by consensus: by his direct address to the spectators and by employing the wisdom of his trade, which allows him to decipher texts and detect errors, the Scrivener is in fact providing the audience with new evidence for Richard's guilt, thus establishing a network of complicity and dissent which extends indefinitely beyond the spatial and temporal confines of the staged events.

A VAGRANT IS WHIPPED

In his *A dyaloge . . . of the ueneration & worshyp of ymages*, Sir Thomas More recounts the episode of a false miracle which, he says, took place 'in kynge Edwardes dayes the fourth'.[86] The story was taken over by Grafton[87] and later by Foxe in the second edition of his *Actes and Monuments*.[88] The aim of More's narrative is mainly to provide an example of what 'some preste to bring up a pylgrymage in hys paryshe may deuise'; as rehearsed by Grafton and Foxe, the episode is obviously aimed to discredit Catholic miracles; they rightly anticipate the episode to the time of Henry VI (1446), for More attributed the discovery of the fraud to Duke Humphrey of Gloucester, stressing the praise of his wisdom in detecting the forgery. Here is how Foxe introduces the story:

I thought here good amongst many other his godly doings, to recite one example, reported as well by the penne of syr Thomas More, as also by M. William Tindall . . . , to the intent to see and note, not only the crafty working of false miracles in the clergy, but also that the prudent discretion of this high and mighty prince, the foresaid Duke Humfrey, may giue us the better to understand what man he was.[89]

In *2 Henry VI* (II.i), returning to the false miracle of St Albans, Shakespeare modifies the focus of interest and introduces details which underscore an aspect which the sources hardly consider: Saunder Simpcox (who is for the first time given a name) and his wife are not presented as an instrument of 'the crafty working of false miracles in the clergy', neither are they simply forgers; they are, technically, two masterless poor belonging to the category of able-bodied vagrants, and therefore representing that menace of which the English ruling class was terrified, 'linking them with a vast range of evils which they thought posed a grave threat to the *status quo*.'[90] More specifically, according to Harrison's classification, they are 'Palliards' (namely, 'male and female beggars traveling in pairs') and Simpcox is a 'sham blind' (there were also 'sham deaf-mutes', called 'dummerers') and also pretends to be lame.[91]

There are relevant modifications in Shakespeare's account of the episode: in the first place, the punishment suggested for Simpcox by the Lord Protector is whipping rather than the stocks; second, although he claims to have recovered his sight, Simpcox still feigns the physical impediment of lameness; third, Simpcox is punished not so much for feigning a miracle as for simulating not being able-bodied; besides, the fact of feigning disability is explained by his wife as being dictated by need; finally, the Lord Protector orders that the couple be taken to their place of origin. These modifications deserve to be discussed for, while characterising Simpcox and wife as vagrants, they cast an unconventional light on the problem of vagrancy. I will argue that these all aim at characterising Simpcox and his wife as a couple of vagrants and that, at the same time, the picture Shakespeare gives of them is aimed at disproving the myth of the vagrants' dangerousness.

After exposing the first of Simpcox's forgeries – the sudden recovery of sight – Gloucester says: 'My masters of Saint Albans, have you not/ A beadle in your town, and things call'd whips?' (II.i.134–5); the Protector's request is promptly answered, and a beadle with whips is summoned. On the kind of corporal punishment that a vagrant must have suffered under Henry VI or Edward IV, the sources are more accurate than Shakespeare, for only after 1531 was the punishment of the stocks replaced by whipping. It is clear, however, that Shakespeare's shift from the stocks to the whip cannot be imputed to ignorance or inaccuracy, for the sources of the false miracle unanimously spoke of the stocks; rather, the change must have been intentional: by updating the scenario, in fact, it makes it more openly allusive of the contemporary vagrancy legislation and therefore more immediately comprehensible to the audience.[92]

But Shakespeare adds feigned lameness to feigned blindness, a detail which reveals what is perhaps the most significant difference between the sources and the play. In the sources, in fact, the beggar (who is not given a name) appears as an instrument of corrupted priests (indeed, his personal motivations for feigning the miracle are difficult to grasp), while Shakespeare focuses on Simpcox and his wife and makes their forgery spring from need ('Alas! sir,' says Simpcox's wife, 'we did it for pure need', 150). This detail is best explained by bearing in mind the basic distinction which was made in all statutes concerning poverty and vagrancy between the 'deserving poor' and the 'idle poor'.

Harrison divides the poor into three categories, which are essentially those contemplated in all statutes and regulations and reported in all the rogue pamphlets, and which affected for centuries the people's perception of poverty: first, there were the 'poor by impotency', namely, 'the fatherless child, the aged, blind, and lame, and the diseased person that is judged to be incurable'; second, there were the 'poor by casualty', namely, 'the wounded soldier, the decayed householder, and the sick person visited with grievous and painful diseases'; third, there were the 'thriftless poor', namely, 'the rioter', 'the vagabond', 'the rogue and strumpet'.[93] Legislation established that the only category of unequivocally deserving poor was the first, who were either helped financially by the local communities or given begging licences; the second category might also include those who were both able and willing to work but could find none, a group which was considered less unequivocally deserving. Simpcox and wife obviously belong to the third category, 'the one which agitated contemporaries most', namely, in contemporary perception, 'those who were fit and able enough to work, but who wilfully refused to do so'; they belonged, in particular, to that category of poor who 'achieved their most pernicious form in the vagrant'.[94] For these people, to demonstrate that they were not able-bodied was a necessity if they did not want to suffer the rigours of the law: 'The able-bodied poor', Paul Slack says, 'fell traditionally among the idle: if they could not support themselves it was their own fault.'[95] It is clear, therefore, that, by feigning disability, Simpcox was trying not only to shun the punishments which were designed for the third category of poor, but also to enjoy the relief which was given to the first. This is why, after simulating the recovery of his sight (maybe in the hope to get some advantage by impressing the saintly king), in Shakespeare's version he still pretends to be lame: if he had been recognised physically healthy he would immediately have been punished as idle poor and vagrant (which is exactly what happens).[96] Simpcox, in Shakespeare's version of the story, is whipped not so much for feigning a miracle (although what impresses the king seems to be mainly this), but for simulating to be unfit for work. Technically, Simpcox is masterless and idle; in addition, he is rootless: he and his wife are among the 12.9 per cent of wandering couples who had no fixed abode,[97] frequently changed residence and migrated from one place to the other until they were discovered and apprehended.[98] The last of the modifications which seem to me significant is precisely the fact that Shakespeare mentions the Lord Protector's order that the two vagrants be taken to their place of origin:

> Let them be whipped through every market-town
> Till they come to Berwick, from whence they came.
>
> (151–2)

Since 1531, in fact, legislation established that vagrants 'were now to be whipped, not stocked, and then returned to the place where they were born or where they last lived for at least three years'.[99] To these was often added the infliction of yet another form of corporal punishment: if the rogue is convicted as vagabond, Harrison says, 'he is then immediately adjudged to be grievously whipped and burned through the gristle of the right ear with an hot iron of the compass of an inch about'[100] (a punishment which 'good Duke Humphrey' does not inflict on the couple). The law was harsh towards the vagrant. Indeed, as Paul Slack says, vagrancy legislation 'helped to create the conditions it was directed against. It was self-confirming. From this perspective, it makes little sense to ask whether vagrants were innocents or criminals, for they had no choice. The circumstances of life on the road prevented them being the first; the law and the constable made them the second.'[101]

The point I should like to make is that, although Saunder Simpcox and his wife are presented as 'professional beggars' of the vagrant kind, nothing in Shakespeare's text implies that they are criminals.[102] The impression we get from their brief appearance on the stage of history places them far from the rogue stereotype divulged by pamphlet literature. They are nearer to the type that historians now recognise to have constituted the predominant reality of the vagrant problem: 'rather than the organized bands of the pamphlets, most vagrants travelled in ones or twos, or at most in a family group'.[103] In depicting them, Shakespeare dismantles the myth of the 'fraternity of vagabonds', that nightmare of the Elizabethan and Jacobean élite which is now recognised to have been largely a fiction; his two vagrants rather resemble those who now appear to historians to have been 'far less threatening than their counterparts in the popular literature of the period'; not 'the professional rogues legislated against in parliament' but the 'unremarkable representatives of the lower, hence more vulnerable, strata of society'.[104]

The company of actors must have felt very near to, and probably in sympathy with, the condition of vagrants, for they were permanently in peril of falling into that category. The 1572 statute, in fact, established that 'common players in interludes and minstrels' were for the law vagabonds, unless patronised by the peerage or the Queen; and that the same applied to 'fencers, bearwards, jugglers and magicians'.[105] What made the difference between belonging to a licensed company and being considered vagabonds, largely depended on the delicate balance of political matters and mutual power relationships, apart, obviously, from the sovereign's very interest in the ritual of courtly playing.

A PORTRAIT OF THREE COMMONERS AS SOLDIERS

And did I not bid you remember that for each protagonist that once stepped on to the stage of so-called historical events, there were thousands, millions, who never entered the theatre – who never knew that the show was running – who got on with the donkey-work of coping with reality?

Graham Swift, *Waterland*

Friday, 25 October 1415. A heavy rain has been falling the whole night on the village of Maisoncelles and on the surrounding countryside. Near the break of day – the rain is still falling and it is bitter cold – the common soldiers John Bates, Alexander Court and Michael Williams are pacing what has become for one night the camp of the English army. They have had little or no sleep, partly because of the wet ground and partly owing to the fear of the imminent battle. They have been far from home and from their homes for a long time and in a few hours they will be engaged in an unequal battle against an enemy, the French, whom they know to be infinitely more numerous than the English. In a few hours, their names and their identities will be dispersed; and by the end of the day they will be reckoned as numbers: the number of those who survived or, more probably, the number of those who died; if they die, they will be counted among those who have no name.[106] It is at this crucial moment in their lives that Shakespeare captures them and gives them an identity that is destined to be perceived and preserved as historical in the minds of the spectators. To hearten each other, our three men have engaged in a conversation – they talk in whispers, though, for the king has ordered absolute silence:[107]

> From camp to camp through the foul womb of night
> The hum of either army stilly sounds,
> That the fix'd sentinels almost receive
> The secret whispers of each other's watch:
> Fire answers fire, and through their paly flames
> Each battle sees the other's umber'd face;
> Steed threatens steed, in high and boastful neighs
> Piercing the night's dull ear; and from the tents
> The armourers, accomplishing the knights,
> With busy hammers closing rivets up,
> Give dreadful note of preparation.
>   (*Henry V*, IV.0.4–14)

We may try to answer a few simple questions in order to get a more precise feeling of that circumstance, of the events that had led to it and of what was bound to follow.

Who are these three soldiers? What did they leave at home; on what compulsion – external or personal – did they join the French campaign; what has their daily pay been during the expedition; what are their material preoccupations; what is their present physical and mental state; what strains have they suffered in the last two months; and what ordeal are they to face on the day we meet them? And finally, what kind of life awaits them when the campaign is over, in case they survive?

All these questions seem improper, since John Bates, Alexander Court and Michael Williams are not historical characters. The sources of the battle of Agincourt have troubled to record a few names of common soldiers or of men who occupied low positions in the English army – one Roger Hunt, archer, who was slain by a French gun, one William Wolf, squire to the Earl of Arundel, who 'put on a little show' of killing French prisoners 'to please Henry' and who is also reported to have kept one important prisoner, the Seneschal of France, instead of delivering him to Henry for ransom, and to have surrendered the prisoner only on his way back home, at Calais;[108] but none of Shakespeare's soldiers is mentioned by name in any record.[109] Technically, they are *invented* characters: why, then, should we care about them and not be content with the limited life that the play allows them? We should, indeed, because the fact that they are not mentioned in the historical sources does not mean that they never existed. On the contrary, we may affirm with assurance that Court, Bates and Williams spent the night of 24 October in or around the village of Maisoncelles in Normandy, that the following day they were deployed in battle in the plain near Agincourt, armed and ready to fight and that they actually fought against the French, presumably as archers, on 25 October, 1415. For thousands who were like them existed in that circumstance, and there are things that may be known of them and that are worthy to be retrieved and discussed.

Obviously, the reason why these three characters are so appealing as to drive one to reconstruct their stories is that Shakespeare chose to represent them in what is perhaps the most intense and problematical moment in the whole play on King Henry V. And we want to know, or wish to figure, why he represented them; why he paused to show the eve of Agincourt through their words and their attitude during their encounter with the disguised king, while he decided on the contrary not to show the actual battle, apart from a comic interlude in which he shows Pistol negotiating with his French prisoner.

The story of Shakespeare's three soldiers, though, is not easy and straightforward to tell, for these men have been made known to us in a peculiar way. Portrayed almost two centuries after their anonymous appearance on the stage of a great event by a playwright with a knack for history but heedless as far as historical accuracy was concerned, they came to share in their author's and in the audience's imagination the physiognomy of later soldiers. Their story, therefore, is – or should be – made up of different and anachronistic elements: those 'facts' that we can glean regarding them from the scene where Shakespeare, picking them out of an army of 6000 nameless creatures, captures their names, their identities and even their opinions, and the facts that we can reconstruct from the historical records of the battle. But the story should also be written in the light of what we know about the condition of soldiers in Shakespeare's time. For, to be sure, the army that fought with Henry at Agincourt had, in Shakespeare's imagination, many of the characteristics of the armies that confronted Elizabeth's enemies in his time. I will, therefore, take the liberty to use indifferently the historical accounts of the battle itself and works published in the sixteenth century, and to refer to the condition of soldiers in Henry's as well as in Elizabeth's time, without pointing out the anachronism. The story I am going to tell, however, is no fiction. It is, rather, the true story of three imagined soldiers.

John Bates, Alexander Court and Michael Williams were 'able-bodied men'.[110] According to what was the common practice by the first decades of the fifteenth century, their recruitment had been made following what was called a contract. These contracts, or 'indentures of agreement' were made with landowners or knights, and detailed a number of obligations on the noble's part as well as on the king's: the period for which the service was required, the number of men-at-arms, archers and other kinds of soldiers, horses, equipment, and so on, and the obligation to be present with the recruited troops on the day established for musters. On his part, the king granted transportation for the contracting noble, his troops, horses and baggage. Then followed the economic details, including the obligations concerning any taking of prisoners and getting of ransoms or of other war booty.[111]

The system of contracts described above had recently superseded both the feudal levy and the so called Commissions of Array, which were the common practice until more or less the end of the fourteenth century. The first was provided by landowners who held a number of 'knight's fees' (the basic unit of land tenure), who were obliged to provide troops and to do military service for forty days every year. The second was a system of assembly by shire. The contracts, which replaced these systems, 'were placed with various leading soldiers . . . who undertook to enlist an agreed number of men-at-arms (that is to say knights and esquires who fought, either mounted or on foot, in full armour) and an agreed number of archers, for a certain period and to bring them together at a muster supervised by officials of the Exchequer'.[112]

Months before (probably around April), our three soldiers had answered the call to arms of a noble. Deemed able, they had been enlisted, armed, trained for a short period and fully equipped.[113] On 1 July they had been taken to musters and supervised by officials of the Exchequer. At musters, soldiers should already display a certain skill in the use of arms and in other aspects of their discipline:

> The Sergeant as they be called, putteth them in araie that euerie man follow his lodseman, placing the shot in vorward and rereward, the ensigne and billes in the middest of the pikes, so be they placed in beautie and strength, as is accustomed, sometimes to receiue a word that shall passe from man to man from the one end to the other, with such silence that none heare the same, but those in araie assembled.[114]

From the moment in which they had been enlisted, they had received a pay of 6d a day, which they would continue to get until they were dismissed (wages in the higher ranks went up to 13s 4d a day). Later on, they were taken to Southampton together with the entire army that was to travel to France, and at 3 o'clock of Sunday, 11 August – it was a bright afternoon – 'with drums beating on deck and trumpeteers blowing their horns, with sailors shouting and priests praying',[115] they sailed south to the coast of Normandy. But before they arrive in view of Harfleur, let us try to know something of what they left at home and try to figure why they left it.

Of their civil life not much can be gleaned. Whether they – or their Elizabethan counterparts – had a family cannot be said for certain. From a reading of the war treatises we learn that there was little agreement on who made a better soldier, whether a married or an unmarried man. While there were theories which affirmed that unmarried men were to be preferred (no doubt because they cared less about losing their lives in battle than those who had families), there were others which argued the contrary, for it was thought that men who had families were less prone to disorder and disobedience.[116] In any case, one of the invitations most frequently repeated to soldiers was that of forgetting all they had left behind and devoting themselves entirely to the war. Here is how devotion to war is advised as one of the chief virtues of the soldier in a treatise by John Norden: 'when they begin to take armes on their backes, and would be called souldiers, whether they bee prest by authoritie, or of their owne forwardnes, they must endeuour to learne . . . speedily, and cast off all thinges that are behinde, namely profite, pleasure, friends, and feare of death. . .'.[117]

In a rather different context, namely, arguing for the employment of 'the natural subjects of the realm' in preference to that of mercenaries or of auxiliaries, Matthew Sutcliffe mentions, as a guarantee of good behaviour, the families and jobs that the soldiers have left behind them, suggesting that these should be a reminder for the soldier's good demeanour: 'Souldiers chosen of this nation . . . haue more reason to fight, hauing not only the defence of their prince and country, but also their religion, lawes, liberty, wiues and children committed to their hands.'[118]

That the commoners who went to the war had possessions to defend, however, can hardly be believed.[119] As civilians, they usually had a job, although this was certainly not such as to grant them a decent life. The fact that they risked their lives for a pay which was unanimously considered miserly and for the prospect of war profits which, if and when obtained, had to be handed almost entirely either to their captains or to the king, suggests clearly that it was poverty that led most of them to embrace, more or less temporarily, the profession of soldier.

However, a recurring war rhetoric – equally perceptible in treatises written during the last decades of the sixteenth century and in books and articles written during or immediately after the Second World War – has affirmed that for men who went to war, either in the time of Henry or in that of Elizabeth, to wage arms against an enemy was a favourite sport, and that each campaign was an exciting adventure (the second motivation being 'profit'): 'For those who went to fight in the war in France there was adventure to be had as well as profit and, although the army had become a professional one, adventure and the opportunity to excel in the most dangerous sport of all were still the principal lures for many of those who joined it.'[120]

In an article written in 1940, after telling of hardship after hardship suffered by the English soldiers during Henry's French campaign, W. B. Kerr describes and evaluates the soldiers' return home in an astonishing passage that deserves to be quoted fully:

When the channel was crossed, hardships were forgotten, casualties became a memory, and the men could look back on a wonderful ten weeks. They had taken a city, made a long march, fought a great battle, and had extraordinary success. They had seen something of France and of a civilization different from their own and more luxurious. They had had all the ups and downs of a soldier's life, – short rations one minute and plenty the next, rain one day and sun the day after, the fields one night and a house the following, with every hour bringing something fresh, agreeable or not. . . . Life for a short space had been full and varied.[121]

Contemporary reports of the campaign are, indeed, more cautious (no writer, for instance, affirms, as Kerr does, that life at Harfleur was for the soldiers 'a military holiday');[122] while Elizabethan war treatises treat the problem of a soldier's motivation from a different perspective – if not with less rhetorical inflation: what we encounter, in fact, is mainly war propaganda rather than the unrealistic description of a soldier's thirst for glory. Generally speaking, and somewhat less hypocritically than certain modern historians, the Elizabethan writers produce arguments to induce in the common soldiers (and in those who led them) the conviction that glory rather than profit should be the unique object of their labour. With this argument we frequently find associated two other issues: the obvious praise of frugality, often corroborated by the examples of antiquity, and the warning against those who join the war simply for profit: 'soldiers would be more desirous of praise rather than gaine', Matthew Sutcliffe prescribes;[123] while John Norden warns them that war is 'the schoole where they shall be taught the substance of honourable vertues indeede, whereas they before imbraced but shadows'; and that the first thing they will learn is that 'in stead of former profit and pleasure, they shall haue continuall honor, the regall riches of Caesar'.[124] Indeed, the portrait of the ideal soldier was often complemented by the suggestion that he should be 'in expences moderate' and temperate in using 'meate or drinke'.[125]

It is remarkable that sobriety is not mentioned in continental treatises as one of the qualities of the perfect soldier;[126] it may, therefore, have been an English invention, aimed to justify the poor pay that was given to soldiers;[127] moreover, the contempt of war profits was advised exclusively to the common soldier, although sobriety was sometimes formally listed among the virtues of the general as well. In fact, things must not have changed considerably from Henry's time, and the Elizabethan writer, apart from justifying the low wages of soldiers, was probably also allowing for the practice of handing the spoils of war to one's captain or to the king.[128] The massacre of French prisoners ordered by Henry at Agincourt was conceived, we are told by a modern historian, 'with a fine eye to profit', for Henry and his staff 'were carefully saving their own prisoners from the consequences of the order'.[129]

Different, more complex but related issues for propaganda were the arguments deployed against a certain category of men: virtually none of the Elizabethan war treatises is without at least a passing mention of rogues and vagabonds, a grim description of their bad behaviour during military service and ample considerations of the inopportuneness of recruiting them. In this case, the propaganda had two targets: in the first place, the 'good soldier', who is both gratified by the praise of his qualities and warned not to fall into the snares of the bad soldier's misdemeanour; and, in the second, the government and all those in power to recruit men. Notwithstanding the passionate invectives of writers, however, it appears that the habit of recruiting masterless men or men taken from jails was hard to die, even in Elizabeth's time. Although the Council, and presumably the Queen, knew well that vagrants did not make ideal soldiers according to formal standards, there were times and circumstances when you were not allowed to be fussy: 'The recruitment of the dregs of society had a long history and, despite its manifest drawbacks, it persisted throughout Elizabeth's reign. It was first seen in her time when prisoners in Newgate were set at liberty to reinforce the troops besieged in Le Havre, a desperate measure to meet a desperate situation.'[130]

Orders to exclude vagabonds were repeatedly issued, although taken to little account, and as late as 1597 it was the Council that 'authorized the levy of vagabonds to reinforce the expedition then in Picardy'.[131] Falstaff's comment on his ragged company of soldiers enlisted for Shrewsbury in *1 Henry IV*, IV.ii.41–2 ('indeed I had the most them out of prison') is, therefore, not unrealistic; and his cynical view that no matter where they came from so long as they were 'food for powder' (65–6) must have been shared by the Council that authorised the recruitment of vagabonds and prisoners. Matthew Sutcliffe is, on the contrary, violently opposed to this recruiting habit. He remarks that no attention is paid in his time to the quality of common soldiers to be preferred when making an enlistment, and complains about the fact that it is frequently ordered 'to the offices of every Parish, to take roges, or masterles men, or inhabitants of prisons, such as if they had their deserts, they were to be sent rather to the gallows, then to the warres for the most part'.[132] In his invective, Sutcliffe does not forget the good soldier, saying that in the company of these 'rogues, loyterers, pikars, and drunkards, and such as no other way can live, . . . there is no honest man but would be loth to be numbered'.[133]

Sutcliffe then proceeds to reveal that bribing was by no means an

unusual habit; often, in fact, a man was recruited either to do him
a favour or for the opposite reason; and for a man who had friends
or money it was easy to avoid being recruited: 'If any other be
chosen, it is for some priuate respect or grudge. And of those who
are chosen, if they haue either friendes, fauour, or money, most of
them are dismissed.'[134] The bribing of commissioners in the *Henry
IV* plays is therefore not Shakespeare's invention. Marching towards
Shrewsbury, Falstaff reveals that he has taken money for recruitment (*1 Henry IV*, IV.ii.13–14); and Mouldy and Bullcalf avoid being
enlisted by bribing Falstaff and Bardolph (*2 Henry IV*, III.ii.236–66).

But now that we know a little more of their profession, let us go
back to our three soldiers, and even venture an evaluation from
what we hear from them. Are they good or bad soldiers, according
to the standards illustrated in war treatises?

Michael Williams gives us more than one hint about what his
situation and probably that of the other two men is when he mentions the case of dead soldiers whose wives are 'left poor behind
them' and whose children are 'rawly left' (*Henry V*, IV.i.141, 146).
Williams is also concerned about the economic situation that those
who go to the war have left behind when he mentions 'the debts
they owe' (142). He and his companions, therefore, do not seem to
belong to the category of rogues or masterless men, neither have
they been taken from jail. However, they are not the portrait of the
ideal soldier, 'more desirous of praise then of gaine' either.[135] What
Shakespeare presents to depict the eve of the battle are three poor
commoners who can by no means be ranked with those of whom
the Chorus to Act Two had spoken, those who 'sell the pasture . . . to
buy the horse' to follow 'the mirror of all Christian kings' (5–6).
Both Elizabethan commentators and the historians of the middle
decades of our century show, as concerns the motivations of men
for going to war, an attitude that is infinitely less articulate and
subtle than that of Shakespeare's soldiers, and the same can be
said about the evaluation of Henry's 'commendable risk' and his
tremendous responsibility in ordering the march from Harfleur to
Calais. Indeed, the great achievement and the audacity of the scene
in which they appear is much more apparent if we contrast their
arguments with the common rhetoric of Elizabethan war propaganda.
Apparently, they have not forgotten their wives and children as
was prescribed; it is clear, on the contrary, that they wish to return
to them, and to pay with the scanty profits that the war will allow
them 'the debts they owe'. Courage is failing them in the hours

immediately preceding the battle: 'we have no great cause to desire the approach of day', says Bates (87–8), indeed, the unfailing
prowess of the perfect soldier has probably never been their characteristic (it is again Bates who says that even the king by this time
'could wish himself in Thames up to the neck', and adds, 'and so
I would he were, and I by him, at all adventures, so we were quit
here', 115–18). Although they are presented as honest men and
although Bates declares that he is determined 'to fight lustily' for
the king (196), they are by no means desirous to approach 'the
perfection of a soldier' as described by Norden: one for whom 'death
is more to be wished in fighting for a just cause, then life by escap-
ing like a coward'.[136] Although they will not fly from the battlefield
during the ensuing battle (apparently no English soldier did), they
are much in doubt that the king's cause be just, as Williams makes
clear to Henry ('that's more than we know', 130), adding: 'But if the
cause be not good, the king himself hath a heavy reckoning to
make; when all those legs and arms and heads, chopped off in a
battle, shall join together at the latter day, and cry all, "We died at
such a place" . . .'. (135–9)

But Williams's speech reveals yet another important point of disagreement, even a conceptual inversion as concerns sin and responsibility. Against statements such as Norden's, that 'it may fal out
that though the Generall be religious, faithfull and fearing God, the
sinnes of the people may procure the confusion both of their
Governour and themselues',[137] Williams dares to affirm the contrary,
namely, that it is the king who will have to answer for his soldiers'
sins: 'I am afeard there are few die well that die in a battle; for how
can they charitably dispose of anything when blood is their argument? Now, if these men do not die well, it will be a black matter
for the king that led them to it . . .'. (143–8).[138]

Henry's answer to Williams's unfailing arguments is unconvincing, and its rhetorical layout is weak: Shakespeare could do much
better when he wanted to confound his audience weighing contrasting arguments with equal force.

The last fragment of Williams's speech deserves a few words of
comment. What can Shakespeare's implications be in technical terms
when he has Williams say that to disobey the king when called to
the arms 'were against all proportion of subjection' (149)?

To what extent, either in Henry's or in Elizabeth's time, was a
man who was considered fit for combat allowed to refuse being
recruited or being sent abroad?

Oman says that by the end of the Middle Ages the almost professional soldier was 'usually not a pressed man, but a volunteer,
raised by one of those barons or knights with whom the king contracted for a supply of soldiers', and he adds that he was 'Led to
enlist by sheer love of fighting, desire for adventures, or hope of
plunder'.[139] It is by no means clear, however, how real the voluntary character of military service was, either in Henry's or in later
times. It is true that formally to go to the war was not compulsory;
however, in all probability there were circumstances (one of which
may well have been Henry's French expedition) in which to recruit
a high number of men was indispensable. Moreover, since recruitment in Henry's time was made by the landowner and since on the
part of the noble the recruiting of troops was an obligation (let
alone the fact that the recruiting noble expected to earn a certain
amount of money from his service), people must have felt that their
liberty to remain at home was conditioned by a more than psycho-
logical form of blackmail. Certainly, then, both in Henry's and in
Elizabeth's time, there existed 'men conscripted more or less against
their will'.[140]

It is understandable, therefore, that soldiers who may not have
been exactly volunteers might conceive some grudge towards their
leaders, and particularly towards the king who led them to war. In
the particular circumstance that I am considering, they had many
good reasons to blame Henry. After the 'military holiday' of Harfleur
was successfully concluded, in fact, it was clear that the army had
suffered many losses. The number of those who had died in battle
was about 500, but many others had contracted a violent form of
dysentery. Of these, about 500 died and more or less as many had
been sent home because sick and therefore useless; of the remain-
ing, about 1500 had to be left at Harfleur to garrison the city.
Moreover, the siege had taken almost two months, and winter was
approaching.

Henry had probably already decided to march to Calais, but he
called a meeting of the Council to discuss in a formal way the
advisability of proceeding in the campaign before making his purpose known. The Council unanimously advised him against proceeding and to make return to England, for they were aware of the
tremendous risk to which the army would be put. Henry ignored
the advice and remained stubborn in his purpose.[141]

The march to Calais had been a disaster. Provisions had not been
taken, nor had plans been made to cross the river Somme, and the

army was forced to take a long detour in order to avoid the French troops deployed on the opposite bank of the river. As a result, the march took 18 days instead of the supposed eight. The soldiers were obliged to cover 15 miles per day, and during the march they had only one day's rest. Meanwhile, the food supplies were soon exhausted, the men were tired and weak, and some of them had to march barefoot (it is even reported that some archers were completely naked during the battle). Even 'non-defeatist' historians admit that 'In their dismay the men could not hide from themselves the error of generalship which was endangering the whole army' and that 'Henry must have felt the eyes of his soldiers turned on him.'[142]

When we meet our three soldiers, the situation is even worse. The previous day, from the crest of a ridge which rose 300 feet above the river Ternoise, they had seen the French army, which numbered – or had seemed to them to number – many thousand men. They were dismayed, and fear was now added to hunger and weakness.

And so, we are back in the rainy night of Maisoncelles. Holinshed spends few words to report how the night preceding the battle was spent in the French and English camps:

> They [the French] were lodged euen in the waie by the which the Englishmen must needs passe towards Calis, and all that night after their comming thither, made great cheare and were verie merie, pleasant, and full of game. The Englishmen also for their parts were of good comfort, and nothing abashed of the matter, and yet they were both hungrie, wearie, sore trauelled, and vexed with manie cold diseases.[143]

The chronicler's report is apparently inaccurate. No 'good comfort', in fact, had come to the English soldiers. The truth is that while the king and the officers had taken what covered refuge they could find in the village and eaten what food was found, the soldiers, who had been eating little but hazel nuts for the last three days, had to spend the night on the wet ground. Shakespeare's account is, in a sense, more accurate:

> The poor condemned English,
> Like sacrifices, by their watchful fires
> Sit patiently, and inly ruminate
> The morning's danger, and their gesture sad
> Investing lank-lean cheeks and war-worn coats

Presenteth them unto the gazing moon
So many horrid ghosts.

(Henry V, IV.0.22–8)

During the night many of them confessed, for they had little
hope of living, others 'tested their weapons and armor and repaired
them as best they could; the archers restrung their bows as the rain
permitted';[144] three of them, at the approach of dawn met a hooded
figure, a soldier who, so he said, served under Sir Thomas Erping-
ham. This man, apparently melancholy, had nevertheless firm convictions about the just and honourable cause of the king, and seemed
curiously passionate when he had to defend the sincerity of the
king's word that if taken prisoner he would not be ransomed. Bates
and especially Williams, on the contrary (Court never took part in
the conversation), much doubted the king's good faith and sincerity; moreover, they did not hesitate to show their fear of the battle,
even revealing a captivating side of what is commonly considered
cowardice. A quarrel followed, which was settled by the exchange
of gages between Williams and the hooded soldier, by which they
reciprocally pledged to settle the business the following day, after
the battle. If they survived. Which they all strongly doubted.

As it happened, they all survived (at least, Williams and the
hooded man did). But the quarrel was never settled; not, at least, in
the way Williams had imagined.

The battle won, our men were sent back home. But their ordeal
had not yet ended.

Demobilisation, in fact, was perhaps an even more thorny problem than recruiting. The war rhetoric prescribed that the common
soldier, on his return home, should not consider 'imbasing', going
back to his former occupation; and that in this he should imitate the
noble Roman soldier, who

thought it no disgrace to returne againe to [his] private estate,
vendicating nothing but the Fame and honour to himselfe, leauing
and contemning the Spoile, and contenting himselfe with his owne
poore possessions. Such noble Presidents and mighty Capitaines
to lay before their Souldiors eies and to beate them from that
corrupt opinion of Riches and Pleasure, whiche are the Enimies
of Vertue, and the very original Causes of the ruine of many
Stately Empires and Common weales.[145]

Clearly, on the soldier's part, it was not a question of thinking it 'no disgrace' to come back to his former occupation. On the contrary, coming back from war, men had to face the problem of unemployment. More often than not, in fact, either their jobs had in the meantime been given to others or their former employers were 'unwilling to have them back when their military service was over', for – as is always the case – 'those who returned from the wars little resembled the men who went away'.[146]

Jorgensen expands on 'the post-war plight of the common soldier' taking as a starting point our three Shakespearean soldiers and the preoccupations that they express. He remarks that Henry 'is uninterested in the economic anxieties of Bates and Williams', and that 'after clearing himself of any responsibility in the matter, he advises both men to look after their own souls so that they may have the comfort of dying well'; and adds that 'Probably neither Henry nor Shakespeare thought of this advice as an irrelevancy.'[147]

It almost invariably happened, then, that disbanded soldiers turned to begging; thus, they became a public nuisance, and ended by being regarded as part of what was thought to be the worse of social menaces. (Falstaff's sentence on the destiny awaiting the survivors of his company, 'they are for the town's end, to beg during life' in 1 *Henry IV*, V.iii.38, is a realistic comment on a huge problem that the government was not able – or willing – to face efficiently.)[148]

Some of the veterans were granted a begging licence for a given time (usually from three to six months), so that in begging they should not incur the punishments that the law prescribed for vagrants; some of the maimed were cured, although inadequately, in hospitals, and very few were granted a meagre temporary pension, although, even when this was officially allowed, it was often hard to obtain.[149] 'The queen', Jorgensen says, 'could not afford much more. Besides, she was apparently quite at ease with her own conscience in the matter. She insisted that the individual counties which had levied the men were responsible for the maimed veterans.'[150]

In short, instead of receiving the thanks of the authorities and of his fellow countrymen for service done, the dismissed soldier faced great trouble: even if he saved his life in battle, this was worth nothing on his return home; moreover, such and so instantaneous was his degradation that he could hardly hope to be recruited again the next time.

The moralistic way in which some of the writers of war treatises

treat the problem is, therefore, patently ungenerous as well as false.
Here is the comment produced by John Norden:

Among many other enormities, proceeding of the want of warres
true discipline, it is not the least that our pretended souldiers returning from the warres, should haue either hearts in themselues,
or sufferance by lawe, to become vagabonds: for their parts, they
bewray their cowardly mindes, in that they will leaue the honourable practise of warre, and betake them to ignominious begging,
whereby the profession of armes is dishonoured, and the magistrates power is thereby discredited, the force of the lawes shewed
to be of finall effect, and the common quiet disturbed.[151]

From the point of view of the retired soldier, Barnabe Rich presents
a more realistic and dramatic picture, which deserves a lengthy
quotation:

First in the times of warres, they spare not in their countries
behalf, to forsake their wife, children, mother, brother, sister, to
leave their friendes, and onely betake them against their enemies:
contented to yeld them selves to continuall watch, warde, fasting,
hunger, thirst, colde, heat, trauell, toyle, over hils, woods, deserts,
wading through rivers, where many sometimes lose their lives by
the way; lying in the fielde in raine, wind, frost, and snow, adven-
turing against the enemy, the lacke of limmes, the losse of life,
making their bodies a fence and bulwark against the shot of the
cannon.
    But the warres being once finished, and that there is no neede
of them, howe be they rewarded, howe be they cherished, what
accounte is there made of them, what other thing gain they then
flounder, misreport, false impositions, hatred and despight. . . .
There be some that haue serued twentie or thirtie yeeres as occasions have happened, and in the warres have spent part of their
blood, and receiued many greeuous woundes, but their estate of
living, I woulde to God were knowne to those that might amend
it. . . . But how ingratefull may that countrye be called, where
those that must fight in the defence, and offer them selues to the
slaughter in their countries quarel, do onely receiue for recom-
pence, but hateful words, slanderous reportes, and are no better
accompted of, then as the abiectes, and holden inferiours to every
other people?[152]

With Rich's sad picture of the destiny awaiting demobilised soldiers we may close our brief inquiry on the margins of a controversial battle. Maybe Shakespeare did not mean to carry us so far. But he certainly stirred our curiosity by allowing three obscure soldiers to enter the theatre of history, step on to the stage of a great event and assume for a while the role of protagonists *vis-à-vis* the mirror of all Christian kings.

Notes

1. C. Ginzburg, *Il formaggio e i vermi. Il cosmo di un mugnaio del '500* (Turin: Einaudi, 1976), p. xi. English transl., *The Cheese and the Worms. The Cosmos of a Sixteenth-century Miller* (Baltimore and London: The Johns Hopkins University Press, 1980), p. xiii. See also, on the necessarily tangential evidence on which scholars of popular culture are obliged to rely, P. Burke, *Popular Culture in Early Modern Europe* (London: Temple Smith, 1978), especially Chapter 3.
2. Sir Thomas Smith, *De republica anglorum*, ed. Mary Dewar (Cambridge: Cambridge University Press, 1982), p. 76. Smith borrowed the passage from Harrison's *Description of England*, which introduced Holinshed's *Chronicles*. See W. Harrison, *Description of England*, ed. Georges Edelen (Ithaca: Cornell University Press, 1968), p. 118. Smith died on 12 August 1577, the year in which the first edition of Holinshed was published. *De republica* was not published until 1583. It should be noticed that the crowd of paupers, vagrants and masterless men is altogether expelled from Smith's *respublica*.
3. *The Arte*, p. 41.
4. Ginzburg, *The Cheese and the Worms*, p. xv.
5. Op. cit., p. 225.
6. Op. cit., p. 12. There are two senses in which the term 'marginal' can be understood in this context, and two categories of persons represented accordingly in Shakespeare's plays. The difference between these two categories lies in their being or not being recorded elsewhere as real persons. Generally, by the term 'marginal' I designate an invented character that has no life outside the play: it is marginal, therefore, in that it lives beyond the margins of recorded history. Obviously, such characters cannot but be marginal also from the social point of view, for socially prominent characters could not be introduced in a historical play without significant modification of the course of events (the Bastard and Falstaff are exceptions to this rule). The second category is that of historical characters that have no real weight in the official recordings of facts, but have a comparatively significant role in the plays. Women who are near to the men in power in the first tetralogy and in *King John* belong to this category. On the role of women in the history plays, see P. Rackin, *Stages of*

History and 'Patriarchal History', and G. Holderness, 'Patriarchy and Gender: *Richard II'*, in *Shakespeare Recycled*, pp. 73–88.

7. Op. cit., pp. 237, 239. Helgerson, it seems to me, makes too much of 'the sympathetic union of high and low' and of what he considers as the popular values of 'ballad history', forcing into his 'history from below' characters that are by no means low (principally Falstaff on the Shakespearean side and, on the side of the rival playwrights, Jane and Matthew Shore, Robert, Earl of Huntington, Sir John Oldcastle, Sir Thomas More and Sir Thomas Wyatt).

8. *The Politics of Shakespeare* (London: Macmillan, 1993), p. 55. To show his point, Cohen obviously evokes Cade and the Cadians.

9. Ibid., p. 65.

10. Ibid.

11. Ibid., p. 56.

12. Ibid., p. 60.

13. Ibid., p. 66.

14. Many voices have spoken against the polarisation of the subversion–containment alternative, suggesting a less monolithic vision of the power structure. Theodore Leinwand has convincingly argued for a model of 'negotiated change', where social conflicts are seen as governed by 'Compromise, negotiation, exchange, accommodation, give and take' and has suggested that 'it is a thorough falsification of historical processes to argue that subversion offers the only alternative to the status quo' ('Negotiation and New Historicism', p. 479). The response of social historians, too, has underscored problems of method and suggested less radical ideological partitions (see D. Cressy, 'Foucault, Stone, Shakespeare and Social History', *English Literary Renaissance* XXI [1991], 121–33).

15. The kind of commentary that Shakespeare's marginal characters produce has on occasions a function that resembles that of choric comment in Greek tragedy, where the voice of the common people, with the credentials of popular wisdom that it presents, expresses an ideal 'norm' of the *pòlis*, which is frequently at odds with the inconsiderate behaviour of the great.

16. Op. cit., p. 68.

17. S. Gosson, *Playes Confuted in Five Actions* (London, 1582), p. 183 (reported in E. K. Chambers, op. cit., vol. 4, p. 216).

18. Helgerson says that 'The mere fact of representing a monarch and a lowly commoner together on stage violated a decorum that was both political and aesthetic' (op. cit., p. 201).

19. The first of these treatises is probably *The Boke of Justices of Peas*, published *circa* 1506; the most famous is *Eirenarcha* by William Lambarde (there are three variants of the first edition, one bearing the imprint 1581 and the other two 1582; my reference edition is one of the last). Lambarde also held a diary of the first eight years (1580–1588) of his experience as member of the Commission of the Peace (*Ephemeris*); by the same we possess a number of 'charges'. See C. Read (ed.), *William Lambarde and Local Government: His 'Ephemeris' and 'Twenty-nine Charges to Juries and Commissions'* (Ithaca: Cornell

University Press, 1962); see also, by the same Lambarde, *The Duties of Constables, Borsholders, Tythingmen, and such other lowe Ministers of the Peace* (London, 1583) and Michael Dalton, *The Country Justice* (London, 1626).

20. C. Read (ed.), *Charges*, p. 77.
21. Ibid., p. 76.
22. *Eirenarcha*, p. 38.
23. *Charges*, p. 107.
24. In the section of *The Duties* dedicated to 'Precepts', Lambarde says that constables must respect scrupulously the instructions of the JPs, who may remove them from their charge if they are 'insufficient'; and adds that lower officers should never dispute the authority of those who pronounce orders, for even though a JP 'should direct a warrant beyond his authoritie', the officer 'be holden excused for executing the same' (p. 20).
25. J. A. Sharpe, *Crime in Early Modern England 1550–1750* (London: Longman, 1984), p. 159.
26. F. G. Emmison, *Elizabethan Life: Disorder* (Chelmsford: Essex County Council, 1970), p. 179.
27. K. Wrightson, *English Society 1550–1680* (London: Hutchinson, 1982), p. 150.
28. E. Moir, *The Justice of the Peace* (Harmondsworth: Penguin, 1969), p. 33.
29. Ibid., p. 30.
30. Ibid., pp. 33–4. Moir does not quote the exact source.
31. Op. cit., p. 150.
32. See in Emmison's book, *Elizabethan Life*, the chapter on 'Assaults on officers', pp. 172–9.
33. Wrightson, op. cit., p. 156.
34. Ibid., p. 158. Leinwand says that 'Personal pressures, applied from below, included shaming, ostracism, noncooperation, and physical violence.' (op. cit., p. 483) See also, on this point, K. Wrightson, 'Two Concepts of Order: Justices, Constables and Jurymen in Seventeenth-Century England', in J. Brewer and J. Styles (eds), *An Ungovernable People. The English and their Law in the Seventeenth and Eighteenth Centuries* (New Brunswick: Rutgers, 1980), pp. 21–46.
35. J. A. Sharpe, ' "Such Disagreement Betwyxt Neighbours": Litigation and Human Relations in Early Modern England', in J. Bossy (ed.) *Disputes and Settlements. Law and Human Relations in the West* (Cambridge: Cambridge University Press, 1983), pp. 167–87, 167. Sharpe also signals an increase in litigiousness and in legal processes, although he stresses the fact that, albeit willing to initiate litigations, people were less willing to bring suits to their conclusion and often accepted arbitration (ibid.).
36. *Crime*, pp. 145, 144.
37. Ibid., p. 143.
38. *English Society*, p. 169.
39. Op. cit., p. 481.
40. Ibid., p. 483.

41. Ibid., pp. 483–4.
42. Ibid., p. 488.
43. 'Vice' is F's reading, while Q has 'vue'. Humphreys (Arden) thinks that 'Q perhaps misread "vice" as "vue"'; Melchiori (New Cambridge) reads 'vue' and explains 'vice' = 'firm grip'; but Fang might here be doubling Quickly's malapropisms.
44. 'Rescue', Emmison says, was the legal term for the forceful liberation of a prisoner (op. cit., p. 172); Quickly is obviously misinterpreting Fang's as a shout for help and echoes 'Good people, bring a rescue or two' (55).
45. On arbitration, see J. A. Sharpe, 'Such disagreement'.
46. A. Fletcher and J. Stevenson (eds), *Order and Disorder in Early Modern England* (Cambridge: Cambridge University Press, 1985), p. 26.
47. Giorgio Melchiori says that 'The recruiting scenes and the moderate revels in Justice Shallow's orchard sanction the birth of what could be called country comedy, a *genre* that breaks down the traditional and conventional, more or less bucolic view of country life, which Shakespeare himself seemed to restate shortly after in *As You Like It*. ('Introduction' to *The Second Part of King Henry IV*, p. 21).
48. The expression is S. T. Bindoff's, *Tudor England*, The Pelican History of England, vol. 5 (Harmondsworth: Penguin, 1977 [1950]), p. 57.
49. Years later we meet Ben Jonson's Adam Overdo in *Bartholomew Fair*. Overdo is a worthy companion of Shallow, although he is affected by the contrary disease of overzealousness. On the social and political function of the JPs and on their literary representation, see L. Curti, A. Mineo and M. Vitale, 'Adam Overdo (*Bartholomew Fair*)', in *Analisi di contenuto della struttura superficiale di alcuni personaggi del teatro comico elisabettiano*, *AION*, XIV (1971), 437–518.
50. Scot's treatise was published in 1584; my reference edition, Brinsley Nicholson (ed.), East Ardsley, E. P. Publishing, 1973.
51. *Malleus maleficarum* was written at the request of Pope Innocent VIII by two Dominican German inquisitors, Heinrich Institor and Jacob Spränger and published in Strasbourg in 1486. On the continent, it was the most influential treatise on witchcraft, going through 34 editions up to 1669 in Germany, France and Italy. Although it was known by the English intellectuals who wrote on the same subject, its influence in England was limited (the first English translation, in fact, appeared in 1928). Although Reginald Scot does not deny the existence of good and bad spirits and of demons, his treatise was meant to expose witchcraft and other magic practices as trickery. Surprising as it was for its demystifying analysis of the phenomenon, *The Discouerie of Witchcraft* was not very influential, for 'by sheer scope and size and weight of critical apparatus, the book took itself out of the popular market and lost the pamphlet audience', B. Rosen, *Witchcraft in England, 1558–1618* (Amherst: University of Massachusetts Press, 1991 [1969], p. 171). One of the main targets of Scot's impassioned critique is the great Jean Bodin, who in his *Démonomanie des Sorciers* (Paris, 1580) showed a complete belief in witchcraft which the sceptical Scot deeply despised.

52. Keith Thomas says that 'Only in the third and final witchcraft statute of 1604 did the full continental doctrine take effect'. *Religion and the Decline of Magic* (Harmondsworth: Penguin, 1991 [London: Weidenfeld and Nicolson, 1971]), p. 526.

53. The connection between witchcraft and mental disorder through possession is obvious, and it influenced both the detection of causes of madness and the healing methods. Michael MacDonald says that 'individual cases of mental disorder might be attributed to divine retribution, diabolical possession, witchcraft, astrological influences, humoral imbalances, or to any combination of these forces'. Richard Napier, the physician whose cases MacDonald discusses in his book, 'treated mentally disturbed people who thought that they were possessed or bewitched with folk magic, astrology, humoral medicine, and earnest prayer'. *Mystical Bedlam. Madness, Anxiety and Healing in Seventeenth-century England* (Cambridge: Cambridge University Press, 1981), pp. 7, 213.

54. The association of mental illness and political radicalism in the seventeenth century is discussed by Christopher Hill in *The World Turned Upside Down* (London: Temple Smith, 1972), Chapter 13.

55. A notable case that occurred in Scotland in 1591 is recorded in a pamphlet published in London the same year. The pamphlet narrates 'what was pretended by' a group of 'wicked and detestable witches against the King's Majesty, as also by what means they sought the same'. The author of the pamphlet says that the same witches declared that his Majesty would never have escaped 'if his faith had not prevailed above their intentions'. *Newes from Scotland . . .* (London, 1591); in B. Rosen, op. cit., pp. 191, 197. During the 1580s and the 1590s, officials discovered dolls representing the Queen which had been stuck through with pins or defaced in other ways. In 1580, an *Act against seditious words and rumours uttered against the Queen's most excellent Majesty* established that to use 'prophesying, witchcraft, conjurations' and so on, either to calculate 'how long her Majesty shall live or continue' or to 'desire the death or deprivation' of the Queen, was considered an act of felony and punished accordingly with death (ibid., pp. 56–7).

56. Harry Rusche, 'Prophecies and Propaganda, 1641–1651', *The English Historical Review* LXXXIV (1969), 752–70, pp. 754. On the use of prophecies as political propaganda, see also R. Taylor, *The Political Prophecy in England* (New York: Columbia University Press, 1911), especially pp. 83–107.

57. Op. cit., p. 551.

58. Barbara Rosen draws a portrait of the English witch as 'almost invariably a woman (more frequently than on the Continent), usually poor, though there are exceptions, and usually elderly. In most cases she has a bad reputation from the beginning – often for unchastity as well as malice – and this is transferred to her descendants' (op. cit., p. 29). On the contiguity of witchcraft and prostitution, see *Richard III*, III.iv.68–72. The authors of *Màlleus maleficarum* list a number of astonishing reasons, which comprise a few extravagant etymologies

of the word *foemina*, to explain why witches are almost exclusively women. Fletcher and Stevenson say that 'The assertive, quarrelsome, scolding, extravagant or immodest woman was perceived as a threat to the social order and as such was to be subject to supervision at home and, if necessary, to intervention and correction by the community in which she lived' (op. cit., p. 32).

59. *Stages of History*, p. 148.
60. L. B. Campbell (ed.), *The Mirror for Magistrates* (Cambridge: Cambridge University Press, 1938), ll. 78–9.
61. *The Union*, p. Cxlvi.
62. Prophecy contrived by means of astrology is mentioned in *The Mirror for Magistrates*: the two priests, it is said, undertook 'To cast and calke the kinges constellation / And then to iudge by depe dyuination / Of thinges to come, and who should next succeede / To Englandes crowne, al this was true in dede.' (ll. 102–5)
63. Op. cit., pp. 69–70. It may be noticed that Shakespeare did not cease to show the 'woman on top' and the female subverter of history after the death of Elizabeth. The type of the disorderly woman who tries to influence or 'deface' the male political project returns in such figures of disorder as Lady Macbeth, Goneril, Regan and even Cleopatra.
64. Ibid., p. 90. Marcus remarks a number of connections between Margaret and Elizabeth, particularly in certain characterisations of Margaret's 'manly' qualities and argues that she is in more than one way connected with Joan; symbolically, she is her daughter, 'in that she is child to Anjou, whom Joan has named among her lovers'; (pp. 89–90). Incidentally, in the chapter dedicated to the connections between Joan and Elizabeth, Marcus remarks that the two noblemen Joan mentions as her lovers, the duke of Alençon and the duke of Anjou, were 'the noblemen Elizabeth had come closest to marrying in the decades before' (p. 68).
65. In the 'Introduction' to *The Misfortunes of Arthur* (1588), Astraea-Elizabeth is addressed as 'She that pronounces oracles and laws' (l. 10).
66. M. Foucault, *L'ordre du discours* (Paris: Gallimard, 1971), p. 13.
67. In *3 Henry VI*, Richard of Gloucester had foreseen that Margaret's most disquieting role in the future would have been the utterance of prophecies. When, together with his brothers, he stabs young prince Edward, he also offers to kill his mother: 'Why', he says, 'should she live to *fill the world with words*' (V.v.44; my emphasis).
68. Prophecy, Keith Thomas says, 'was not a straightforward prediction, but an elusively vague or ambiguous piece of prose or verse, resting on no clearly defined foundation, either magical or religious' (op. cit., p. 461). The prophecy divulged by Richard, 'which says that "G" / Of Edward's sons the murderer shall be' (*Richard III*, I.i.39–40) is of this kind. It will be the ruin of Clarence, whose name is George, but it obviously referred to Gloucester.
69. M. Garber, ' "What's Past is Prologue": Temporality and Prophecy in Shakespeare's History Plays', in B. Levalsky (ed.), *Renaissance Genres* (Cambridge, Mass.: Harvard University Press, 1986), pp. 301–31, 321.

70. Ibid., pp. 331, 324.
71. 'O thou, well skill'd in curses, stay awhile/ And teach me how to curse mine enemies' (*Richard III*, IV.iv. 116–17) is Queen Elizabeth's prayer to Margaret.
72. B. Rosen, op. cit., p. 49.
73. 'Lying like Truth', p. 36.
74. Op. cit., pp. 103–4.
75. In Holinshed, the withering of bay-trees which is mentioned by the Welsh Captain among the omens occurs in England (*Chronicles*, 496.II.66–70).
76. Op. cit., p. 104. Although in circulation long before, political prophecy was rife under the Tudors, who used the Arthurian legend and Merlin's prophecies to trace their ancestry back to Arthur. The most complete account of political prophecy is, to my knowledge, Rupert Taylor, op. cit.; but see also M. Hope Dodds, 'Political Prophecies in the Reign of Henry VIII', *MLR* XI (1916), 276–84; C. W. Previté-Orton, 'An Elizabethan Prophecy', *History* II (1918), 207–18; R. F. Brinkley, *Arthurian Legend in the Seventeenth Century* (New York: Octagon Books, 1932); H. Rusche, 'Prophecies and Propaganda'. The source of Merlin's prophecies is Geoffrey of Monmouth's *Historia regum Britanniae*; the first version of the Moldwarp prophecy is found in the *Prophecy of the Six Kings to follow King John*, written about the middle of Edward II's reign. According to the prophecy, the sixth king (Henry IV) would be the Moldwarp or Mole, who would be defeated by a Dragon, a Wolf and a Lion. These would divide England into three parts (see Taylor, op. cit., pp. 48–50). The ant, fish, raven and cat which Hotspur mentions are not part of the same prophecy.
77. *Chronicles*, 521.II.67–74.
78. On the Moldwarp prophecy, see K. Thomas, op. cit., pp. 473–4. Glendower's belief is in the Galfridian, that form of obscure prediction of human affairs in which human beings are represented as animals. This form, Hope Dodds says, 'is an inheritance from the Welsh bards and is characteristic of a nation still retaining some of the savage beliefs which in an earlier state of society produced totemism' (op. cit., p. 278).
79. G. Martella, 'Tradimento e profezia in *King John*', in M. Tempera (ed.), '*King John*' *dal testo alla scena*, pp. 111–32. Showing in the play the transition from prophecy to empirical prognosis, Martella argues that *King John* inaugurates a process of secularisation of historiography.
80. That prophecy might stir rebellion was demonstrated during the trial of the Duke of Norfolk in 1572 for his involvement in the Ridolfi plot (see Thomas, op. cit., pp. 479–80). As late as 1626, Michael Dalton said that JPs were entitled to imprison 'such as advisedly shall publish any false prophecies . . . to the intent thereby to make any rebellion, insurrection, or other disturbances within the kings dominion' (op. cit., p. 104). The best known example of a prophecy which was used to the advantage of the regime is that pronounced by the German astronomer Johann Müller of Königsberg (*alias* Regiomontanus) about

the 'octogesimus octavus mirabilis annus'. Although the prophecy spoke of disasters, it was interpreted after the event as foretelling the defeat of the Spanish.

81. See again Martella, 'Tradimento'.

82. Thus defined by Ralph Berry, *Shakespeare and Social Class* (Atlantic Highlands: Humanities Press International, 1988), p. 1.

83. The usual way to deal with hired murderers is an attitude of complicity and the praise of their courage. Macbeth adds a fairly long speech to convince those who are to murder Banquo that they are going to take a personal revenge, for Banquo, he says, 'hath bow'd you to the grave/ And beggar'd yours for ever' (III.i.89–90).

84. The scene starts with a long dialogue in which Clarence tells his keeper the premonitory dream he has dreamt. The keeper is gentle and sympathetic to him. Keepers are another of the categories of commoners in which is shown a humane attitude which contrasts with the inhumanity of power.

85. Foucault said that 'dans toute société la production du discours est à la foi contrôlée, sélectionnée et redistribuée par un certain nombre de procédures qui ont pour rôle d'en conjurer les pouvoirs et les dangers, d'en maîtriser l'événement aléatoire, d'en esquiver la lourde, la redoutable matérialité' (*L'ordre du discours*, pp. 10–11).

86. *A dyaloge . . .* (London, 1529), p. xviii. The episode is reported in Chapter xiiii, pp. xviii–xviii[v].

87. *A Chronicle at Large* (London, 1569), pp. 597–8.

88. *Actes and Monuments* (London, 1583).

89. Foxe, 5th imprint (1596), vol. I, p. 648.I.1–8. For my use of this edition, see Chapter 9, note 14. Grafton and Foxe repeat almost verbatim More's account. Tyndall wrote *An Answere unto sir Thomas Mores Dialoge* (1530) which, however, does not mention the episode.

90. A. L. Beier, *Masterless Men* (London: Methuen, 1985), p. 48.

91. W. Harrison, *Description*, pp. 184–5. Paul Slack reports the case of a woman vagrant in the Shropshire village of Myddle in the 1660s. Sina Davies was a 'crafty, idle, dissembling woman' who 'did counterfeit herself to be lame, and went hopping with a staff when men saw her, but at other times could go with it under her arm'. *Poverty and Policy in Tudor and Stuart England* (London: Longman, 1988), p. 63. Slack also quotes cases of 'counterfeit Bedlams', counterfeit cripples and a 'dummerer' in Salisbury, pretending he had no tongue (ibid., p. 96). All these types of counterfeiters are described in numerous tracts and pamphlets on vagrancy. The most famous is the one by Thomas Harman, *A Caveat or Warening for Common Cursetors* (1566?); see also John Awdeley, *The Fraternitye of Vacabondes* (1560–61). Harman treats all vagabonds as impostors; see, in particular, the story of Nicholas Gennyns, a 'counterfeit cranke', who is also shown in two of the illustrations: first in stocks and then on his way to the gallows. Greenblatt connects Harman's pamphlet to Shakespeare's *Henry IV* plays holding that as Harman, by betraying his confidential sources with the publication of his pamphlet, served the purpose of maintaining order in the community, so the small acts of betrayal

and subversion performed by Hal, Falstaff and Shallow are functional to securing order and supporting authority ('Invisible Bullets').

92. The problem of vagrancy must have been present to the mind of all kinds of spectators; in fact, historians generally agree that the last decade of the century was that in which vagrancy was 'approaching its peak' (P. Slack, op. cit., p. 101). In Harman's pamphlet there are illustrations of both whips and stocks.

93. *Description*, p. 180. The basic distinction was formulated much earlier: in the dialogue *Dives et pauper* (1493), attributed to the Dominican Henry Parker, the Poor who gives his precepts to the Rich states that some 'be pore agenst their wylle' and 'sume been pore only by synne and for the loue of syn' ('The nynth Precepte', p. Hi).

94. J. A. Sharpe, *Early Modern England. A Social History, 1550–1760* (London: Edward Arnold, 1987), p. 217.

95. Op. cit., p. 28.

96. The Act of 1531 gives a definition of the 'masterless man' which, Beier says, was slightly altered only by the 1597 Statute. A vagabond is 'any man or woman being whole and mighty in body and able to labour, having no land, master, nor using any lawful merchandise, craft or mystery whereby he might get his living' (op. cit., p. 9). Harman tells the story of a 'dummerer', a man who pretended to be both deaf and dumb and who 'could in short time both hear and speak' because 'hoisted . . . up over a beam, and there let' to 'hang a good while'. After the discovery, the 'dummerer' was sent to a Justice and punished by whipping. Harman calls this episode a 'merry miracle' (op. cit., p. 133). The passage suggests that two different traditions (the religious one and the one concerning vagrancy) may have joined in the framing of Shakespeare's Simpcox episode.

97. Sharpe, *Early Modern England*, p. 219.

98. Even seasonal shifts were common during the period. Sharpe says that some vagrants were a kind of 'primitive tourists', for they travelled with a map of England (*Crime*, p. 101).

99. Slack, op. cit., p. 118.

100. *Description*, p. 185.

101. Op. cit., p. 100.

102. Slack calls 'professional beggars' those who counterfeited some kind of inability (op. cit., p. 96).

103. Sharpe, *Early Modern England*, p. 218. 'Masterless men', Manning says, 'inspired a fear of ungovernable multitudes which was out of all proportion to their numbers and actual potential for mischief.' B. Manning, *Village Revolts* (Oxford: Clarendon Press, 1988), p. 158.

104. Sharpe, *Crime*, p. 100. Jean Howard holds a different view of Simpcox, whom she considers as 'the tetralogy's most blatant example of a simple charlatan, someone who uses deception to gain power for himself' and as 'a sign of the pernicious effects of clerical deceit'. *The Stage and Social Struggle in Early Modern England* (London: Routledge, 1994), pp. 132, 134.

105. Beier, op. cit., p. 96. Beier also says that the 1597 statute repeated these provisions. He also recalls that finally in 1648 'Parliament

declared all players to be vagrant, while during the Protectorate a law ordered fiddlers and minstrels summarily to be branded' (ibid.). Lambarde lists among rogues 'every Fensor, Bearward, Minstrel, or cunning player of Enterlude (other then such player of Enterlude as belongeth to a Baron or other Honorable person of greater degree, and bee authorized under his hand and seale of Armes)'. The passage appears for the first time in the 1599 edition of *The Dueties*, p. 39.

106. In Shakespeare's play, the losses of the English army are announced by Henry as follows:

> Edward the Duke of York, the Earl of Suffolk,
> Sir Richard Kikely, Davy Gam, esquire;
> None else of name;
>
> *(Henry V, IV.viii.102–4)*

The historical accounts of the battle, contemporary as well as subsequent, follow the same pattern. See also the opening scene of *Much Ado*:

> *Leon.* How many gentlemen have you lost in this action?
> *Mess.* But few of any sort, and none of name.
>
> (I.i.5–6)

107. The order was given because the French army had camped hardly a mile away. Silence, however, was one of the 'principall points belonging to the souldiers', as is stated by Thomas Styward: 'In all places of seruice such silence must be used, that soldiers maie heare friends, and not be heard as well in watch, ward, ambush, camisado, or else where: in which pointe consisteth oftentimes the safetie or perdition of the whole Campe.' Thomas Styward, *The Pathwaie to Martiall Discipline* (London, 1581), p. 46. Contemporary historians say that such was the silence in the English camp that night that the French thought the English might have run away.

108. W. B. Kerr, 'The English Soldier in the Campaign of Agincourt', *Journal of the American Military Institute*, IV (1940), 8–29 and 209–24, pp. 220, 221–2.

109. The contemporary accounts of the battle are, in the first place, an anonymous chronicle probably written by a priest who said to have accompanied the expedition. The text (in Latin) is in the British Library, Cottonian Ms. Julius E.iv. and Sloane Ms. No. 1776. (The part relating the expedition is found in translation in H. Nicolas, *History of the Battle of Agincourt* (London, Johnson & Co., 1832), Appendix. The second manuscript source is the anonymous *Chronicles of London*, also held in the British Library (Harleian Ms. 565, 'Cleopatra C iv'; the manuscript has been edited by C. L. Kingsford in *Chronicles of London* (Oxford: Clarendon Press, 1905). Of the printed sources, mention should be made of the *History of Charles VI* by Jean Le Fèvre, who affirms that he was with the English army (*Chronique de Jean Le*

Fèvre, Seigneur de Saint Rémy, ed. F. Morand (Paris: Société de l'histoire de France, 1876); also Titus Livius, *Vita Henrici Quinti, Regis Angliae*, is a valuable source.

110. Recruitment in Elizabeth's time was made among all able-bodied men between the ages of 16 and 60. However, there were some who thought that the age between 20 and 45 better suited a soldier. See Matthew Sutcliffe, *The Practice, Proceedings and Lawes of Armes* (London, 1593), p. 63. From 19 to 45 is the age indicated by Leonard and Thomas Digges, *An Arithmeticall Militare Treatise, named Stratioticos* (London, 1579), p. 81. A useful, although not extensive, introduction to Elizabethan war treatises is the book by H. J. Webb, *Elizabethan Military Science. The Books and the Practice* (Madison: University of Wisconsin Press, 1965).

111. In one of these indentures, agreed with a certain Thomas Tunstall, it is said that 'respecting other profits or "Gaignes de Guerre," our said Lord the King shall have as well a third part of the "gaignes" of the said Thomas, as the third of the third part of the "gaignes" of the people of his retinue in the said voyage taken, as the "gaignes" of the prisoners, booty, money, and all gold, silver and jewels, exceeding the value of ten marks'. *Indenture of Thomas Tunstall*, in H. Nicolas, op. cit., 'Appendix', p. 10; translated from the French, *Foedera*, vol. IX, p. 233. It should also be remarked that those who occupied the lower ranks were obliged to give part of the war booty conquered by them to the nobleman who had recruited them. C. Hibbert says that 'Usually the captor received only a fraction of the money paid, a large proportion going to the noble or knight under whose banner he served and this leader in turn had to divide his share with the king', and adds that 'certain men, if captured, had to be handed over to the king anyway'. *Agincourt* (London: Batsford, 1964), p. 33.

112. Hibbert, op. cit., p. 32. In Elizabeth's time, the recruitment was made by the Lord Lieutenant and the JPs acting as commissioners of muster, from whom the Council required a certain number of soldiers ready by a certain date; see C. G. Cruikshank, *Elizabeth's Army* (Oxford: Clarendon Press, 1966), p. 23. In *2 Henry IV* (III.ii) the recruiting is made by a commission of JPs (Shallow and Silence) and supervised by a knight (Sir John Falstaff).

113. The ideal equipment of archers or long-bowmen was the following:

> Necessarie it is that euerie man haue a good and meete Bowe according to his draught and strength, light and easie: a iacke with a skull, sword and dagger, nothing uppon his armes, whereby in time of seruice he maie easilie draw the arrow to the head, that they maie deliuer the same with strength and arte as Englishmen be accustomed. They must haue also braser and shooting gloue, their stringes whipped and wared ouer with glew, their feathers drie: so be they seruisable in anie weather to serue against the enimie to slaughter and execution. (Styward, op. cit., p. 44)

114. Ibid., p. 45.
115. Hibbert, op. cit., p. 49.

116. 'A soldier is better accommodated than with a wife' is Bardolph's sententious statement in 2 *Henry IV*, III.ii.65–6.
117. *The Mirror of Honor* (London, 1597), pp. 42–3. Norden's book, a mixture of religious and military fanaticism, is dedicated to Essex.
118. M. Sutcliffe, op. cit., p. 71.
119. Falstaff describes his soldiers' poverty saying: 'There's not a shirt and a half in all my company, and the half shirt is two napkins tacked together and thrown over the shoulders...' (1 *Henry IV*, IV.ii.42–4).
120. C. Hibbert, op. cit., p. 25.
121. Op. cit., p. 224.
122. Ibid., p. 13. On the tendency 'to place the ideological power of "Shakespeare" at the service of the national war effort' during the Second World War, see G. Holderness, 'Agincourt 1944: Readings in the Shakespeare Myth', *Literature and History* X (1984), 24–45. Holderness discusses three texts produced in 1944: G. Wilson Knight's *The Olive and the Sword*, Olivier's film *Henry V* and Tillyard's *Shakespeare's History Plays*.
123. Op. cit., p. 67.
124. Op. cit., p. 43.
125. L. and T. Digges, op. cit., p. 82.
126. See Niccolò Machiavelli, *Dell'arte della guerra* (1519–20), transl. Peter Whitehorne in 1560 as *The Art of Warre*; see also, Raimond Beccarie de Pavie, Baron de Fourquevaux, *Instructions sur le faict de la guerre* (Paris, 1548), where the author insists on the fact that 'il faut recompenser les hommes après avoir bien servi' (p. 107). The English translation of the treatise, *Instructions for the Warres* (London, 1589), wrongly attributes its authorship to Guillaume du Bellay.
127. Thomas Styward lists sobriety among the six principal virtues of a soldier, together with silence, obedience, secretness, hardiness and truth (op. cit., pp. 46–7); the same quality is indicated by William Garrard, *The Arte of Warre* (London, 1591), pp. 30–1. Sutcliffe says that 'lesse pay doth content our souldiers, then any forreine nation' (op. cit., p. 71). The poverty of the English soldier is discussed as a point of fact by Barnabe Rich, *Allarme to England* (London, 1578), passim.
128. That soldiers' wages were still miserly in Elizabeth's time is mentioned by Matthew Sutcliffe, who advises that the pay should be such as to avoid that soldiers, for want of money, 'spoyle their friends and associates, yea their companions, and commit many outrages' (op. cit., p. 74).
129. W. B. Kerr, op. cit., p. 220. Kerr adds that 'Many soldiers and the few tradesmen sold their men to Henry and the nobles' (ibid., p. 221). It is easy to imagine what profitable negotiations the soldiers were able to make with the king and his circle. John Hardyng, who was at Agincourt, obviously justifies the massacre, although he says that it was executed 'in fell and cruell wise'. Hardyng also says that 'dukes and erles' were spared (owing, no doubt, to Henry's 'fine eye to profit'): *The Chronicle of John Hardyng*, ed. H. Ellis (London, 1818), the CCxiiii Chapter, p. 375.

130. Cruikshank, op. cit., p. 27.
131. Ibid., p. 28.
132. Op. cit., p. 62.
133. Ibid., pp. 62–3.
134. Ibid., p. 63.
135. M. Sutcliffe, op. cit., p. 67.
136. J. Norden, op. cit., p. 42.
137. Ibid., p. 6.
138. The argument of the king's responsibility which is produced by Williams was in fact used by Henry in the actual speech that, according to at least one of the contemporary sources, he delivered to the troops before the battle: 'But I would no blood were spilt Christ help me so now in this case, but though that hath been cause of this trespass; when thou sittest in judgment, there hold me excused tofore thy face, as thou art God omnipotent' (*Chronicles of London*, p. 120).
139. C. W. C. Oman, *The Art of War in the Middle Ages*, revised and edited by John H. Beeler (Ithaca: Cornell University Press, 1953), p. 126; my emphasis.
140. Cruikshank, op. cit., p. 25. G. J. Millar says that the voluntary character of conscription, especially in the case of waging war in foreign countries, was easily overcome by the crown by invoking national emergency. *Tudor Mercenaries and Auxiliaries* (Charlottesville: University Press of Virginia, 1980), p. 15. That the voluntary character of military service was a fiction is also hinted at in a passage by Norden quoted earlier: 'whether they bee prest by authoritie, or of their own forwardnes' (op. cit., p. 43). Machiavelli's idea on this point is that soldiers should be neither wholly pressed nor wholly volunteers – 'né al tutto forzati né al tutto volontarii' – but rather led by the respect they feel for their prince – 'tirati da uno rispetto ch'egli abbiano al principe'. *Dell'arte della guerra*, in *Opere*, ed. Antonio Panella (Milan: Rizzoli, 1939), vol. II, p. 495.
141. A. H. Burne comments approvingly on the 'immensity of the risk' that Henry was conscious of running and on the atmosphere of 'defeatism' that determined the Council's recommendation, saying that to decide to proceed 'required some moral courage', and argues against the verdicts that have been pronounced against Henry by some historians. His idea is that 'In war if you risk nothing you gain nothing', that a return to England 'would be construed as failure in both countries, the king's prestige would fall, there might even be a revolution and he might be supplanted by the legitimate heir to the throne, the earl of March'. *The Agincourt War* (London: Eyre and Spottiswoode, 1956), pp. 49 and 52.
142. Kerr, op. cit., pp. 25, 26. There are historians who evaluate Henry's decision to march to Calais as 'a rash and unjustifiable undertaking' (Oman, op. cit., p. 133).
143. *Chronicles*, 552.II.59–66.
144. Kerr, op. cit., p. 29.
145. L. and T. Digges, op. cit., p. 83.
146. Cruikshank, op. cit., p. 26.

147. P. A. Jorgensen, *Shakespeare's Military World* (Berkeley and Los Angeles: University of California Press, 1956), pp. 209–10.

148. In his monologue, where he declares 'bawd I'll turn,/ And something lean to cutpurse of quick hand' (*Henry V*, V.I.89–90), Pistol is foreseeing a future of begging and trying to imagine some expediency in order to avoid it.

149. Jorgensen reports a letter written by the Council to the Justice of Monmouth about one William James, 'a poore maimed souldier' to whom the local authorities should have granted a pension for a year and who had protested with the government because the pension was 'wrongfully and without cause with the certificate of his mayms and hurtes (his maims being apparent) deteyned from him.' (op. cit., p. 211; from the *Acts of the Privy Council, New Series*, ed. J. R. Dasent (London, 1890–), XXV, 249.

150. Ibid., p. 211. Jorgensen argues that 'The sincerity of this conviction is evident in the injured tone of frequent letters from her council to county officials complaining that their responsibilities had been neglected.' (ibid.)

151. Op. cit., p. 57.

152. Op. cit., pp. E ii–E iii.

Index

Abraham, 88, 91–2, 93
Actes and Monuments, by John
   Foxe, 174, 175, 213, 239 (n. 88,
   89)
Agincourt, battle of, 137, 138, 144,
   207, 217–32 (passim), 241–5
   passim
Alençon, Duke of, 237
Allarme to England, by Barnabe
   Rich, 231, 243
Altman, J. B., 43, 44, 55 (n. 6, 7),
   56
ambiguity, 138–9, 151–2. *See also*
   ambivalence, *amphibologia*,
   complementarity, contrariety,
   doubleness, duplicity, *in
   utramque partem, jeu parti*
ambivalence, 42, 43, 45, 46, 54, 55,
   139, 151–2. *See also* ambiguity,
   amphibologia, complementarity,
   contrariety, doubleness,
   duplicity, *in utramque partem,
   jeu parti*
amphibologia, 47, 50, 55, 139,
   151–2. *See also* ambiguity,
   ambivalence, complementarity,
   contrariety, doubleness,
   duplicity, *in utramque partem,
   jeu parti*
Anjou, Duke of, 237
Annales, by William Camden, 94,
   100–1
*Answer to the First Part of a Certain
   Conference, Concerning Succession,
   An*, by Sir John Hayward, 39
*Answere unto Sir Thomas Mores
   Dialoge, An*, by William Tindall,
   239
Antony and Cleopatra, 135

Apology for Actors, An, by Thomas
   Heywood, 61, 67
Aquinas, Thomas, 100
*Arithmeticall Militare Treatise, named
   Stratioticos, An*, by Leonard and
   Thomas Digges, 242, 243, 244
Aristotle, *Poetics*, 36–7, 41, 69–70, 73
Armada (battle): and the rise of
   historical plays, 1–2, 4, 8–9 (n. 2,
   4), 11; and Shakespeare's initial
   steps in the theatre, 2–5, 9
Aron, Raymond, 56
Arte of English Poesie, by George
   Puttenham, 30, 38, 47, 55, 56–7,
   71, 139, 151, 182, 188
Arte of Warre, The, by William
   Garrard, 243
Arthur, King, 238
Arthur, of Brittany: 32, 88–9, 101;
   character in *King John*: 78, 79,
   83, 85, 86, 87, 90–1, 94–7
   passim, 100, 206, 207; character
   in *The Troublesome Raigne*: 89–90,
   100
Arundel, Earl of, 218
Ascham, Roger, *A Report and
   Discourse . . . of the Affaires and
   State of Germany*, 47, 58
audience: 24, 28, 44, 49, 61, 62, 64,
   67 (n. 5, 6, 8, 9, 10, 11), 78, 80,
   97, 104, 105, 106, 113, 121, 122,
   126, 130, 131–2, 133, 141–2, 148,
   149, 150, 163, 174, 186, 188, 195,
   196, 201, 202, 205, 213, 218, 219;
   Elizabethan: 7, 12, 36–7, 50, 64,
   82, 143, 173, 187
Auerbach, Eric, 122
Augmentis scientiarum, De, by Sir
   Francis Bacon, 40